LAW, HISTORY,
THE LOW COUNTRIES AND EUROPE

LAW, HISTORY,
THE LOW COUNTRIES
AND EUROPE

R.C. VAN CAENEGEM

EDITED BY
LUDO MILIS, DANIEL LAMBRECHT,
HILDE DE RIDDER-SYMOENS AND
MONIQUE VLEESCHOUWERS-VAN MELKEBEEK

THE HAMBLEDON PRESS
LONDON AND RIO GRANDE

Published by The Hambledon Press 1994
102 Gloucester Avenue, London NW1 8HX (U.K.)
P.O. Box 162, Rio Grande, Ohio 45674 (U.S.A.)

ISBN 1 85285 088 4

© R.C. Van Caenegem 1994

A description of this book is available from
the British Library and from the Library of Congress

Typeset by York House Typographic Ltd
Printed on acid-free paper and bound in
Great Britain by Cambridge University Press

Contents

Acknowledgements		vii
Preface		ix
Bibliography of R.C. Van Caenegem		xiii
1	History and Experiment	1
2	Modern Historiography: A Science without Experiment	15
3	Clio and the Humanities: Alma Mater and Prodigal Sons?	27
4	Reflections on the History of England	37
5	Parliament: A European Deviation?	55
6	The Sources of Flemish History in the *Liber Floridus*	71
7	Considerations on the Customary Law of Twelfth-Century Flanders	97
8	The Ghent Revolt of February 1128	107
9	The Pacification of Ghent	113
10	Bookish Law and Customary Law: Roman Law in the Southern Netherlands in the Late Middle Ages	119
11	Witchcraft in the Low Countries	135
12	Chivalrous Ideals and Religious Feeling	145
13	Henri Pirenne: Medievalist and Historian of Belgium	161
14	F.L. Ganshof	179
Index		191
Tabula Gratulatoria		199

Acknowledgements

The essays reprinted below first appeared in the following places and are reprinted by the kind permission of the original publishers.

1   First published under the title 'Geschiedenis en experiment', *Economische geschiedenis van België: behandeling van de bronnen en problematiek. Handelingen van het colloquium te Brussel, 17-19 Nov. 1971* (Archief – en bibliotheekwezen in Belgie, extranummer 10), ed. H. Coppejans-Desmedt (Brussels, 1973), pp. 117-37.

2   Lecture given on 16 March 1964. Slightly revised text published under the title 'De moderne geschiedschrijving: een wetenschap zonder experiment', *Studia philosophica Gandensia*, 7 (1969), pp. 91-103.

3   Translated from 'Clio en de menswetenschappen: alma mater en verloren zonen?', *Tijdschrift voor geschiedenis*, 87 (1974), pp. 321-29.

4   Lecture given at the Royal Academy of Sciences in Brussels on 13 February 1982 and published under the title 'Beschouwingen bij de geschiedenis van Engeland', *Medelingen v.d. Koninklijke Academie voor Wetenschappen, Letteren en Schone Kunsten van België, Academiae analecta, Kl. Lett.*, 44 (1982), pp. 53-71.

5   First published under the title 'Het parlementarisme: een Europese afwijking?', *Forum der letteren*, 13 (1971), pp. 191-209.

6   *Liber Floridus Colloquium: Papers Read at the International Meeting Held in the University Library, Ghent on 3-5 September 1967*, ed. A. Derolez (Ghent, 1973), pp. 71-85.

7   First published under the title 'Beschouwingen over het gewoonterecht in het graafschap Vlaanderen in de twaalfde eeuw', *Tijdschrift voor Rechtsgeschiedenis – Revue d'histoire du droit*, 35 (1967), pp. 485-99.

8   First published under the title 'De Gentse Februari-Opstand van het jaar 1128', *Spiegel historiael*, 13 (1978), pp. 478-83.

9   Lecture given in the Pacification Room, Ghent Town Hall, on 8 September 1976 to commemorate the 400th anniversary of the signing of the Pacification of Ghent. First published under the title 'De Pacificatie van Gent, 1576-1976', *Handelingen der Maatschappij voor geschiedenis en oudheidkunde te Gent*, new series, 30 (1976), pp. 3-7.

10 Lecture given to the Historisch Genootschap, Utrecht, 2 November 1965. First published under the title 'Boekenrecht en gewoonterecht: het Romeinse recht in de zuidelijke Nederlanden op het einde der middeleeuwen', *Bijdragen en mededelingen van het Historisch Genootschap*, 8 (1966), pp. 12-37.

11 Final address at a Brussels colloquium on witchcraft. First published under the title 'Hekserij in de Nederlanden', *Standen en landen – Anciens pays et assemblées d'états*, 86 (1987), pp. 203-16.

12 *Hoofsheid en devotie in de middeleeuwse maatschappij: de Nederlanden van de 12e tot de 15e eeuw. Handelingen van het wetenschappelijk colloquium te Brussel, 21-24 Oktober 1981*, ed. J.D. Janssens (Brussels, 1982), pp. 240-59.

13 First published under the title 'Henri Pirenne: een evaluatie naar aanleiding van de honderdste verjaardag van zijn benoeming te Gent', *Mededelingen van de Koninklijke Academie voor Wetenschappen, Letteren en Schone Kunsten van België, Academiae analecta, Kl. Lett.*, 49 (1987), pp. 85-105. Subsequently published in *Illustere historici: leven, werk en invloed van toonaangevende geschiedschrijvers*, ed. M. Smits (Nijmegen, 1988), pp. 79-104.

14 In Memoriam delivered before the Class of Letters of the Belgian Academy of Sciences, 1980. First published under the title 'In Memoriam F.L. Ganshof (14 March 1895-26 July 1980)', *Jaarboek 1980 v.d. Koninklijke Academie voor Wetenschappen, Letteren en Schone Kunsten van België*, 42 (1980), pp. 231-42. The text printed there is followed by a bibliography of F.L. Ganshof, pp. 243-51.

Preface

At the end of September 1992 Professor Raoul C. Van Caenegem retired from the university of Ghent, having entered it in 1946 as a student. Guided in the field of legal history by the late Professor F.L. Ganshof, he studied in both the Law and Arts Faculties. He became a Doctor of Law in 1951 and a Doctor of Philosophy in 1953. Van Caenegem pursued his training in Paris (at the Sorbonne, the École Pratique des Hautes Études and the École Nationale des Chartes) in 1951–52, and in London (the London School of Economics and the Institute of Historical Research) in 1952–54. Such international contacts were not common in the harsh post-war period. The British contacts, in particular, were to endure: they influenced his career, his scientific interests and, not least, his private life. In 1958 he achieved his *Hoger Aggregaat* — until its recent abolition the highest-ranking academic degree in Belgium. In the meantime he worked as a research assistant and research associate of the National Fund for Scientific Research, and as the research assistant and *geaggregeerde* of Professor Ganshof. At the university of Ghent, where he spent his professional career, he became a lecturer in 1960 and a full professor in 1964.

We will not attempt to describe Van Caenegem's career in detail or the prizes he has won, the functions he has assumed in his university and in learned societies, and his invitations to lecture at foreign universities. We mention here only the most outstanding: the highly prestigious Francqui Prize (1974) and the Solvay Prize of the National Fund for Scientific Research (1990); his presidency of the Koninklijke Academie voor Wetenschappen, Letteren en Schone Kunsten van België (Royal Academy of Sciences, Arts and Fine Arts of Belgium) (1988); his honorary degrees at the universities of Tübingen (1977), Leuven (1984) and Paris (1988); his Arthur L. Goodhart Professorship of Legal Science at Cambridge (1984–85); his Sir Henry Saville Fellowship at Merton College, Oxford (1989); and his Erasmus Lectureship at Harvard (1991). The essential and constant feature in his career, however, has been his ardour for his own alma mater, especially as head of the Seminar for the General and Institutional History of the Middle Ages in the Arts Faculty at Ghent. An important part of his teaching has also taken place in the Law Faculty.

Raoul Van Caenegem's inaugural lecture of 1964 was on the theme of 'Western Middle Ages and Universal History'.[1] In his perception the middle ages engendered two unique features which were to be 'of essential and permanent importance for the development of mankind: modern science and the constitutional parliamentary state'. His work of thirty years ago contains the themes of his later work. The first topic, science and scientific thought, was not pursued further. His diffidence, caused by his self-avowed *ignorantia*, prevented this. The other topic, the history of institutions, has continued to attract his full attention: the slow and cumbersome process of growth from authoritarian expressions of power to democratic ways of power-sharing fill many pages of his writings. In one way his work can be seen as the mature expansion of books on penal law and penal law procedure in medieval Flanders.[2] Looked at from another angle, the hallmark of his work is its breadth: considerable even in his early work, his scope, feeding on growing experience, has become exceptionally great. Here lies his strength. His profound knowledge of European continental law has enriched time and again his study of the English common law, making him a leading expert in that field.[3] Even in regional studies his constant urge to compare and to cross borders is everywhere apparent.

Van Caenegem is strongly taken by the idea of the importance of law and institutions as determining factors of historical development, rather than being the mere results of economic and social situations and conditions – for many other historians the prime movers of history.[4] In his view, however, institutions and law stem more from a kind of internal dynamics than from great individuals, 'legislators'. Van Caenegem, we know, is not blind to what figures of exceptional stature have meant to history. Yet he has never been attracted to portraying these figures or presenting them in full detail. Kings and bureaucrats alike, each rather typified than personified, have caught his full attention. Their interactions have captivated him more and more. This broad approach explains the success of many of his publications.

At one time Van Caenegem became fascinated by the theme of chance in history, when Jacques Monod published *Le hasard et la nécessité* (Paris, 1970), but he has never come to see chance as an explanation for specific changes. Like every great historian, he has recoiled from what would essentially prove the impotence of *le métier d'historien*.

[1] *De plaats van de westerse geschiedenis in de universele geschiedenis* (Bruges, 1964).
[2] *Geschiedenis van het strafrecht in Vlaanderen van de XIe tot de XIVe eeuw* (Brussel, 1954); *Geschiedenis van het strafprocesrecht in Vlaanderen van de XIe tot de XIVe eeuw* (Brussel, 1956).
[3] *Royal Writs in England from the Conquest to Glanvill: Studies in the Early History of the Common Law* (London, 1959); *The Birth of English Common Law* (Cambridge, 1973; 2nd edn, 1988); *English Lawsuits from William I to Richard I*, 2 vols (London, 1990–91).
[4] *Over koningen en bureaucraten: oorsprong en ontwikkeling van de hedendaagse staatsinstellingen* (Amsterdam, 1977); *Judges, Legislators and Professors: Chapters in European Legal History* (Cambridge, 1987; 2nd edn, 1988), translated into Italian (*I signori del diritto: guidici, legislatori e professori nella storia europea* (Milan, 1991)) and Japanese (Tokyo, 1990).

Van Caenegem has let himself become deeply involved in his teaching. Time and again those close to him have marvelled at his ability to mesmerise a large audience by fascinating syntheses. They have also seen how he can intrigue his audience by the painstaking and meticulous analysis of detail. Many of his publications have sprung directly from his professorial teaching. Imposing summaries developed out of his lectures on legal history in the Law Faculty;[5] and out of his lectures on the history of England and on medieval sources in the Arts Faculty.[6] His handy *Guide* has been kept up to date in each of its consecutive translations.[7] A distinctive mark is the care he bestows on his writing, whether in Dutch, French or English. He always writes concisely, yet the exact expression of his arguments does not prevent gracefulness.

A rumour survives amongst Ghent medievalists that the immediate successors of Henri Pirenne agreed in 1935 not to accept a festschrift when they in turn retired. That generation kept its agreement well and allowed at the most the gathering of a selection of their own articles. The current generation has chosen differently: some of Van Caenegem's articles in Dutch, illustrative of his historical interests and scientific approach, have been translated and gathered, in order to emphasise his international stature. This volume aims at being a complement to Van Caenegem's *Legal History: A European Perspective*, published by the Hambledon Press in 1991.

Those who have graduated under his supervision have appreciated Van Caenegem's scholarly openness and the belief in intellectual freedom he has always advocated, endorsing by actions ideals that often unfortunately remain just words. His ideas have made an even deeper impression on those who have worked closely with him. Imposing his own ideas is completely alien to him, even if he is convinced that his view is the only correct one. His colleagues have enjoyed his confidence, which has allowed them to get on independently with their own research and to develop their own personal views. Out of this sense of mutual respect friendship has grown. This feeling has rarely blossomed inside the austere Arts Faculty building; it has come more easily at social evenings where Raoul and Patricia Van Caenegem have acted as amiable hosts or as charming guests.

To a greater extent than they are willing to acknowledge Raoul's wife, Patricia Carson – a celebrated author herself who has presented the

---

[5] *Geschiedkundige inleiding tot het privaatrecht* (Ghent, 1981); revised edition: *Geschiedkundige inleiding van het recht*, i, *Privaatrecht* (Brussels, 1989); translated into French: *Introduction historique au droit privé* (Brussels, 1988); and into English, *An Historical Introduction to Private Law* (Cambridge, 1992). *Geschiedkundige inleiding tot het recht*, ii, *Publiekrecht* (Brussels, 1988).

[6] *Geschiedenis van Engeland* (The Hague and Antwerp, 1982).

[7] *Encyclopedie van de geschiedenis der middeleeuwen: inleiding tot de geschreven bronnen van de geschiedenis der westerse middeleeuwen* (Ghent, 1962) [in collaboration with F.L. Ganshof]; translated into German: *Kurze Quellenkunde des Westeuropäischen Mittelalters* (Göttingen, 1964); and into English: *Guide to the Sources of Medieval History* (Amsterdam, New York and Oxford, 1978).

'Fair Face' of her adoptive Flanders to the world, and their three children have contributed to mould Raoul's character. His many friends here and abroad, in and outside Europe, will undoubtedly share this view.

We wish Raoul and Patricia many productive years during which, at the peak of their maturity, they may fully realise their creativity, freed from the administrative routine which increasingly devours the time of academics. From the depth of our hearts we toast them: *ad multos annos*.

Ludo Milis

Hilde De Ridder-Symoens

Daniël Lambrecht

Monique Vleeschouwers-Van Melkebeek

Bibliography of R.C. Van Caenegem
(1951–94)

BOOKS

1   *Geschiedenis van het strafrecht in Vlaanderen van de XIe tot de XIVe eeuw* (= History of Criminal Law in Flanders from the Eleventh to the Fourteenth Century) (Brussels, 1954) (Verhandelingen van de Koninklijke Vlaamse Academie, Klasse der Letteren, 19), 399 pp.

2   *Geschiedenis van het strafprocesrecht in Vlaanderen van de XIe tot de XIVe eeuw* (= History of Criminal Procedure in Flanders from the Eleventh to the Fourteenth Century) (Brussels, 1956) (Verhandelingen van de Koninklijke Vlaamse Academie, Klasse der Letteren, 24), 370 pp.

3   *Royal Writs in England from the Conquest to Glanvill: Studies in the Early History of the Common Law* (London, 1959) (Publications of the Selden Society, 77), xlix + 556 pp.

4   *Encyclopedie van de geschiedenis der middeleeuwen: inleiding tot de geschreven bronnen van de geschiedenis der westerse middeleeuwen* (= Introduction to the Written Sources of the History of the Western Middle Ages) [in collaboration with F.L. Ganshof] (Ghent, 1962), 356 pp.
    German edition: *Kurze Quellenkunde des westeuropäischen Mittelalters* (Göttingen, 1964), 365 pp.; English revised edition: *Guide to the Sources of Medieval History* (Amsterdam, New York and Oxford, 1978) (Europe in the Middle Ages. Selected Studies, 2), 428 pp.

5   *Les Iles Britanniques* (Brussels, 1963) (J. Gilissen, Introduction bibliographique à l'histoire du droit et à l'ethnologie juridique, C/5), 87 pp.

6   *Monarchie franque* [in collaboration with F.L. Ganshof] (Brussels, 1964) (J. Gilissen, Introduction bibliographique à l'histoire du droit et à l'ethnologie juridique, B/6), 52 pp.

7   *De plaats van de westerse middeleeuwen in de universele geschiedenis*

(= The Place of the Western Middle Ages in World History) (Bruges, 1964) (Werken Faculteit Letteren en Wijsbegeerte, Rijksuniversiteit Gent), 24 pp. (inaugural lecture).

8   *Les arrêts et jugés du Parlement de Paris sur appels flamands conservés dans les registres du Parlement*, i, *Textes (1320–1453)* (Brussels, 1966) (Commission des Anciennes Lois et Ordonnances de Belgique: recueil de l'ancienne jurisprudence, 1st series), 657 pp.

9   *Le droit romain en Belgique* (Milan, 1966) (Ius romanum medii aevi, v, 5b), 65 pp.

10 *Les institutions féodo-vassaliques* [in collaboration with F.L. Ganshof] (Brussels, 1972) (J. Gilissen, Introduction bibliographique à l'histoire du droit et à l'ethnologie juridique, B/8), 57 pp.

11 *History of European Civil Procedure* (Tübingen, The Hague, Paris and New York, 1973) (International Encyclopedia of Comparative Law, xvi, 2), 113 pp.

12 *The Birth of the English Common Law* (Cambridge, 1973; 2nd edn, 1988), 160 pp.

13 *Les arrêts et jugés du Parlement de Paris sur appels flamands conservés dans les registres du Parlement*, ii, *Textes (1454–1521)* (Brussels, 1977) (Commission Royale des Anciennes Lois et Ordonnances de Belgique: recueil de l'ancienne jurisprudence, 1st series), 882 pp. in–4°.

14 *Over koningen en bureaucraten: oorsprong en ontwikkeling van de hedendaagse staatsinstellingen* (= Kings and Bureaucrats: Origins and Development of Contemporary Political Institutions) (Amsterdam and Brussels, 1977), 383 pp.

15 *Galbert van Brugge en het Recht* (Galbert of Bruges and the Law) (Brussels, 1978) (Mededelingen van de Koninklijke Academie voor Wetenschappen, Letteren en Schone Kunsten van België, Klasse der Letteren, xl, no. 1), 35 pp.

16 Editor of, and author of historical introduction to, *Galbert van Brugge: de moord op Karel de Goede. Dagboek van de gebeurtenissen in de jaren 1127–1128* (= Galbert of Bruges: The Murder of Charles the Good. Diary of the Events in the Years 1127–1128) (Antwerp, 1978), 274 pp. in–4° (Historical Introduction. pp. 13–17). French edition, *Galbert de Bruges: le meurtre de Charles le Bon* (Antwerp, 1978).

17 *Geschiedkundige inleiding tot het privaatrecht* (Historical Introduction to Private Law) (Gent, 1981), 184 pp (2nd edn, 1985, 259 pp). Revised edition, *Geschiedkundige inleiding tot het recht*, i, *Privaatrecht* (Brussels, 1989), 259 pp.

18 *Geschiedenis van Engeland* (= History of England) (The Hague and Antwerp, 1982; reprint, 1985), 502 pp.

19 *Het Common Law herbezocht: voordracht gehouden aan de Rijksuniversiteit te Leiden op 23 maart 1983* (= The Common Law Revisited: Conference held at the State University of Leiden on 23 March 1983) (Leiden, 1983) (Thorbecke-Colleges: voordrachten gehouden in het kader van de uitwisseling tussen de juridische faculteiten te Gent en te Leiden, 9), 28 pp.

20 *Judges, Legislators and Professors: Chapters in European Legal History* (Cambridge, 1987 and 1993) (Goodhart Lectures 1984−85), 205 pp. Italian transl.: *I signori del diritto: guidici, legislatori e professori nella storia europea* (Milan, 1991) (Giuristi stranieri di oggi, dir. C.M. Mazzoni and V. Varano, 8), xii + 170 pp.; Japanese transl.: Tokyo, 1990.

21 *Introduction historique au droit privé*, translated from the Dutch by A. Wijffels (Brussels, 1988), 261 pp.

22 *Geschiedkundige inleiding tot het recht*, ii, *Publiekrecht* (= Historical Introduction to the Law, ii, Public Law) (Brussels, 1988), vii + 304 pp.

23 *Max Weber: historicus en socioloog* (= Max Weber: Historian and Sociologist) (Amsterdam, 1988) (Koninklijke Akademie van Wetenschappen: mededelingen van de Afdeling Letterkunde, new series, SI, no. 3), 27 pp.

24 *Legal History: A European Perspective* (London and Rio Grande, 1991), xi + 242 pp.

25 *English Lawsuits from William I to Richard I*, i, *William to Stephen*; ii, *Henry II and Richard I* (London, 1990−91) (Selden Society Publications, 106, 107), 1 + 710 + 710 + 81 pp.

26 *An Historical Introduction to Private Law*, transl. by D.E.L. Johnston (Cambridge, 1992), viii + 215 pp.

ARTICLES

1 'Note sur la date de la première charte de Philippe d'Alsace pour la ville d'Arras', *Revue belge de philologie et d'histoire*, 29 (1951), pp. 481−86.

2 'Een onuitgegeven Brugse keure uit 1229' (= An Unedited Borough Charter of Bruges from 1229), *Bulletin de la Commission Royale des Anciennes Lois et Ordonnances*, 17 (1952), pp. 1−13.

3 'Nota over de terechtstelling van Willem de Deken te Parijs in 1328'

(= Note on the Execution of Willem de Deken in Paris in 1328), *Handelingen van de 'Société d'Emulation' te Brugge*, 90 (1953), pp. 140–2.

4 'Problemen van historische interpretatie' (= Problems of Historical Interpretation), *Bijdragen voor de geschiedenis der Nederlanden* (1953), pp. 259–64.

5 'De rationalisatie van het procesrecht in het crimineel proces in Vlaanderen in de XIIe eeuw' (= The Rationalisation of Procedure in the Criminal Courts in Flanders in the Twelfth Century), *Handelingen van het XXe Vlaams filologencongres* (1953), pp. 47–53.

6 'De appèls van de Vlaamse rechtbanken naar het Parlement van Parijs' (= The Appeals from Flemish Courts to the Parlement of Paris), *Handelingen van het XXVIe Congres van de Federatie der Kringen voor Geschiedenis* (Ghent, 1956), pp. 191–92.

7 'Recente onwikkeling van een net County Record Offices in Engeland' (= The Recent Development of a Network of County Record Offices in England), *Handelingen van het XXIIe Vlaams filologencongres* (1957), pp. 312–16.

8 'Note sur le premier traité anglo-flamand de Douvres' [in collaboration with F.L. Ganshof and A. Verhulst), *Mélanges R. Monier* (Paris and Lille, 1958), pp. 245–57.

9 'Les appels flamands au Parlement de Paris au moyen âge', *Etudes d'histoire du droit privé offertes à P. Pétot* (Paris, 1959), pp. 61–68.

10 'Ouvrages de droit romain dans les catalogues des anciens Pays-Bas méridionaux (XIIIe–XVIe siècles)', *Revue d'histoire du droit*, 28 (1960), pp. 297–347, 403–37.

11 'Les études médiévales: quelques réflexions', *Studi medievali*, 1 (1960), pp. 627–59.

12 'La paix publique dans les Iles Britanniques du XIe au XVIIe siècle', *La paix*, ii, Brussels (1961), pp. 5–26 (Recueils de la Société Jean Bodin, 15).

13 'Méthodes et problèmes actuels de la recherche historique, particulièrement dans le domaine de l'histoire du moyen âge', *Revue de l'Institut de Sociologie*, 4 (1963), pp. 769–800.

14 'Le diplôme de Charles le Chauve du 20 juin 877 pour l'abbaye de Saint-Bertin', *Revue d'histoire du droit*, 31 (1963), pp. 403–26.

15 'La preuve dans l'ancien droit belge des origines à la fin du XVIIIe siècle', *La preuve* (Brussels, 1965), pp. 375–430 (Recueils de la Société Jean Bodin, xvii).

16 'La preuve dans le droit du moyen âge occidental, rapport de synthèse', *La preuve* (Brussels, 1965), pp. 691–753 (Recueils de la Société Jean Bodin, xvii).
English translation, with up-to-date bibliography *Methods of Proof in Western Medieval Law* in *Mededelingen van de Koninklijke Academie van Wetenschappen, Letteren en Schone Kunsten van België. Academiae Analecta, Klasse der Letteren*, 45 (1983), pp. 83–127.

17 'Universitair onderwijs in de geschiedenis der wetenschappen in de Verenigde Staten' (= Academic Teaching of the History of Science in the USA), *Scientiarum historia*, 7 (1965), pp. 202–12.

18 'Psychologische geschiedenis' (= Psychological History), *Tijdschrift voor geschiedenis*, 78 (1965), pp. 129–50.

19 'The Law of Evidence in the Twelfth Century', *Proceedings of the Second International Congress of Medieval Canon Law* (Vatican, 1965), pp. 297–310 (Monumenta iuris canonici, series c, 1).

20 'Cartografie en institutionele geschiedenis' (= Cartography and Institutional History), *Tijdschrift voor rechtsgeschiedenis*, 33 (1965), pp. 525–37.

21 'L'histoire du droit et la chronologie: réflexions sur la formation du "Common Law" et la procédure romano-canonique', *Etudes G. Le Bras*, ii (Paris, 1965), pp. 1459–65.

22 'Boekenrecht en gewoonterecht: het Romeinse Recht in de zuidelijke Nederlanden op het einde der middeleeuwen' (= Bookish Law and Customary Law: Roman Law in the Southern Netherlands in the Late Middle Ages), *Bijdragen en mededelingen van het Historisch Genootschap*, 80 (1966), pp. 12–37.

23 'De slag van Hastings' (= The Battle of Hastings), *Spiegel historiael*, 1 (1966), pp. 130–40.

24 'Notes on Canon Law Books in Medieval Belgian Booklists', *Studia Gratiana* (= Collectanea Kuttner, ii), 12 (1967), pp. 265–92.

25 'Note sur la date de la donation de Charles le Chauve pour l'abbaye de Saint-Bertin', *Miscellanea mediaevalia J.F. Niermeyer* (Groningen, 1967), pp. 71–78.

26 'Beschouwingen over het gewoonterecht in het graafschap Vlaanderen in de twaalfde eeuw' (= Considerations on the Customary Law of Twelfth-Century Flanders), *Tijdschrift voor rechtsgeschiedenis*, 35 (1967), pp. 485–99.

27 'Le droit romain dans les anciens Pays-Bas au moyen âge', *Recueil de mémoires et travaux publiés par la Société d'Histoire du Droit*, 6 (Montpellier, 1967), p. 63.

28 'Coutumes et législation en Flandre aux XIe et XIIe siècles', *Les libertés urbaines et rurales du XIe au XIVe siècle* (Brussels, 1968), pp. 245–79.

29 'Nieuwe wegen: psychologische geschiedenis' (= New Roads: Psychological History), *Spiegel historiael*, 4 (1969), pp. 47–56.

30 'The State, Society and Private Law', *Tidschrift voor rechtsgeschiedenis*, 37 (1969), pp. 235–45.

31 'De moderne geschiedschrijving: een wetenschap zonder Experiment' (= Modern Historiography: A Science without Experiment), *Studia philosophica Gandensia*, 7 (1969), pp. 91–102.

32 'De Moord op Thomas Becket' (= The Murder of Thomas Becket), *Spiegel historiael*, 5 (1970), pp. 664–72.

33 'Het Parlementarisme: een Europese afwijking?' (= Parliament: A European Deviation?), *Forum der letteren*, 13 (1971), pp. 191–209.

34 'Considérations sur l'ordonnance comtale flamande connue sous le nom d' "Ordonnance sur les baillis" ', *Actes du congrès international de la Société Italienne de l'Histoire du Droit* (Florence, 1971), pp. 133–52,

35 'Karel de Grote' (= Charlemagne), *Spiegel historiael*, 7 (1972), pp. 286–93.

36 'The "Reception" of Roman Law: A Meeting of Northern and Mediterranean Traditions', *The Late Middle Ages and the Dawn of Humanism outside Italy* (Louvain and The Hague, 1972), pp. 195–204 (Mediaevalia Lovaniensia, series 1, studia 1).

37 'Kanttekeningen bij een periodiseringsprobleem: de evolutie van het burgerlijk procesrecht' (= A Problem of Periodization: The Evolution of Civil Procedure), *Opstellen R. Victor*, ii (Antwerp, 1972), pp. 1075–85.

38 'Geschiedenis en experiment' (= History and Experiment), *Economische geschiedenis van België* (Brussels, 1973), pp. 119–37.

39 'The Sources of Flemish History in the *Liber Floridus*', *Liber Floridus Colloquium* (Ghent, 1973), pp. 71–85.

40 'Henri Pirenne: An Historian at the Cross-Roads', *De Brug*, 3 (1974), pp. 152–58.

41 'De feodaliteit in Engeland van Willem de Veroveraar tot Magna Carta' (= Feudalism in England from William the Conqueror to Magna Carta), *Bijdragen en mededelingen betreffende de geschiedenis der Nederlanden*, 89 (1974), pp. 212–24.

42 'Clio en de menswetenschappen: Alma Mater en verloren zonen?'

(= Clio and the Humanities: Alma Mater and Prodigal Sons?), *Tijdschrift voor geschiedenis*, 87 (1974), pp. 321–29.

43 'Nieuwe biografie van Henri Pirenne: interview met Prof. B. Lyon' (= A New Biography of Henri Pirenne: An Interview with Prof. B. Lyon), *Spiegel historiael*, 9 (1974), pp. 532–37.

44 'Belgien: C. Geschichte', *Reallexikon der Germanischen Altertumskunde*, ii, 2/3 (Berlin and New York, 1974), pp. 227–32.

45 'Ghent and Bruges, History of', *Encyclopaedia Britannica* (1974).

46 'Philippe d'Alsace, comte de Flandre et législateur', *Actes des journées du Néerlandais organisées . . . à l'occasion du 25e anniversaire de l'introduction des études néerlandaises . . .* (Lille, 1976), pp. 79–96.

47 'In memoriam Prof. Dr. H. van Werveke (1898–1974)', *Bijdragen en mededelingen betreffende de geschiedenis der Nederlanden*, 90 (1975), pp. 80–83.

48 'De middeleeuwse vorstendommen' (= The Medieval Principalities) [in collaboration with R. van Uytven and J. Buntinx], *Vlaanderens Roem* (Brussels, 1975), pp. 28–54.

49 'Public Prosecution of Crime in Twelfth-Century England', *Church and Government in the Middle Ages: Essays Presented to C.R. Cheney*, ed. C.N.L. Brooke et al. (Cambridge, 1976), pp. 41–76.

50 'Le problème des chartes de libertés', *Album E. Malyusz* (Brussels, 1976), pp. 3–15.

51 'De Pacificatie van Gent (1576–1976)' (= The Pacification of Ghent), ed. J. Decavele, *Eenheid en scheiding in de Nederlanden, 1555–1585* (Ghent, 1976), pp. 13–17 (*Handelingen der Maatschappij voor Geschiedenis en Oudheidkunde te Gent*, new series, 30 (1976), pp. 3–7).

52 'Procédure civile anglaise et continentale: problèmes de périodisation', *La formazione storica del diritto moderno in Europa*, i (Florence, 1977), pp. 149–56.

53 'Kritische uitgave van de "Grote Keure" van Filips van de Elzas, graaf van Vlaanderen, voor Gent en Brugge (1165–1177)' (= Critical Edition of the "Great Charter" of Philip of Alsace, Count of Flanders, for Ghent and Bruges (1165–1177)) [in collaboration with L. Milis], *Handelingen van de Koninklijke Commissie voor Geschiedenis*, 143 (1977), pp. 207–57.

54 'De Gentse Februari-Opstand van het jaar 1128' (= The Ghent Revolt of February 1128), *Spiegel historiael*, 13 (1978), pp. 478–83.

55 'La tradition juridique en tant que limite aux réformes du droit', *Rapports belges au Xe congrès international de droit comparé: Budapest, 23–28 août 1978* (Brussels, 1978), pp. 11–35.

56 'In memoriam Prof. Dr. L. Th. Maes', *Rechtskundig weekblad*, 42 (17 February 1979), columns 1676–77.

57 'Kritische uitgave van de "Precepta" van graaf Filips van de Elzas voor de stad Gent (1178)' [in collaboration with L. Milis] (= Critical Edition of the "Precepta" of Count Philip of Alsace for the Town of Ghent (1178)), *Handelingen van de Maatschappij voor Geschiedenis en Oudheidkunde te Gent*, new series, 33 (1979), pp. 99–116.

58 Preface to: ed. G. Peeters, *België, een verhaal over land en volk* (= Belgium: A Story about Country and People) (Brussels, 1980).

59 'Das Recht im Mittelalter', ed. W. Fikentscher, H. Franke and O. Köhler, *Entstehung und Wandel Rechtlicher Traditionen* (Freiburg and Munich, 1980), pp. 609–67 (Veröffentlichungen des Instituts für Historische Anthropologie, 2).

60 'Common Law: una deviazione dal modello europeo', *Studi Senesi*, 92 (1980), pp. 55–77.

61 'De bronnen voor de staatsrechtsgeschiedenis: enkele overwegingen' (= The Sources of State Law History: Some Considerations), *Verslagen en mededelingen van de Stichting tot Uitgaaf der Bronnen van het Oud-Vaderlandse Recht*, new series, 2 (Zutphen, 1980), pp. 69–80.

62 'Slotbeschouwing' (= Epilogue), *Apologie van Willem van Oranje* (= Apology of William of Orange) (Tielt, 1980), pp. 83–93.

63 'Law in the Medieval World', *Tijdschrift voor rechtsgeschiedenis*, 49 (1981), pp. 13–46 (= translation of no. 59).

64 'In memoriam F.L. Ganshof (1895–1980)', *Tijdschrift voor rechtsgeschiedenis*, 49 (1981), pp. 5–12.

65 'Recht en politiek: De "Precepta" van graaf Filips van de Elzas voor de stad Gent uit het jaar 1178' (= Law and Politics: The "Precepta" of Count Philip of Alsace for the Town of Ghent in the Year 1178), *Recht en instellingen in de Oude Nederlanden tijdens de middeleeuwen en de nieuwe tijd: Liber amicorum Jan Buntinx* (Leuven, 1981), pp. 51–62 (Symbolae facultatis litterarum et philosophiae Lovaniensis, series A, vol. 10).

66 'In memoriam J. Van Rompaey, 1935–1981', *Tijdschrift voor rechtsgeschiedenis*, 49 (1981), pp. 431–32.

67 'Edition critique des versions françaises de la "Grande Keure" de Philippe d'Alsace, comte de Flandre, pour la ville d'Ypres' [in collaboration with L. Milis], *Bulletin de la Commission Royale d'Histoire*, 147 (1981), p. 1–44.

68 Concluding lecture, ed. J.D. Janssens, *Hoofsheid en devotie in de*

middeleeuwse maatschappij: de Nederlanden van de 12e tot de 15e eeuw (= Chivalrous Ideals and Religious Feeling) (Brussels, 1982), pp. 240–59 (Handelingen van het wetenschappelijk colloquium te Brussel, 21–24 Oktober 1981).

69 'De keure van Sint-Omaars van 1127' (= The Borough Charter of Saint-Omer of 1127), *Tijdschrift voor rechtsgeschiedenis*, 50 (1982), pp. 253–62.

70 Reflections on the Place of the Low Countries in European Legal History', *Festschrift für Helmut Coing*, i (Munich, 1982), pp. 3–17.

71 'In memoriam F.L. Ganshof (met Bibliografie)' (= In Memoriam F.L. Ganshof (with Bibliography)), *Jaarboek 1980 [van de] Koninklijke Academie voor Wetenschappen, Letteren en Schone Kunsten van België, 42e jaar* (Brussels, 1982), pp. 231–51.

72 'Inleiding' (= Introduction) [with H.P.H. Jansen], *Algemene geschiedenis der Nederlanden*, ii (Haarlem, 1982), pp. 9–16.

73 'Beschouwingen bij de geschiedenis van Engeland' (= Reflections on the History of England), *Mededelingen van de Koninklijke Academie voor Wetenschappen, Letteren en Schone Kunsten van België, academiae analecta*, 44 (1982), pp. 53–71.

74 'Oud recht, goed recht?' (= Old Law, Good Law?), *Hulde aan René Dekkers* (Brussels, 1982), pp. 153–65.

75 'Criminal Law in England and Flanders under King Henry II and Count Philip of Alsace', *Diritto e potere nella storia Europea: atti in onore di Bruno Paradisi. Quarto congresso internazionale della Società Italiana di Storia del Diritto*, i (Florence, 1982), pp. 232–54.

76 'Skriptinterview', *Skript: historisch tijdschrift*, 5 (1983), pp. 14–23.

77 'Punctuatie-perikelen in het polyptiek van de St. Bertijnsabdij' (= Punctuation Problems in the Polyptych of the Abbey of Saint-Bertin), *Pascua mediaevalia: studies voor Prof. Dr. J.M. De Smet* (Leuven, 1983), pp. 510–17 (Mediaevalia Lovaniensia, series I, studia B, x).

78 'Het charter van graaf Gwijde van Dampierre over de Gentse rechtspraak (10 juli 1294)' (= The Charter of Count Guy of Dampierre concerning the Jurisdiction of Ghent, 10 July 1294), *Handelingen van de Koninklijke Commissie voor Geschiedenis*, 150 (1984), pp. 415–36.

79 'Egied-Idesbald Strubbe, 1897–1970', *Handelingen van de Koninklijke Commissie voor Geschiedenis*, 150 (1984), pp. 135–42.

80 'Willem de Zwijger en de opstand der Nederlanden: een proeve van plaatsbepaling' (= William the Silent and the Revolt of the

Netherlands: An Attempt to Define their Place in History), *Herdenking Willem van Oranje, 1584–1984, Brussel, Paleis der Academiën 12 oktober 1984* (Brussels, 1985), pp. 43–54.

81 'De mediëvistiek in de 20ste eeuw' (= The Middle Ages in Twentieth-Century Historiography), ed. H.B. Teunis and L. Van Tongerloo, *Middeleeuwen tussen Erasmus en Heden: bundel aangeboden aan Prof. Dr. F.W.N. Hugenholtz* (Amsterdam, 1986), pp. 107–20.

82 'Inleiding' (= Introduction), *Handelingen IXe Nederlands-Belgisch rechtshistorisch congres. "Rondom Feenstra". Zaterdag 2 november 1985* (Leiden, 1986), pp. 1–7.

83 'Slotwoord' (= Summary) van het colloquium *Hekserij in de Nederlanden* (= Witchcraft in the Low Countries), *Standen en landen*, 86 (1987), p. 203–16.

84 'Henri Pirenne: een evaluatie naar aanleiding van de honderdste verjaardag van zijn benoeming te Gent' (= Henri Pirenne: Medievalist and Historian of Belgium), *Mededelingen van de Koninklijke Academie voor Wetenschappen, Letteren en Schone Kunsten van België, academiae analecta, Klasse der Letteren*, 49 (1987), pp. 85–105.

85 'F.L. Ganshof', *Nationaal biografisch woordenboek*, xii (Brussels, 1987), columns 263–73.

86 'Government, Law and Society', ed. J.H. Burns, *The Cambridge History of Medieval Political Thought, c. 350–c. 1450* (Cambridge, 1988; paperback, 1991), pp. 174–210.

87 'De Gentse justitiekeure van 1294: een commentaar' (= The Borough Charter of Ghent of A.D. 1294 on the Administration of Justice: A Commentary), *Liber amicorum Achiel De Vos* (Evergem, 1989), pp. 189–95.

88 'Galbert of Bruges on Serfdom, Prosecution of Crime, and Constitutionalism', ed. B.S. Bachrach and D. Nicholas, *Law, Custom, and the Social Fabric in Medieval Europe: Essays in Honor of Bryce Lyon*, pp. 89–112 (Kalamazoo and Michigan, 1990) (Studies in Medieval Culture, 28).

89 'Reflexions on Rational and Irrational Modes of Proof in Medieval Europe', *Legal History Review*, 58 (1990), p. 263–79.

90 'Orderic Vitalis and the Criminal Law', ed. F. Stevens and D. Van Den Auweele, *Xenia iuris historiae G. van Dievoet oblata* (Leuven, 1990), pp. 561–72.

91 'De Rechtsstaat: een Europese verworvenheid', ed. M. Storme, *Recht en macht: Colloquium Koninklijke Academie voor Wetenschappen, Letteren en Schone Kunsten, Brussel, 16 dec. 1988* (Brussels, 1990), pp. 269–77.

92 'Réflexions historiques sur l'état de droit', *La sistematica giuridica, storia, teoria e problemi attuali: atti del convegno internazionale, Roma, 1–5 aprile 1986* (Rome, 1991), p. 239–51 (Biblioteca internazionale di cultura, 22).

93 'De Vrede van Gent van 1814', *Handelingen Maatschappij voor Geschiedenis en Oudheidkunde te Gent*, new series, 44 (1990), pp. 7–12.

94 'La peine: exposé introductif', *La peine*, i, *Antiquité* (Brussels, 1991), pp. 9–20 (Recueils de la Société Jean Bodin, 55).

95 'La peine dans les anciens Pays-Bas (12e–17e s.)', *La peine*, ii, *Europe avant le XVIIIe siècle* (Brussels, 1991), pp. 117–141 (Recueils de la Société Jean Bodin, 56).

96 'Historical and Modern Confrontations between Continental and English Law', ed. B. De Witte and C. Forder, *The Common Law of Europe and the Future of Legal Education* (Deventer, 1992), pp. 621–38.

97 'Democratie en rechtsstaat in het twaalfde-eeuwse graafschap Vlaanderen', *Tijdschrift voor rechtsgeschiedenis*, 61 (1993), pp. 205–15.

98 'Lawyers and Holy Books', *Index quaderni camerti di studi romanistici. International Survey of Roman Law*, 22 (1994), pp. 419–31 (= Omaggio a Peter Stein).

1
History and Experiment

In the humanities all disciplines are now historical. Making use of the enormous amount of factual material uncovered by archaeologists and historians, all students now see their respective fields in a historical perspective. It is generally recognized that such great classic disciplines as theology, philosophy, law and philology acquired a historical dimension under the impact of nineteenth-century ideas on evolution and progress. Younger social sciences also pay tribute to the historical approach. I refer to the cyclical theories of the economists, who continually push the frontiers of their research further back into the past. Similarly the sociology of Max Weber, who started as a historian, is steeped in the study of past civilizations.[1] Even the most recent sociology stresses the importance of history.[2] The interest of modern psychology in historical research is considerable, and various attempts at a historical approach have been undertaken by psychologists and psychiatrists. I refer, for instance, to the celebrated books of the neurologist and professor at Leiden J.H. van den Berg, *Metabletica of leer der veranderingen: beginselen van een historische psychologie* (Nijkerk, 1957) and *Het menselijk lichaam: een metabletisch onderzoek* (Nijkerk, 1959), and to the recent book *Waanzin in de middeleeuwen* (Nijkerk, 1969) by the psychiatrist H.H. Beek. It is somewhat surprising that some people even forecast that modern logic will become more historical.[3] However, nothing should sur-

---

[1] See his doctoral dissertation *Zur Geschichte der Handelsgesellschaften im Mittelalter* of 1889. His dissertation for the habilitation concerned the legal history of Antiquity: 'Die römische Agrargeschichte in ihrer Bedeutung für das Staats-und Privatrecht' (Heidelberg, 1891).

[2] See an appeal for more historical interest among sociologists in R.A. Nisbett, *Social Change and History: Aspects of the Western Theory of Development* (New York, 1969), with the justification that social reality is history. N. Elias, *Sociologie en geschiedenis en andere essays* (Amsterdam, 1971), p. 79, speaks of sociologists in the nineteenth-century industrial countries who 'looked for a confirmation of their wishes and expectations by studying the direction and the driving forces of social development until then'; on p. 58 he speaks of the 'addition of a sociological dimension, by which the science of history could obtain a "continuous advance"'.

[3] Thus S. Toulmin, *The Uses of Argument* (Cambridge, 1958), p. 257: 'Not only will logic have to become more empirical, it will inevitably tend to become more historical'; cf. D.H. Fischer, *Historians' Fallacies: Toward a Logic of Historical Thought* (London, 1971), p. ix.

prise us any more, as even outside the framework of the familiar humanities historical research is being carried out. An instance is the historical work of the Oxford professor and biologist C.D. Darlington, published in 1969 under the title *The Evolution of Man and Society*, a book based on research by biologists, anthropologists, archaeologists and even ordinary historians.

The professional historian cannot fail to be flattered by this enormous success among so many disciplines, but it cannot escape his notice that it contains certain risks. Economists, linguists, jurists and many other scholars practise history not for its own sake but for the advancement of their own science, in order to obtain a more exact and deeper insight into economic, linguistic, legal and other problems. It is understandable that the economist who studies the present-day Gross National Product, and the factors on which it is based, wonders how this G.N.P. reached its present size and how it developed in the course of the years. Thus he naturally places his economic analysis in an historical perspective and may even draw a graph of the G.N.P. going back a few centuries. This might be a positive gain for our historical knowledge but is mainly, from the economist's point of view, done to enhance the study of economic expansion and cycles.

Similarly, the lawyer wonders what is the meaning and origin of a particular, somewhat puzzling, article of the civil code. He wants to know when the rule was first formulated, in what circumstances and for what purpose. He starts enquiring and, from jurist to jurist or from case to case, delves ever deeper into the past, as if he were composing his genealogy and constantly discovering new ancestors. But, however far our scholar goes back, he remains a lawyer, his aim is to reach a better understanding of a juridical concept or to solve an anomaly in the code. A classic example of this form of research is afforded by the article which the leading lawyer and legal historian E.M. Meijers devoted in 1907, as a young barrister, to art. 584 of the Dutch Civil Code of 1838.[4] Meijers had been struck, like others before him, by the quaint enumeration of six real rights in art. 584, while there clearly were others which, for some obscure reason, had been left out (such as right of surface, emphyteusis, tithes and ground rent). Lawyers used to explain away the problem by guessing that the lawgiver had suffered from diminished consciousness when he drafted the guilty article: 'it happened by chance rather than with a clear understanding of what was being done' Meijers was dissatisfied with this facile explanation and wanted to find out what had really happened. He discovered that history, and history alone, could explain the anomaly of art. 584: it stemmed, via the several authors and drafts of codes analysed by Meijers, from a doctoral dissertation submitted in 1639 at Helmstädt by Heinrich Hahn under the title *De jure rerum et juris in re speciebus* – a dissertation which remained influential until

---

[4] 'Art. 584 B.W. en de zakelijke rechten', *Rechtsgeleerd magazijn: tijdschrift voor binnen- en buitenlandse rechtsstudie*, 26 (1907), pp. 271-99.

well into the nineteenth century, a rather surprising distinction for that sort of publication.[5]

In such cases we are confronted not with history, properly speaking, but with economics or jurisprudence with an historical dimension, in other words historical economics, historical jurisprudence, historical psychology and so on. The great success which these specializations enjoy nowadays is undeniable. Their names are also changing in a typical way: historical economics, historical econometrics or even historiometrics instead of economic history, and history as 'une économétrie et une sociométrie rétrospectives',[6] and instead of historical geography scholars now talk of 'retrospective human geography'. In this same vein one could speak of a retrospective science of the press or retrospective politics, and historic psychology rather than psychological history (this is more than a quibble about words).[7]

If this tendency continues there may soon be a moment when all aspects of social life will be studied in their historical dimension by sociologists, economists, psychologists and jurists. We will then have historical economics, historical psychology, historical jurisprudence and historical linguistics, practised by economists, psychologists, jurists and linguists with an interest in history or at least the historic dimension of their craft. They will be equipped with the scientific techniques and terminology of their respective disciplines, all of which no individual historian could master or even apprehend, so that he will be unable to equal the technical quality of their work,[8] or even to assimilate and appreciate it.

What will be left for us, 'ordinary' historians to do? Shall we still be needed, or will every discipline have absorbed so much history that history itself will explode and Clio, after many centuries of obedient service, be dismissed? Will historians be offered a pension if they are willing to give up their craft, like some farmers in the European Community? Or might only a few ancillary sciences be left for us unfortunate historians – such as the tracing, classifying and editing of old documents – so that we will be no more than 'de simples auxiliaires des sciences juridiques, politiques ou économi-

---

[5] Hahn distinguished five real rights: *dominium, pignus, servitus, possessio* and *hereditas*; in art. 584 a sixth was added, at a late stage, i.e. usufruct. The latter is not introduced by the term 'right', as are the other five, an anomaly of drafting which was also explained by Meijers's discovery.

[6] R. Marx, *L'Angleterre des révolutions: courants et monuments* (Paris, 1971), pp. 14-15: 'A l'heure présente, des historiens économistes, tels Ph. Deane et W. Cole en Angleterre, et des économistes purs s'efforcent de pratiquer une économétrie et une sociométrie rétrospectives et de reconstituer, à partir des données partielles et en s'inspirant du connu, des tableaux statistiques relatifs à des périodes de plus en plus anciennes.'

[7] See my article 'Psychologische geschiedenis', *Tijdschrift voor geschiedenis*, 78 (1965), pp. 129-49.

[8] There will hardly be a historian who could improve on the historical work of the economist Tinbergen, in his *Business Cycles in the United Kingdom, 1870-1914* (Amsterdam, 1951).

ques'?[9] Might this be 'the end of history'?[10] A remarkable work by Hedemann on nineteenth-century private law demonstrates, for example, how some jurists visualize legal history exclusively in an ancillary role.[11] Legal history, according to him, should not concern itself with the distant past, which is of academic interest only. What are the Egyptian papyri to us? The bridges between the law of Antiquity and that of the twentieth century have been blown up: 'die mächtigen Tagesfragen die uns heute bewegen, werden nicht aus den Papyri gelöst'. Legal history that starts in Antiquity or the middle ages is out; the present should be our vantage-point. We must, Hedemann concludes: 'von der Gegenwart aus zurückbauen' in order to provide young twentieth-century law with a credible historical foundation (pp. vii-viii).

Even though I have not conjured up this phantom crisis of historiography without good reason, I believe that much important work still remains to be done by an autonomous historical discipline, if Clio goes on believing in her own aim and method and avoids running after various other disciplines and trying to put other people's feathers in her cap.[12] There are two essential functions I would like to mention.

It will, firstly, remain the task of history to describe the events of the past in the direction in which they occurred, i.e. proceeding from the past to the present. History did not move backwards, like crabs do, retreating from the present to the past. Taking the present as a starting-point in order to follow in the past one line of development is in fact unhistorical, as it creates the illusion that the past was directed towards the present; it closes the eyes to the innumerable other roads which history could have taken, and to the fact that the present result is no final achievement and often not even intended or pursued by our ancestors.

Secondly, the historian's role will become more important as more specialized studies are published by non-historians on diverse aspects of the past. It will be the historian's task to produce a synthesis of these specializations and their results, to shape them into a general picture of society and to interpret it. It will be his task to weigh the roles of the numerous material, psychological, institutional and religious elements (on which so many specialists concentrate and for which they may claim precedence) and to order them into a comprehensive survey. It is indeed possible to analyse these elements separately, but they have not occurred separately. We can read on the doors of our seminar rooms 'economic history' or 'legal history', but these are no more than educational devices and artificial divisions by which we separate

---

[9] A. Demichel, 'Plaidoyer pour l'histoire', *Mélanges L. Falletti* (Paris, 1971), p. 100.
[10] See some variations on this theme in H. Lefebvre, *La fin de l'histoire* (Paris, 1970).
[11] J.W. Hedemann, *Die Fortschritte des Zivilrechts im XIX Jahrhundert: Ein Überblick über die Entfaltung des Privatrechts in Deutschland, Österreich, Frankreich und der Schweiz* (Berlin, 1910).
[12] See the noteworthy, although somewhat extreme position of R. Cobb, 'Historians in White Coats', *Times Literary Supplement* (3 Dec. 1971), pp. 1527-28.

what was in reality closely linked. The past must be studied by scholars who are trained to comprehend in a panoramic survey the most diverse phenomena of a given period: to think synchronically and not only diachronically.

It is also necessary to trace causal relations between these phenomena: the impact of the Protestant ethic on modern capitalism is not simply a econometric problem. Of course, the historian can restrict himself to a descriptive approach, collecting and neatly classifying in a chronological order important and less important facts such as 'the knights of the Golden Fleece held a banquet here' or 'Queen Victoria slept here' and other bits of information which are showered upon the visitors to historic mansions. This is how the careful Linnaeus classified the species of the biosphere, without entering upon the question of their origin and evolution. This antiquarian approach, however, does not satisfy the historian, who aims at some form of generalization.[13] He wants to see causal connections, trace factors, explain as well as describe: he not only wants to identify the parts of a clock, he wants to know what makes it tick. This curiosity entails risks: the more complex and interesting a historical problem, the smaller the degree of certainty will be. We know with certainty when the battle of Waterloo took place, but we will never know with that sort of certainty why Nazism triumphed in Germany in the thirties. The scholar who demands absolute certainty condemns himself to studying the least important and least interesting problems, something for which few historians can muster enthusiasm. On the contrary, their ambition is usually to discover the causes that explain the complex growth of our society.

This leads us to problems of method. Practising historians seldom write on the method of their craft: they often are content just to practise it. After all, few creative artists have felt an urge to expatiate on the methodology of painting or building, and Gottfried Hermann (1772-1848) even maintained that 'wer nichts über die Sache versteht, schreibt über die Methode'.[14] If, nevertheless, by way of exception, I venture here on the path of the theory of history, it is only to try and help historians to situate their discipline correctly. Amongst the characteristics of the scientific method we find, besides objectivity, precision, controllability and communicability, the use of

---

[13] See the remark in H. Poincaré, *La science et l'hypothèse* (Paris, 1935), p. 168 on *Einmaligkeit* and the historian: 'Carlyle a écrit "Le fait seul importe: Jean sans Terre a passé par ici, voilà ce qui est admirable, voilà une réalité pour laquelle je donnerais toutes les théories du monde". Carlyle était un compatriote de Bacon, mais Bacon n'aurait pas dit cela. C'est là le langage de l'historien. Le physicien dirait plutôt: "Jean sans Terre a passé par ici; cela m'est bien égal, puisqu'il n'y repassera pas"'. P. Veyne, 'Contestation de la Sociologie', *Diogène*, 75 (1971), p. 19 writes: 'Il demeure qu'histoire et sociologie sont sur le même plan: mieux encore, l'histoire n'est qu'un cas particulier de la sociologie générale', referring to his *Comment on écrit l'histoire: essai d'epistémologie* (Paris, 1971). Just as Poincaré, he quotes Carlyle's saying and takes it as the starting point of his discussion.

[14] Quoted in H. Fuhrmann, 'Die Sorge um den rechten Text', *Deutsches Archiv*, 25 (1969), p. 13.

the (repeatable) experiment. Systematic experimentation slowly developed in the late middle ages and became generally accepted in modern times. It is a scientific technique in which the researcher does not restrict himself to the observation of what nature happens to produce, but creates by a conscious intervention a situation where one particular element is added or eliminated (the 'complicating factor') in order to discover or to demonstrate which role the factor in question plays or does not play. An experiment is therefore different from an experience, which is something one has gone through or observed (but observed without deliberate conditioning). In his remarkable history of modern biology F. Jacob has shown that the transition from pure observation to active experiment only took place in that discipline in the middle of the nineteenth century. As he puts it: 'Jusqu'au milieu du XIXe siècle on observait les êtres vivants, mais on ne cherchait guère à en déranger l'ordonnance pour l'analyser . . . Seuls les physiologistes intervenaient parfois pour modifier délibérément les conditions de vie et observer les effets produits.' Things changed, however, and there was 'non plus une physiologie d'observation, mettant en jeu ce que Claude Bernard appelle une "expérimentation passive", où le biologiste se borne à constater les variations . . . , mais une science "active" où l'expérimentateur intervient directement, prélève un organe, l'isole, le fait fonctionner, change les conditions, analyse les variables'.[15]

This experimental method, so fundamental to the natural sciences, is closed to historians because of the very nature of their object: the past. Bygones are bygones: we cannot resuscitate the past, adding or eliminating a factor selected by way of experiment. We cannot produce a fourteenth-century Flanders without the Van Arteveldes. We cannot even establish – to cite a more recent example – how Dutch public opinion would have reacted in the past to a certain poster, which is now received with as much indifference as it would probably then have led to a scandalized outcry.[16] It is a great pity, but there is nothing we can do about it. As Woolman put it: 'The most reliable and precise method is controlled experimentation; the historian, however, is at a definite methodological disadvantage in comparison with other research workers' (some disciplines, however, such as astronomy and

---

[15] F. Jacob, *La logique du vivant: une histoire de l'hérédité* (Paris, 1970), pp. 198-99. Whereas in English and Dutch there is no confusion between experience and experiment, the French word *expérience* is sometimes used in one sense and sometimes in the other.

[16] See the amusing remarks in I. Schöffer, 'Nieuwe methoden in de geschiedkundige wetenschappen', *Handelingen v.h. 28e Vlaams Filologencongres* (Leuven, 1971), p. 64: 'We cannot, as happens in the natural sciences, repeat in an experiment all that happened now, replaced in an identical surrounding as existed five years ago; in other words, show by the experimental method the effect of the poster if it had been put up five years ago.' One could compare this with Deutscher's example (in connection with a polemic against Trotsky): 'the historian cannot re-enact the revolution, keep Lenin out of the spectacle, and see what happens', quoted in C. Hill, 'The Theory of Revolutions', *Isaac Deutscher: The Man and his Work*, ed. D. Horowitz (London, 1971), pp. 25-26.

ethnology, are in the same situation). 'Historical time', Woolman continues, 'knows no mercy, whatever happened happened once and does not exist any longer – obviously history is not an experimental science'.[17] Another author complains similarly: 'We are not able to confirm a hypothesis that a given event occurred as the outcome of another specified event, or set of events, by making an experiment under laboratory conditions.'[18]

Such, nevertheless, is the fascination of the experiment that historians – consciously or not – try to find a substitute, an *Ersatz*. They use a method which could be described as quasi-experimental, but is in fact based on comparison. Whereas the historian cannot create a situation by adding or eliminating certain elements, he looks for comparable situations in the past or the present where a particular element occurs or is missing. The historian who wants to examine the cause of a certain evolution looks for an analogous one (in another country and/or period), where the essential ingredients are similar, except for a single factor. The latter's absence in a similar situation eliminates it as the causal factor. Inversely, the presence of the same factor in different situations proves that it cannot have played a determinant role.[19]

Let us select some examples of similar phenomena where a particular factor is present in one case and absent in another. We note in western civilization an attitude towards sex which can be described as one of rejection and repression; it seems to have culminated in the nineteenth century, to the extent that the qualification of an 'antisexual syndrome' has been used. How can this be explained? Is it, as Van Ussel believes, all the fault of the bourgeoisie, which did indeed reach the summit of their power in that century and undoubtedly played an important role in European

---

[17] B.B. Woolman, 'Sense and Nonsense in History', *The Psychoanalytic Interpretation of History*, ed. B.B. Woolman (New York, 1971), pp. 81-82.

[18] P. Gardiner, *The Nature of Historical Explanation* (Oxford, 1952), p. 40. Cf. R.C. Van Caenegem, 'De moderne geschiedschrijving: een wetenschap zonder experiment', pp. 91-103, in this volume: 'Modern Historiography: A Science without Experiment', p. 15. Compare this with the following opinion of C. Hill: 'Analogies and historical parallels are the nearest the historian can get to *laboratory experiment*: his problem is to be sure that he is comparing comparable phenomena, so that the *variables* can be usefully analysed' (Hill, 'The Theory of Revolutions', p. 116).

[19] A recent article describes Max Weber's method as follows: 'On sait que, pour Weber, si l'on veut démontrer l'efficacité causale d'un antécédent, il faut supposer que cet antécédent n'a pas existé ou a été différent, et imaginer alors l'évolution possible. La comparaison de cette évolution irréelle avec le cours réel des événements permet de savoir si l'élément antécédent, que l'on a éliminé ou modifié par la pensée, a été une des causes du phénomène étudié ou plutôt une des causes des caractéristiques que l'on retient de ce phénomène construit comme "individu historique". S'agissant de l'efficacité causale de l'éthique protestante dans le développement du capitalisme moderne, la méthode comparative fournit à Weber un *substitut de cette expérimentation mentale* . . . Le régime économique capitaliste ne s'est développé qu'en Occident malgré la présence dans d'autres civilisations de nombreuses conditions nécessaires à ce développement'. Ph. Bernard, *Protestantisme et capitalisme: La controverse post-wébérienne* (Paris, 1970), pp. 19-20.

history?[20] In order to verify this hypothesis we look for comparable civilizations, with a similar anti-libertine, sexually strict tradition, which we find, *inter alia*, in Russia, both before and after 1917 (with a brief period of relaxation in the years immediately after the October Revolution). As the bourgeoisie has played a minor role in historic Russia and as Soviet society, which is anything but libertine, is markedly anti-bourgeois, it is at once clear that the bourgeoisie cannot be held responsible for the aforementioned puritan strain in western civilization. Other factors, such as Christianity, conservatism and stern forms of government claim our attention as possible explanations.[21]

Another example is afforded by Max Weber's thesis that modern capitalist entrepreneurship stems from the religious tenets of the Calvinists.[22] Gerschenkron studied a comparable phenomenon in the Russian *Raskolniki* or Old Believers, an heterodox religious community which played an important entrepreneurial role in Russian economy, comparable to that of their puritan colleagues in the West, although the substance of their religious doctrine was not in accord with their economic activity. The conclusion must be that it is not their specific religious convictions which explains the importance of the Calvinists. The fact is that deviant social groups, living as it were in the margin of their communities, are pushed into a specific economic role, not because of their beliefs but because they are a distinctive section of society.[23]

---

[20] J.M.W. Van Ussel, *Geschiedenis van het seksuele probleem* (Meppel, 1968).

[21] I owe thanks to Dr. H. De Ridder-Symoens and Dr. C. De Maegd-Soëp, who very kindly provided me with information on this point. See some remarks on prudishness in Soviet society in A. Gerschenkron, *Economic Backwardness in Historical Perspective* (Cambridge, MA, 1962), pp. 318, 331ff. More data in K. Geiger, 'The Family and Social Change', E.C. Black, *The Transformation of Russian Society* (Cambridge, MA, 1960), pp. 458ff.; R. Schlesinger, *The Family in the U.S.S.R.* (London, 1949); K. Mehnert, 'Changing Attitudes of Russian Youth', Black (ed.), *The Transformation of Russian Society*, pp. 513ff.; P. Sorlin, *La société soviétique, 1917-1964* (Paris, 1964), pp. 98ff.

[22] For a recent survey of the controversy surrounding the 'Weber thesis', see the introduction and collection of texts in Besnard, *Protestantisme et capitalisme*, and W.G. Runciman, *A Critique of Max Weber's Philosophy of Social Science* (Cambridge, 1972). An excellent presentation of Weber's historical vision can be found in G. Abramowski, *Das Geschichtsbild Max Webers: Universalgeschichte am Leitfaden des Oczidentalen Rationalisierungsprozesses* (Stuttgart, 1964), with particular attention for the rise of the *rationale Verfassungs- und Verwaltungsstaat* as a unique western contribution, and with a description of Weber's work as 'soziologisch-typologische Geschichtsschreibung'.

[23] A. Gerschenkron, *Europe in the Russian Mirror: Four Lectures in Economic History* (Cambridge, 1970), pp. 17ff., esp. p. 37: 'Thus the Old-Believing entrepreneur on the whole did reveal traits which Max Weber was willing to regard as the specific capitalist spirit . . . But the fount and origin of this value system cannot be found in his religious tenets. It stems with great clarity from the specific social position of the group of which he was a member. In fact, the religious teachings were contrary to the motivations which kept transforming Old-Believing serf peasants into successful entrepreneurs.' See also on these *raskolniki*: P. Pascal, *Avvakum et les débuts du raskol* (1938); V. Pleyer, *Das russische Altgläubigentum* (1961) and P. Hauptman,

Continued

Another example is provided by the work of the medievalist Herlihy, who found that in certain areas, such as Brittany, Wales and Scotland, the solidarity of the family group was exceptionally strong. He explains this by the pastoral way of life of these peoples, herdsmen being particularly dependent on the protection of kinship. I believe, however, that a comparison with medieval Flanders shows the weakness of this interpretation: scholars who are familiar with medieval Flemish law know how exceptionally strong were the ties of kinship, yet Flanders was not a country of herdsmen or cattle-breeders but of arable farming with a high degree of urbanization and industrialization.[24]

The aforementioned economist Gerschenkron scrutinized the nineteenth-century hypothesis that an initial accumulation of private capital was an essential precondition of modern heavy industry.[25] Such an accumulation was indeed present in eighteenth-century England, yet Gerschenkron found that in Russia it was not accumulated private wealth but public money, obtained by taxation, which provided the necessary initial capital. According to Gerschenkron this was a substitute for private capital, but one could equally maintain that private capital was a substitute for lacking state funding, as there is no intrinsic reason why private and not state industrialization should be the norm. The Russian experiment is proof to the contrary and makes clear that accumulated private capital was no essential precondition for industrialization.

Gerschenkron used this same, quasi-experimental method in his study of mercantilism. Taking as his starting point the fact that England, the more economically developed country, displayed a smaller degree of mercantilism than France, he posed the question of a possible correlation between economic underdevelopment and mercantilism, in the sense that 'historically seen, the phenomenon of mercantilism can be usefully regarded as a function of the degree of economic backwardness of the countries concerned'.[26] By way of counter-experiment, a third country, Russia, was examined and it appeared indeed that, as expected, mercantilism was even stronger there than in France.[27]

The ups and downs of serfdom are one of the fundamental themes of European history. Slicher van Bath devoted to this phenomenon a very

---

Continued
Altrussischer Glaube (1963). I refer to Gerschenkron's study to illustrate a particular method without making any pronouncement on the substance of the question: the 'Weber thesis' is too complex for that. I would nevertheless like to remind the reader that Weber himself had noticed the general attraction of minorities towards economic activities, because of their exclusion from positions of politial influence: 'Die protestantische Ethik und der "Geist" des Kapitalismus', *Archiv für Sozialwissenschaft und Sozialpolitik*, 20 (1904), p. 38; cf. Besnard, *Protestantisme et capitalisme*, pp. 40-41.

[24] D. Herlihy, *The History of Feudalism* (London, New York, 1970), p. 68.
[25] A. Gerschenkron, *Economic Backwardness in Historical Perspective*, pp. 31-51.
[26] Idem, *Europe in the Russian Mirror*, p. 62.
[27] Ibid., pp. 62-96; idem, *Economic Backwardness*, pp. 5-30.

stimulating and well documented study.[28] The following general picture emerged from it, with due allowance for the generalization and simplification concomitant to the treatment of so complex a development. Between the twelfth and the sixteenth century freedom was gaining ground strongly in western Europe, whereas in central and eastern Europe the period from the fifteenth to the eighteenth century witnessed an increase of bondage, with a peak in the sixteenth and seventeenth. How can this finding be explained? Slicher van Bath subjected the question to a comparative examination, which may be cited as a model of the quasi-experimental method. As soon as in a given country a particular correlation and therefore a possible 'cause' appeared, he examined whether this factor was also present in other countries going through a similar development of bondage. By so doing he eliminated a number of 'factors', and incidentally indicated how inefficient the search for causes, limited to a single country, is bound to be. Could the evolution of the grain price be responsible for the increase in servitude? One could conceive a priori that rising prices would incite landowners to push for higher production, increase the workload of their peasants and worsen the conditions of bondage. Yet the opposite reasoning seems equally plausible, that lower grain prices forced landowners to increase production in order to keep their income intact. The paradoxical consequence is that 'Lütge sees both the high grain price of the fifteenth and sixteenth centuries and the low grain price of the second half of the seventeenth as an important factor in the worsening position of serfs'.[29] How could two opposing developments be responsible for the same 'consequence' and the same 'factor' lead to two opposite 'consequences'? Moreover, the secular rise of the grain price, which took place from the second half of the fifteenth to the first half of the seventeenth century and is blamed for the increase in serfdom in eastern Europe, had in western Europe in the twelfth and thirteenth centuries been accompanied by a striking increase of freedom. Numerous historians, particularly in eastern Germany and Poland, have explained the increase in bondage and the strengthened position of the landowners by the fact that grain was produced for the export market – undoubtedly a key element in the economy of these countries. Yet for this market theory a comparison with other countries is also fatal: in Russia, Hungary and Bohemia the factor of 'massive export of grain to the west' did not play a role and nevertheless the same worsening of the peasants' lot can be observed there. Some scholars have found the answer in the changing position of the nobility, whose military role was taken over by mercenary armies and who therefore paid more attention to the exploitation of their manors and peasants. But in western Europe also, in the twelfth and following centuries, the old military role of the armies of feudal knights was reduced and that of mercenaries

---

[28] B.H. Slicher van Bath, 'Vrijheid en lijfeigenschap in agrarisch Europa (16de-18de eeuw)', *A.A.G. Bijdragen*, 15 (1970), pp. 75-100.
[29] Ibid., p. 85.

increased, without on the contrary any loss of freedom being involved. Could the weakening of the monarchy be to blame and the correlated strengthening of the nobility? Against this at first sight plausible theory one could point out that serfdom had increased under strong regimes, as in Bohemia after 1620 and in Russia under Peter the Great. If the results of this enquiry are rather negative,[30] they nevertheless show how tracing comparable situations where specific elements are absent can lead to fruitful conclusions, in any case to the elimination of a number of apparent 'factors'.[31]

The modern West is unique in world history and has produced unparalleled achievements in the most diverse fields. How this can be explained is one of the great historiographical problems of our time. A few years ago a book was published which tried to answer the question from an economic point of view. Its author examined what caused the unique technological and industrial rise of modern Europe. He more specifically wondered why this astonishing development had taken place in only one civilization (not counting less speedy imitations), and why precisely in the western and not in one of the other, older and in many ways better prepared civilizations of world importance.[32] His method could be called quasi-experimental in the sense that he time and again isolates one particular factor and looks for civilizations where that factor is also present (which eliminates it) or is absent, which indicates a possible explanation for specific western development. He formulates his twofold question as follows: why was Europe the first to experience the industrial revolution; and why has the latter taken place in Europe at all (p. 12)? He describes his method as follows: 'By holding Europe up against the mirror of the most advanced non-European societies, we should be able to discern some – surely not all – of the critical elements in her economic and technological precedence' (p. 15). This comparative and eliminatory method points at some specifically western factors, such as the importance of private enterprise, the value attached to the rational manipulation of man and nature, the presence of political and ecclesiastical powers vying with each other (in other words, the fragmentation of power instead of the monolithic domination of universal empires), legal and constitutional guarantees of personal liberty and ownership, the desire to master nature and the European inclination to learn and borrow from others. One will naturally question one or other of these specific

---

[30] The author finds, on a rather sceptical and disappointed note, that 'the same material was quoted both to explain the end of serfdom and its origin and worsening' (p. 95).

[31] See the review by P.R. Hyams, *English Historical Review*, 85 (1970), p. 608, of R.H. Hilton, *The Decline of Serfdom in Medieval England* (London, 1969). Hilton's explanation of the retreat of serfdom (the Black Death having strengthened the peasants' resistance against intenser exploitation) is hardly acceptable, as 'similar economic difficulties led to the hardening of servitude elsewhere'.

[32] D.S. Landes, *The Unbound Prometheus: Technological Change and Industrial Development in Western Europe from 1750 to the Present* (Cambridge, 1969).

western factors. I am, for example, far from convinced that 'there is good reason to believe that already in the middle ages, Europe was freer of superstition and more rational in behaviour than other parts of the world' (p. 22). More rational and freer of superstition than China? This is doubtful, to say the least, when one considers the general *diesseitige* attitude of the classical Chinese world and its high degree of scientific and technological attainment.[33] How one can explain that even in science western Europe eventually surpassed all other civilizations, including China, is the theme of studies by Dr. Needham.[34] Here again the search is on for factors that might explain the European pre-eminence. The latter is all the more surprising as China's eminent and old culture seemed in fact predestined to be the harbinger of modern science.[35] The author eliminates several factors, which were or are present in China as well as Europe (such as a moderate climate and innate intelligence), to which one might attach great importance if one limited one's horizon to Europe alone. It strikes me as revealing that the author, who was trained as a scientist, uses the terminology of the experimental method, in such phrases as: 'The comparison between China and Europe is particularly instructive, almost a test-bench experiment one might say, because the complicating factor of climatic conditions does not enter it.'[36]

Tracing up comparable situations demands patience. Instead of creating the required situations himself, as does a real experimentalist, the historian must look for analogies in the enormous and variegated treasure-house of human experience past and present, in the great cultures and elsewhere. There are tribes which live nowadays in some prehistoric phase and can be used as comparative material for past as well as present cultural stages. The historian here leaves the strict limits of his discipline in order better to understand and interpret his proper subject. He asks ethnologists and sociologists for a service in return for all they have borrowed from him. Fortunately the past is so immense and so thoroughly studied that the chance of finding comparable structures is excellent: see for example, the numerous feudalisms that have been discovered and compared with each other.[37] It is even conceivable that history, ethnology and sociology may one

---

[33] The author notes himself that numerous inventions 'came originally from China, which enjoyed at various times during the T'ang (618-907) and Sung (960-1279) dynasties the most advanced technology and economic organization in the world' (p. 27), a pre-eminence that seduced the Chinese into 'crippling self-sufficiency' (p. 28).

[34] Slicher van Bath, 'Vrijheid', p. 76 also poses the question whether the West-European history of peasant freedom is a 'deviation from a usual pattern'.

[35] J. Needham, *The Grand Titration: Science and Society in East and West* (London, 1969); idem, *Clerks and Craftsmen in China and the West: Lectures and Addresses on the History of Science and Technology*, (Cambridge, 1970). Dr. Needham's main work is, of course, his *Science and Civilisation in China*.

[36] Idem, *The Grand Titration*, p. 190.

[37] R. Coulborn, *Feudalism in History* (Princeton, 1956).

day come together into one comprehensive transdisciplinary anthropology, where man is studied in the past and the present, and in which certain antitheses, as economics versus history, may be reconciled in a higher synthesis.

It may reasonably be assumed that the quasi-experimental method offers practical opportunities. It is not really new, as it is based on observation and comparison, and on deductions made from that comparison.[38] As a method of isolating one particular factor, as in a real experiment, it sharpens the scholar's insight and demarcates the field of research more clearly. Instead of discussing possible factors within the horizon of only one country or one civilization, as often happens, the scholar looks elsewhere, and sometimes far afield, for his material. Instead of wondering – in a purely speculative way – what would have happened if certain factors had been absent ('counter-factual history'),[39] it is more fruitful to search for comparable situations which really existed: a more solid foundation of enquiry. The comparative approach of accepting or eliminating specific causal factors, the historian's quasi-experimental method, holds the possibility of interesting results. Historians should apply it more frequently.

---

[38] The comparative historical method is, however, still in its infancy and holds some disappointments for the reader. I refer to the fact that the volumes of the *Recueils de la Société Jean Bodin* all too often get no further than the juxtaposition of self-contained papers without any real comparison. I also refer to the recent book *The Economic Decline of Empires*, edited by C.M. Cipolla (London, 1970), which offers much less than its title promises and contains no stirring conclusions, based on thorough comparative research, on the causes of the economic decline of empires.

[39] Gerschenkron, *Europe in the Russian Mirror*, p. 127, speaks of 'history in the conditional mood'. In reality 'counterfactual history' is not so different from the traditional causal explanation: if I say 'the Black Death is the cause of the rise in wages' or 'if there had been no Black Death, wages would not have risen', I express exactly the same thing. Every explanation is, in a way, a form of 'counter-factual' reasoning.

2

Modern Historiography:
A Science without Experiment

In this essay I propose to examine the particular position in which historical research today finds itself. History is, of course, a fully-fledged scientific pursuit, with all the relevant formal characteristics and with a proper place in the circle of scientific disciplines, but, in contrast with many others, it does not use experiment as a technique of research.

I. Modern Historiography as a Science

The following characteristics give historical research a truly scientific character. They are all associated with science in general.

1. Precise observation and description of its object, the human past

As not the past itself, but testimonies about and relics of it are observed, we ought properly to speak of a reconstruction, as precise and accurate as possible, of the past on the basis of the available sources. Any shortcoming in certain elements has to be corrected by confrontation with others, so that the witnesses and material relics of various sorts lead with the greatest possible accuracy to one total picture.

2. The critical method

This entails the examination and definition of the value of the sources, and is carried out in function of two essential questions, namely 'what is the degree of information of which the witness disposed?' and 'what is his degree of reliability?' To this critical appraisal of the source as witness we should add the criticism of the tradition of the text, from the original or autograph product to the present (textual criticism).

3. Unprejudiced approach, objectivity

This is an attitude which precludes all polemical argument or defence of preconceived conceptions, theories on ideologies, or at most accepts them as hypothetical starting-points. The historian must at all times be prepared to give them up when they are contradicted by the facts. These first three characteristics should lead to the greatest possible certainty in the elaboration of the facts of the past.

4. Controllability

The historian must indicate the basis of his assertions so that they can be verified. Others must be able to repeat his argumentation and consultation of the source material; in other words, the process of information or interrogation of the sources is repeatable. The historian does not expect his findings to be accepted by an act of faith, based on his authorities, but by an act of understanding and appreciation of his documents and arguments.

5. Communicability

The results of historical research are communicable: they are expressed in a language accessible to all educated readers and not in some esoteric, symbolic medium which only makes sense to the initiated.

6. Specific methods and techniques

Historians have produced their own adequate methods for various needs and aspects of their research. Thus several 'auxiliary sciences' have arisen, with specific methods and finalities for various elements of research (numismatics, palaeography and so on). Hence history and its auxiliary disciplines use a technical language of their own, as necessary tools for an adequate treatment of technical problems. However, this technical language is neither closed nor esoteric, but is open and can be assimilated by anyone with the necessary intelligence and time.

7. A certain degree of abstraction and generalization

Through abstraction and generalization the historian strives to comprehend a multitude of facts as indicative of great coherent movements, comprehensive social phenomena. Thus he may understand, describe and summarize a large mass of facts and phenomena in the political institutions of twelfth-century Europe, which occurred in very diverse milieus and countries, as aspects of a few fundamental processes, such as centralization, organization, rationalization and bureaucratization. The progress in church and state of the central organs, the rise of specialized services for the financial, judicial and other functions of the administration, the abandonment of numerous irrational usages and representations and the increase of writing by the government were common to all of Europe. The description in general and abstract terms of these innumerable facts unites them in one meaningful whole. Scholars used to attach less importance to this in the past, when the best historians were deemed to be those who had observed demonstrable characteristics most sharply; nowadays we most admire those who discover the connection between the greatest number of seemingly unrelated facts and phenomena.

8. A certain degree of prevailing schematization

When dealing with very complex problems, one finds that persons, places, dates, political and military events tend to disappear from historical studies – a striking contrast with the days of the *histoire événémentielle*. Historians nowadays use types of social structures (feudal, capitalist etc.). They operate with a few main *Idealtypen* (M. Weber) and they attempt to analyse these types in detail, to describe the transition from one to the other, to define the chronology more precisely and to establish the causal nexus. One thus arrives at a chronological typology. So much effort is devoted nowadays to tracing the stages and phases of human development that one is inclined to speak of a real 'phaseology' (an unattractive neologism), meaning the art of discovering ever more stages and phases and of describing and explaining their succession.

9. Mathematics

Whenever possible we nowadays introduce figures into all sorts of studies, including history. The possibilities are limited, because not every aspect of the past lends itself to calculation and for many fields there simply are no figures available. Taking these restrictions into account, the use of calculation and statistics has recently made great progress in historical research. Where one used to be content with such approximations as 'considerable' or 'little', one tends nowadays to demand and obtain figures. This is obvious enough for economic and demographic research, but applies also to textual criticism and social history: the crime rate, the degree of democratization of government, or the impact of serfdom are all expressed in graphs and statistics. This desire for the relative certainty of figures is far from new, as may be gathered from a quotation from Roger Bacon: 'Probatur per rationem quod omnis scientia requirit mathematicam' (*Opus maius*, ed. J.H. Bridges, i, p. 103).

10. Causal nexus and coincidence

The historian is careful to distinguish chance coincidence from the relation of cause to effect. Positively speaking, this entails the search for the impact of various factors and the attempt to explain the facts as well as describing them. Negatively speaking, it means that he will point out the role of chance, i.e. the mere coincidence of facts in time and space without a causal or functional nexus, whenever it appears from an analysis of historical events.

11. Historical laws

The historian does not hesitate to reveal the apparent operation of historical laws whenever he finds a revealing pattern. We have in mind certain cyclical movements, or the recurrent succession of certain stages in various political or intellectual developments: for example, the occurrence of feudalism whenever certain conditions are combined. However, the 'laws of history' are as little absolute as those of other sciences; as Professor Groenewold put it, about his own discipline: 'In physics every law is provisional and liable to be revised or shown to be relative'.

So far this presentation of some characteristics of modern historiography as a science. In reality no one ever attains an absolute degree of scientific perfection, the requirements of science are never absolutely satisfied. It is impossible because the historian, being only human, cannot avoid a certain degree of subjectivity, and also because the very choice of the subject, the problems selected for research, the sources one consults and the 'significant facts' one quotes all contain an arbitrary element. A final difficulty is, of course, that the historian is at the same time the observer of the flow of history and part of it: he stands in the midst of what he observes. This is the general condition of the social sciences, where man is at the same time object and subject of study and knowledge.

II. Importance of Historical Research

Interest in history moves on very diverse levels and in very different contexts. It may, for example, serve to satisfy a simple curiosity about one's genealogy or the past of one's village. At the highest level, however, the importance of history lies in the fact that it provides the richest source of information for the study of the origin and the development of mankind. Is it necessary to point out that this knowledge of society, its development and structure, is indispensable for a correct assessment of its needs and for making the correct decisions for the future? Ignorance about human society is as damaging as ignorance about the forces of nature. Ignorance and incompetence often go hand in hand, with fatal consequences.

III. The Place of History in Contemporary Cultural Life

Many years ago C.P. Snow regretted the lack of understanding and contact between the 'two cultures', the scientific and the literary. The author clearly had drawn a somewhat exaggerated picture: not all disciplines and ways of thinking can easily be allotted to one or other camp. There is, indeed, a third group of sciences which belongs neither to mathematics and physics nor to literature – a 'third culture'. Not so long ago C.P. Snow presented and defended the idea of a 'Third Culture'.[1] Whatever the lasting value of this distinction may be, it is obvious that the historical muse used to be a form of literature or *belles lettres,* whereas nowadays it belongs – with economics, sociology, human geography and so on – to a sort of no man's land between the domains of literature and physics. There is indeed a field of study there which has society as its subject – in its various aspects and approached from various points of view – and which has its own face and methods, by which it is distinguished from mathematics and physics as well as literature.

IV. History: A Science without Experiment

So far, we hope we have indicated that history is a science with a place and a method of its own. It is, however, a science without experimentation. The technique of experiment, applied by countless disciplines, is as such not available to the historian. This is necessarily so, as it follows from the very nature of the object of historiography, which is past, human behaviour which has taken place and is over, so that it by definition eludes experimental techniques. One can subject present-day man and society, but not those of the past to experiments.[2] It is admittedly difficult to define the past. In the strict chronological sense the past is everything that is neither the

---

[1] C.P. Snow's 'The Two Cultures and the Scientific Revolution', *Rede Lectures* (1959) and his 'Second Look', *Times Literary Supplement* (25 October 1963) were published in one volume by the Cambridge University Press under the title *The Two Cultures: And a Second Look.*

[2] At most a historian-politician could carry out a social experiment in order to draw conclusions by analogy from the result concerning a comparable situation in the past. As a scholarly technique this seems an unrealistic proposition.

present nor the future. Every minute that goes by belongs automatically to the past. This is no sufficient criterion, however, to define the past as an object of historical research, because this entails a certain degree of being complete and finished, essential in order to make an event or period fit for serious historical study, as opposed to a sociological enquiry, an opinion poll or a journalistic report.

The situation is somewhat paradoxical. Whereas human history might be considered as one protracted experiment, it is precisely the historian who is precluded from the use of experiments on this bygone part of the human odyssey. Indeed, scientific experiment can be described as the repeatable observation of a phenomenon in special conditions, which were selected or created in advance as a function of a specific problem (often the tracing of cause and effect). It is in other words an interference with ordinary conditions, in the unconstrained course of events. It may be useful to remind the reader that 'experiment' is also used in the much wider sense of a trial, an attempt, a new formula (a literary or linguistic 'experiment'), whose results are still uncertain.

Scientific experiment is mainly useful confirming or rejecting a causal nexus, suggested by the observation of certain coincidences, by the creation of conditions where all factors are similar except one, which has been changed or eliminated. Unfortunately, I cannot make the past come back, having cut out or added certain factors, persons or circumstances. However fascinating it would be to know the course of world history if Cleopatra had had an ugly long nose, this will forever be a mystery.[3] Could the speculation on what would have happened if William of Normandy had not conquered England be a form of historians' nostalgia for the experimental method which is denied them?

Historiography is not the only science without experiment, for in this it resembles astronomy, which also finds it impossible to carry out experiments on its object of study, the heavenly bodies; while biology seems until the twentieth century not to have gone beyond the observation of what nature produced, without experimental intervention.

It follows that history is condemned to stick to observation if it wants to be scientific. This does not mean that it is necessarily restricted to a mere accumulation of precisely described facts from the past (the *histoire historisante*). On the contrary, like every other true science it attempts to trace causal relations and comprehensive connections. The painful absence of experimentation is partly compensated by the extreme refinement of the methods of observation (archaeological and historical) and the enormous extension of our knowledge of the conditions of the past. Indeed, the mass of data accumulated by modern archaeology and history has taken on fantastic proportions.

There exists a more important technique which can be used as a – very

---

[3] See, for example, J.B. Bury, 'Cleopatra's Nose', (1916); repr. in Bury's *Selected Essays* (1930).

imperfect – replacement for the experiment, namely the comparative method. We mean the search for comparable situations and structures, where one element is different or missing. If a situation in which historians are interested also appears where a particular factor is absent, it is at once clear that that factor cannot have been a determining one for the situation under study. In other words, the historian who cannot recreate a past situation or structure, looks for one – if possible in the same period – that is comparable or even similar except for one factor. Although no historical comparison is ever perfect, comparative research is at present flourishing,[4] even though so far its results have admittedly been modest. Whereas comparable material has been gathered on a considerable scale, the real task of comparison, let alone the formulation of conclusions has hardly started. Nevertheless, the method is obviously fruitful. Suppose that a particular phenomenon is attributed to feudalism. It suffices to trace a comparable non-feudal country (if possible from the same period, in order to eliminate a number of variants straightaway), where the phenomenon under scrutiny also occurs in order to conclude that feudalism cannot be blamed for it. Suppose again that a particular situation on the Continent of Europe in the late middle ages is attributed to the reborn Roman law (which *inter alia*, strongly influenced private law): comparative history will enquire whether in England, where private law escaped romanization, the phenomenon is indeed absent.

A recent article by a leading American medievalist, Professor Bryce Lyon, on the social decline of English peasants in the thirteenth century, has shown how useful this method can be. The historians Postan and Kosminsky attributed this worsening situation to the rise of the towns, which pushed up the demand for food and therefore food prices, thus encouraging the landowners to demand ever higher payments – particularly in kind – from their serfs. This thesis seemed plausible enough, but Professor Lyon's comparative research has shown that in various countries, which enjoyed an urban development at least equal to England, the social position of the peasants improved and serfdom was reduced.[5] How difficult the problem of the causal nexus is can be gathered from the controversy on the true nature of the iconoclastic onslaught in the Low Countries of 1566, as expressed in the question 'hunger year or wonder year'? Traditionally the activity of the iconoclasts was viewed as a purely religious phenomenon, both in its character and in the factors that created it. But in Amsterdam in 1949 E. Kuttner published his *Het hongerjaar 1566*, suggesting a new interpretation: the violence of that turbulent year consisted of food riots; the breaking of

---

[4] See the massive tomes of comparative-historical studies in the *Recueils de la Société Jean Bodin*.

[5] B. Lyon, 'Encore le problème de la chronologie des corvées', *Le moyen âge*, 69, (1963), pp. 615-30.

the images had been a social revolt. The fact is that in July and August 1566 the grain price was somewhat higher than the average of the 1560s/1570s and even small price rises caused great nervousness because a recent hunger period was still in people's minds.[6] It also appeared that in Ghent in August 1566, at the time of the breaking of the images there, there had been food riots, including the looting of the grain market.[7] Moreover although this was less significant, quite a few poor people had joined the ranks of the iconoclasts there.[8] Several questions remain unanswered. Were other years of dearth in the period under review, without any extension, let alone explosion of Protestant activism. And when the chronology is checked with precision, it appears that in Ghent the food riot took place on 21 August in front of the St. Nicholas church, which was left untouched, that the breaking of the images did not start until the 22nd and that on the 23rd, another day of iconoclasm in Ghent, activity in the grain market took place undisturbed.[9] It is also noteworthy that a not inconsiderable number of well-to-do persons and leading members of the community took part in the breaking, which leads to the conclusion that there were indeed two distinct developments, one religious and the other social in character, which went ahead one beside the other but without any real connection – the iconoclasts acting according to their own plan and aim and ignoring the nervous mob which plundered the grain market. Or was there a causal connection after all, the market being left in peace on 22 and 23 August because of severe control by security forces and the hungry being free to take their revenge on the unguarded churches? On 23 August, after all, the town authorities provided a supply of cheap grain.

So far the debate at present. The final answer will depend on the results of even more refined and detailed prosopographical, topographical and chronological research. Thus very gradually and tentatively, through the formation of hypotheses, debate and the discovery of new facts, reality can be grasped ever more closely, and refined observation, confrontation and comparison lead to deeper insight and wider knowledge.

---

[6] A connection between the obstruction of the grain import and the iconoclasm had already been suggested by E.C.G. Brunner, 'Die dänische Verkehrssperre und der Bildersturm in den Niederlanden im Jahre 1566', *Hansische Geschichtsblätter*, 33 (1928), pp. 97-110.

[7] The chronology of the events in Ghent is as follows. Markets on 19, 21 and 23 August. On 19 August the grain price went up, and again on 21 August. On 17 August the news of the breaking of the images in the West Quarter of Flanders was received in Ghent; there was a food riot there on 21 August; the breaking of the churches took place on 22 and 23 August.

[8] See the study by M. Delmotte, 'Het Calvinisme in de verschillende bevolkingslagen te Gent (1566-1567)', *Tijdschrift voor geschiedenis*, 76 (1963), pp. 145-76.

[9] I owe many thanks to Mr. J. Scheerder who very kindly provided me with some data from his unpublished Brussels lecture of 17 November 1963 on 'The Problems of the Wonder-Year, 1566-1567' and who checked these lines to make sure that I had rendered his ideas correctly.

V. History and Human Self-Knowledge

History as a means of self-knowledge is one of man's oldest intellectual preoccupations. It is also one of the most universal and variegated: primitive warrior songs orally transmitted from a misty past as well as imposing learned tomes in modern libraries, polemical and metaphysically engaged writings as well as antiquarian and erudite studies without a trace of disquiet. It seems possible to us to distinguish three main types of historical narrative amongst this great variety; all three are very old, though possibly not equally so. Their character deserves to be described.

A first great historical way of thinking could be called meta-historical (the phrase meta-history is used nowadays as we used to speak of metaphysics as the philosophy of the ultimate reality and of research on meta-structure as that dealing with the ultimate secrets of nature). Here we find the great mythologies, revelations, prophetic visions and historical-philosophical systems that pretend to answer the question of the origin of the universe and mankind, and the explanation of the *condition humaine*. This form of history attempts to describe and explain the totality of human genesis and history and to discover the sense of its evolution (goal) in one swoop, in a short and comprehensive way. Not infrequently even the future and more precisely the end of the world is encompassed or a paradisiacal apotheosis of history extrapolated: the fascination of the millennium for western thought is well known. These religious or philosophical representations are ancient and ever young; they are clearly permanent and can boast of an uninterrupted tradition.

The critical, scholarly study of the past is very different. Its domain is the humble analysis of a causal nexus which is viewed as complex. Here nobody pretends to know the future or to have discovered the universal laws of history, let alone to discern its ultimate goal. The message here is patiently to harvest firm and controllable data, slowly to advance knowledge and understanding, *inter alia*, concerning certain regularities, cyclical developments or recurrences, and to discover the connections between numerous seemingly isolated phenomena. This is the long way: progress and exploration comes piecemeal, nobody explains and knows everything at once, nobody immediately holds the key to all secrets. This way is of scientific value because it believes less in intuition and more in controllable observation. One should compare, for example, what the great world mythologies and revelations have to say on the earliest history of man with the fumbling progress of palaeontology, anthropology and archaeology, with their slow collection of data and hesitant formulation of provisional conclusions.

These two systems are indeed very different, and it is not surprising that they utterly fail to understand each other. The adepts of the first way of thought blame the others for senselessly stringing together isolated facts – as a child catches butterflies to stick them on a cushion – without understanding anything about their connection, the underlying forces and the finality of history. The thinkers in the latter group reproach the former with basing themselves on faith and intuition and the generalization of a very limited amount of facts; they also blame them for producing simplifications and abstraction to the point of falsifying the complex reality.[10]

One example of the explanation of historical events in the light of a single factor is the attribution of the central role to the class struggle in all aspects, even the most divergent, of human history, be it the medieval origin of the English parliament,[11] the rise of the centralized monarchies in western Europe in the twelfth and thirteenth centuries,[12] or all religious and ecclesiastical phenomena in history.[13] The distinction between the two approaches goes back, to a certain extent, to personal aptitude (the contrast, say between Hegel and Russell) and national traditions. The most pronounced example of the pragmatic, fact-finding type of historiography is found in Britain; the most ideologically inspired has been seen in the Soviet Union (where one was strongly reminded of C. Schmid's observation that modern thought is secularized theology).[14] Both extremes have great disadvantages, because they are both in danger of coming to a dead end, the latter ending up in the maze of mere assertions and state-controlled ideology, the former in the quagmire of an undifferentiating enumeration of significant and insignificant facts and dates.

The third model of historiography is the utilitarian, devoted to the exaltation of 'greatness' of all sorts, national, dynastic, to the justification of various initiatives, the satisfaction of simple curiosity or the discovery of memorabilia and anecdotes.

---

[10] A typical example of scholars talking at cross purposes on this sort of problem can be found in the critical review of S.J. De Laet's *L'archéologie et ses problèmes* by A. Mongaut in *Sovietskaia Archeologia*, 4 (1957), pp. 195-98.

[11] E.A. Kosminsky, 'Les ouvrages des historiens soviétiques sur l'histoire des assemblées représentatives de l'Europe occidentale', *Anciens pays et assemblées d'états*, 18 (1959), pp. 177-96.

[12] V. Birioukovitch and I. Levitski, *Le moyen âge*, Recherches internationales à la lumière du marxisme, 37 (Paris, 1963), pp. 18-19 (= transl. of the Introduction to Vol. III of the *Vsemirnaia Istoria* (Moscow, 1957).

[13] Ibid., p. 21: 'Les différents systèmes religieux et les différentes organisations ecclésiastiques avaient un seul et même but: renforcer la domination des féodaux sur les masses opprimées et exploitées.' The authors add that the numerous medieval heresies were social revolts. According to their thesis the latter should have had an anti-religious or at least an areligious character, but, as they admit themselves, the opposite was true, for those movements adopted a religious, 'heretical' dress. Religious sentiment clearly was something else than a mere technique in the hands of the oppressors.

[14] See the interesting considerations by T.J.G. Locher, 'De Nieuwe Tijd', W. Den Boer, F.W.N. Hugenholtz and T.J.G. Locher (ed.) *Gestalten der geschiedenis* (The Hague, 1960), pp. 168-244. The author talks, *inter alia* of 'ideological servitude'.

VI. History an 'Applied Science'?

The idea that society can be transformed by learning the lessons of history is a powerful one. Politicians and social prophets have often used history as an intellectual tool. An important role is played here by the belief in the repetitive character of history and by the idea that the study of history allows the detection of noxious elements which it suffices to eliminate in order to produce a better society. There is no doubt that the study of history and its impressive catalogue of errors can contribute to the enlightenment of man and help him to take his decisions on the basis of better information and clearer insight than was previously the case.

3

Clio and the Humanities: Alma Mater and Prodigal Sons?

Whenever historians appear in the media the general public may well wonder what their role in society really is and what the meaning is of their involvement with the great events of our time. 'Involvement' here means political involvement. Is it right or even obligatory for the historian to engage his pen without restriction in the service of a great cause or some establishment, or should he merely study the facts according to the scientific rules of historical criticism and publish his conclusions and arguments, even if they fly in the face of powerful interest groups and official doctrines, with all the unpleasant consequences that may follow? These are the terms in which the public sees the problem of historians' involvement, and that of scholars in general. The professional historian is also faced with quite different choices, which require his decision and involvement, and this is the theme of this essay. The reason is not that I want to elude the problem of ideological and political freedom and of historical objectivity, but to avoid it monopolizing our attention. Indeed, even within the limits of strictly objective scholarship,[1] the historian faces a number of fundamental choices, that make his craft more problematical than in the time of Bernheim's *Lehrbuch der historischen Methode*.

A first choice confronting the historian at the outset lies between the collective and the individual method. This decision is usually taken unconsciously, but is nevertheless a decision: whoever embarks on a project by himself implicitly rejects the collective approach. This is still 'id quod plerumque fit', a fact that may cause some amazement, as it seems obvious that historical research really ought to be team work. What scholar alone can examine all aspects of a given situation with the techniques developed by so many disciplines? Whoever wants to understand the main problems of our time, naturally consults specialists of various disciplines; for example, the reports of the 'Club of Rome'. Why is it not done for the equally complex events of the past? What historian is still capable of mastering the relentless

---

[1] Strict objectivity, as many norms, is difficult to accomplish, but it is an ideal worth striving for; the alternative, unbridled subjectivity, has nothing to do with science.

flood of publications on his own discipline?[2] We nevertheless continue to work on our own and we find that 'seminal books' are still produced by individual scholars, whereas the large collective enterprises seldom go further than the notorious *Buchbindersynthese*. Whether we are thinking of the Unesco World History, the *Algemene geschiedenis der Nederlanden* or the grandiose series of comparative-historical volumes of the Société Jean Bodin,[3] we find time and again that they have not proceeded much beyond a collection of valuable individual contributions, written by authors who have had only a minimal contact with each other or none at all, so that a comprehensive picture or general conclusions seldom emerge. How will the situation develop? The publication of large 'bookbinders' syntheses', produced by pleiads of eminent specialists, will no doubt continue, but as balance-sheets of hard facts and as presentations of the *status quaestionis* rather than as instruments of innovation; individual work will, of course, also continue to be published. We moreover expect useful results from colloquia, in which a distinct, well-defined theme – possibly inspired by some present concern – is put before a group of historians and non-historians of various disciplines and, after due preparation, discussed until a publishable conclusion is reached.[4] It is advisable for every historian to think carefully about this problem at the start of a research project.

A second choice, which faces the historian more frequently, concerns the place of social history. It has for a long time been a sort of appendix of economic history, so that the formula 'social and economic history' has become a standard expression about which few people raise questions. Nevertheless, the matter is not so straightforward. If social history is nothing other than the study of the way of life of various social classes and their standard of living one can understand the traditional attitude, but there are eminent historians who see things differently. To them social history is the most comprehensive form of historiography, as it by definition includes the whole human *societas*, in its structure and aspirations, its political institutions as well as its system of production and distribution, its science and its scale of values.[5] In that perspective people and groups of people are the principal objects of study, so that a traditional discipline like

---

[2] Where will it all end? That is the anxious question many users, for example, of the tenth edition of the famous Dahlmann-Waitz will ask themselves. This monster-bibliography of German history (to 1960) is so enormous and appears so slowly that its six stout volumes planned with *c.* 120,000 titles in 430 sections may only be ready by the year 2000. See some remarks in *Deutsches Archiv*, 29 (1973), p. 242 and in *Tijdschrift voor rechtsgeschiedenis*, 39 (1971), pp. 485-87.

[3] See the balance of more than thirty-five years of achievement presented by its secretary-general: J. Gilissen, 'Histoire comparée du droit: l'expérience de la Société Jean Bodin', M. Rotondi, *Inchieste di diritto comparato* (Padua, 1973), ii, pp. 257-97.

[4] More on this later on.

[5] See G. Duby's innovative remarks in his inaugural lecture at the Collège de France: *Des sociétés médiévales* (Paris, 1971). Karl Bosl and Otto Brunner have expressed similar ideas.

constitutional history develops into social-constitutional history (people and social groups operating in the framework of political institutions), and economic history into social-economic history (people and groups operating in the economic framework). Man and society always holding the centre of the stage.

Value judgment is the third option that historians should consider, even though most of them are horrified at the thought. We all 'know' that it is not 'the historian's task' to pronounce value judgments on the past, and everyone is aware of numerous good reasons for that attitude – anyone who does not is certainly convinced that he ought to know them and is careful not to enquire about them. The paradoxical consequence is that the historian is condemned to silence precisely on those questions which his fellow citizens ask him with the greatest urgency. There are, for example, innumerable books on the history of political institutions. We know in incredible detail which councils, courts, benches and chambers of all sorts have functioned in every state, city and borough, from the most illustrious to the most obscure. We know when they arose and disappeared, who manned them, what they earned, how and when they were appointed, what they read and where they lived, whether they followed Roman or Germanic law and much else besides; we even know what predecessors these institutions had and by which others they were absorbed. But what we seldom or never hear is how well or how badly the men in these institutions ruled the people. The legitimate question, 'When was Europe ruled in the best, or the least bad way, and what lessons can we draw from this?' – what could be considered the focal problem of institutional history and one of direct social utility – is not even considered by most historians: everyone knows that this implies a value judgment and introduces a subjective element, incompatible with the true pursuit of the strict man of science. It is indeed true that we can find out precisely, objectively and in a controllable and even measurable way which books a certain councillor had in his library and what stipend he received (or should have received if his king had not been short of cash); but such research raises the option of whether it is better to answer questions to which current public opinion is wholly indifferent, or to give tentative, and approximate answers (involving a risk of subjectivity) to questions relevant to our time and posed by non-professionals? Or is it unreasonable that the public wants historians to say what 'we can learn from history' about the most just and human form of government and the most adequate administration of justice? 'Good government' concerns us all, so why should the historian keep silent about it?

A further scientific choice concerns the historian's attitude towards the other social sciences and their significance for his own discipline. What can we historians do with political theory, psychology, economics, sociology, ethnology and anthropology? Shall we just continue along the well-tried paths of historical research – as the legendary peasant who went on ploughing his plot of land while empires came and went – in the conviction that the other social sciences have nothing to offer us or, worse still, can only serve to poison the pure well of historical knowledge? Shall we go on studying past societies as if the concepts of sociology – the 'science of society' – did not exist? Shall we write political history in blissful ignorance of what modern political science teaches on the behaviour of man, defined by Aristotle as a '*zoön politikon*'? Whether historians care for other disciplines or not, it is clear that the opposite movement is in full swing and that psychologists, sociologists and others are studying the past with methods and questions which are not those of historiography, but of their own discipline and that they even stress the fact that they are not writing 'history' (and are not even trying to). A psychologist or philosopher may study the reactions of a group of eighteenth-century chemists to a certain theory in order to check an aspect of the theory of cognition, declaring expressly that he is not pursuing historical research at all, only checking a psychological model through the behaviour of an experimental group of people, who happen to be eighteenth-century Europeans, but might just as well have been twentieth-century Americans.[6] Thus the professional historian is robbed of whole areas by scholars of whose psychological theories and cognitive models he has never heard. What can the historian do? He cannot run after every other discipline, but he can put certain problems before a symposium of scholars of various disciplines – a practice that is still unusual. What he ought certainly not to do is deliberately to select one historical factor, omitting other important ones. That an economist decides to study a phase of the past purely as an economist, and without going into the psychology of the time, seems reasonable enough (even though every economist knows the role of market psychology), but that a historian decides to study the economic history of the early middle ages and declares expressly that he will take no notice of psychological factors is hard to accept.[7] As a historian he knows – or ought to know – that the psychology of the early middle ages and in particular of the leading circles of ecclesiastical and lay landowners was a factor of importance in economic life. It is from the historian that one may expect particular attention to be paid to the

---

[6] I am referring here to the defence in Ghent in 1973 of an unpublished doctoral dissertation by F. Verbruggen, 'Cognitieve dissonantie en phlogistoncontroverse'. See, by the same author, 'De receptie van Lavoisiers theorie', *Tijdschrift voor geschiedenis*, 86 (1973), pp. 293-309, where the author proposes that 'the Phlogiston controversy should no longer be viewed as a purely historical event, to be studied by means of the historical method, but as a current event, to be approached with laboratory techniques' (p. 294).

[7] R.S. Lopez, *The Commercial Revolution of the Middle Ages, 950-1350* (Englewood Cliffs, 1971), p. 11: 'Why did the Roman will and ability to resist wear out? If we leave aside the possible impact of psychological changes, which cannot be adequately explored in the framework of economic history . . .'; this is all the more strange since the author, on the same page, talks of the heavy charges the late Roman empire placed on its citizens, causing them 'to lose interest in its preservation and turn their best efforts and hopes increasingly towards the Kingdom of Heaven' – unmistakably a psychological explanation.

mutual influence of economic, institutional and intellectual elements and powers.[8]

Even though twentieth-century man is used to fast mutations, nevertheless the recent change in the situation of historical research seems to me quite amazing. It was only in the last century that history received its autonomous and universal recognition as a great scientific initiator and catalyst and became the discipline *par excellence* which transformed and revolutionized all others. Yet there are already certain indications that it could be turned into the great imitator, decomposed into the retrospective study of mentalities, retrospective geography, historiometrics, retrospective sociology, historical linguistics and historical-comparative jurisprudence. The historian who does not jump on the bandwagon of the other humanities in time could find himself out of business, and might be reproached for studying the economy of the past without knowing modern economics, so that he is only a pseudo-economist and cannot be taken seriously as a scholar.

What the proper role and goal of historical science will be in perspective of the future (a future that has already begun) is a question every historian should ask himself, unless he prefers to go on ploughing without looking back and to act as if there were no cloud on the horizon.[9] History has for centuries played an ancillary, when not a purely narrative role. Its purpose was to illustrate providential interpretations or to sing the praise of the dynasty; history was in the service of Reformation and Counter-Reformation, and provided leading circles with the desirable aristocratic genealogies. In no university was history taught except in the margin of classical languages and of Roman law. In the nineteenth century things changed significantly. Historical criticism became a perfected technique and an autonomous science which stopped at nothing, not even the Bible, in whose shadow historians had so long and humbly worked. Historical evolution conquered all disciplines and put an end to the ancient static conception of philosophy, linguistics, jurisprudence, anthropology, zoology, biology and astronomy. Chairs of history belonged to the most illustrious scholars in universities, and leading historians exerted a political influence on students and public opinion, which we can nowadays hardly imagine, but can be judged from the biographies of a Mommsen, a Treitschke or a Pirenne. In the same century history became, especially in England, the discipline *par excellence* for the general education of young people, in preparation for the responsibilities they would one day carry in public life: in 1928 one out of

---

[8] Among authors who have managed to give economic history its proper place in the general development are A. Gerschenkron, on whom more later, and D.S. Landes, *The Unbound Prometheus: Technological Change and Industrial Development in Western Europe from 1750 to the Present* (Cambridge, 1969).

[9] See in this volume p.1-13.

four of all undergraduates in Cambridge studied history (compared with today about one out of twelve).[10]

The historian who wonders about the meaning of his craft nowadays faces real problems. It is not even obvious any more what the position of his discipline is in the spectrum of the social sciences. At the end of the nineteenth century P.J. Blok spoke of 'History as a Social Science' (*De geschiedenis als sociale wetenschap*)[11] and to many it will seem evident, even today, that historical research is eminently a social science, a main source of data for and a valuable method of study of human society. But not everyone feels so. One reads nowadays under the name of a well-known historian that for him 'sociology alone is left as the social science, which has made the very existence of its conceptual apparatus the subject of reflection', opposing, in the line of Huizinga 'the science of history to systematic humanities' (we are talking of social sciences).[12] Thus the circle is complete. In the nineteenth century two famous philosophers and social thinkers said: 'Wir kennen nur eine einzige Wissenschaft, die Wissenschaft der Geschichte',[13] but today a historian finds that it is sociology which has become the only social science.[14] Is it surprising that many a historian is perplexed? Is he an individual and autonomous researcher or a scientific official who has been told to carry out a particular enquiry as a piece of team-work? Is he an independent thinker, who freely selects his problems and presents his arguments and criticisms, or is he a soldier at the ideological and political front? Is his discipline a social science or not? If so, in what is it different from the others? And should the historian receive sociological, political or ethnological schooling before he hears the 'dignus es intrare' of his fellow-historians (supposing that this *doctum corpus* still consists of historians and not of sociologists, political theorists and ethnologists with a 'retrospective' interest)?

The perplexed historian is confronted with even more choices. The choice between history and sociology goes further than a problem of method and accent: it concerns the fundamental question whether it is the task of the historian to discover supposed 'inexorable laws' or whether the undetermined character of events is what concerns him, as he is interested

---

[10] G.R. Elton, *The Future of the Past* (Cambridge, 1968), p. 10.
[11] An inaugural lecture (Leiden, 1984).
[12] A.M. Van Der Woude, 'Het gebruik van begrippen ontleend aan de sociale wetenschappen bij het analyseren van economische en sociale verschijnselen in het verleden', *A.A.G. Bijdragen*, 18 (1973), pp. 4, 5; the author consequently talks, logically if not elegantly, of 'turning historical science into a social science'.
[13] K. Marx and F. Engels, *Werke* (Berlin, 1958), iii, p. 18, quoted in P. Landau, 'Karl Marx und die Rechtsgeschichte', *Legal History Review*, 41 (1973), p. 361 (from the *Deutsche Ideologie* of 1845).
[14] So the roles are exactly reversed: the nineteenth century turning everything into historical science gives way to the 'turning everything into social science' of the second half of the twentieth.

in what is *einmalig*.[15] A closely connected question is whether the course of history is dominated by 'obscure mass movements' and 'impersonal forces' (if this is the case, it is impossible by definition to detect historical factors, and the historian might as well give up the search for a causal interpretation and a rational historiography), or by decisions taken by individuals or groups who knew what they were doing and what they wanted, even if they could not foresee what would happen in the end or prevent events from going badly wrong.[16] Is the course of history determined by an ineluctable succession of phases and stages, following an iron dialectic, or is it the result of human calculations and miscalculations, a chain of improvised and chance-related solutions for recurrent problems and dilemmas, whereby each solution contains the seed of new problems and conflicts? Here again the historian has to decide: even acting as if the problem did not exist and writing purely descriptive history, *histoire historisante*, is a decision.

It is with some remarks on this *histoire historisante* that I would like to conclude. The straightforward description and narrative of the facts — particularly in the political, dynastic and military sphere, has disappointed those who had hoped that history would uncover the laws of world events, as the great physicists of the seventeenth century discovered the mechanism of the material universe. The pioneer of cultural history, Giambattista Vico (1668-1744), was strongly influenced by the great mathematicians and physicists of the century of his birth.[17] Whoever expects history to provide a comprehensive social doctrine, with universal categories, concepts, laws and main lines of development — which can hopefully even be extrapolated into prognoses — will be bitterly disappointed by the massive output which the gild of professional historians produces year in year out. Certainty is seldom attained — at least on the more important and interesting questions; tentative conclusions are formulated after much hesitation; and working hypotheses are prudently suggested but not without reference to contradictions in the sources. Some authors even restrict themselves to a 'presentation of the problem' and the indication of various elements that may 'start a discussion'. This is no adequate nourishment for the hungry who demand to know the 'grand design' of history. But it is not only the traditional professionals who have disappointed the hungry, it seems obvious to me that the grand

---

[15] A.J. Jongkees, 'Une génération d'historiens devant le phénomène bourguignon', *Bijdragen en mededelingen betreffende de geschiedenis der Nederlanden*, 88 (1973), pp. 231-32: 'Il est bien tentant, lorsque nous avons ordonné les faits du passé de sorte qu'ils s'arrangent dans une connexion compréhensible, de considérer alors cette connexion des faits comme une nécessité inhérente. L'historien doit se garder de cette tentation. Il lui importe avant tout d'être *in*déterministe, de se représenter, à chaque moment, que les événements auraient pu tourner autrement.'

[16] The interesting pages devoted to this problem in I. Berlin, *Historical Inevitability* (Oxford, 1954) retain all their relevance.

[17] A symposium was organised on the occasion of the 300th anniversary of his death: *Giambattista Vico: An International Symposium* (Baltimore, 1969) (containing forty papers).

systems of universal history conceived by the social and cultural philosophers of the previous century – historically minded philosophers or philosophical historians and vulgarizers – are today read very critically.[18] Several 'terrible simplifiers' had the ambition, in their vast monistic interpretations, to reveal what made the clock of history tick. Professional historians rejected these simplifications and refused to reduce the very complicated play of factors, which their detailed research revealed, to a single *causa determinans*; few even took the trouble to familiarize themselves with the great theories, let alone to respond to them – they were rather inclined to find everything relative and to carry scepticism to the point of denying absolute values and judging everything in the light of past circumstances. The general reader, however, loved these grand, total interpretations, some of which even became inspiring dogmas for great political movements and led the world into uncharted territory.

Is the conclusion of all this that the choice we face lies between a historical *science*, eschewing valid general conclusions useful to society and dedicated to relativity, and a monistic historical *philosophy*, elevated to the status of the official political doctrine (with the dire consequences of lost freedom and one-sided thought)? If the two children of modern historiography are 'value-free' relativity and socially involved dogmatism, the question must be: 'Clio, what have you done to us?'. It is clear that public opinion, as opposed to professional circles, does indeed pose this disgruntled question. People reproach Clio, who is in a dilemma, that she gives technically perfect answers according to the highest professional norms to questions which the modern world does not pose,[19] and that she leaves those which are insistently posed unanswered, or provides only partial and misleading replies, which have not profited society or have even been noxious.

If history wants to be something else than the staging of some dramatic episode from the multifarious repertory of the theatre of the world ('retrospective news flashes' of undoubted 'entertainment value'), it will have to break through this dilemma. Two conditions seem necessary for this. It should be made clear what is the place of historical writing in the concert of the modern humanities, so that there is an exchange of information, but without any confusion (the economist imagining that he is a better historian than the historians, or the historian a better sociologist than the sociologists). The dialogue between the followers of the social sciences is imperative and will induce many scholars to question the traditional limits of their own disciplines. Why, for example, is the student of the Merovingian *reges criniti* a historian and the student of the role of the beard of nineteenth-century

---

[18] See the survey of their interpretations in B. Mazlish, *The Riddle of History: The Great Speculators from Vico to Freud* (New York and London, 1966).

[19] As I listened to the papers at the Second International Congress of Medieval Canon Law, in Boston in 1963, it struck me that apparently nobody had thought of referring to the legal themes on the programme of the Second Vatican Council, then being held.

tribal chiefs an ethnologist? Furthermore, society should ask historians the right sort of questions and they should make every effort to answer them. Public opinion should understand that just as alchemists failed to find the philosophers' stone, historians are unable to produce a golden key which will unlock the mysteries of the world. But it is legitimate to expect historians to provide by their exact and objective analysis a better insight into the structure of society and the latter's inherent dangers and possibilities. They may, moreover, be expected not to close their eyes to the problems of their own time, but to take part in the great debates of the moment armed with their specific expertise.[20] This also is a choice confronting the historian and also poses the question of his involvement.

---

[20] The research of Gerschenkron is directly relevant for the present-day problems of developing countries. See on his varied oeuvre: I. Schöffer, 'Gerschenkrons theorie van "The Great Spurt"', *Tijdschrift voor geschiedenis*, 82 (1969), pp. 282-88; one should now add to the books reviewed there, A. Gerschenkron, *Europe in the Russian Mirror: Four Lectures in Economic History*, (Cambridge, 1970), a most stimulating and revealing book, containing, *inter alia*, the pronouncement by the author, speaking as 'an economic historian' that 'any interpretation of Soviet industrialization which ignores the primacy of the political factor in Soviet history must be inadequate and misleading' (p. 121).

4

Reflections on the History of England

Having studied in the course of some thirty years various aspects of medieval English law,[1] I have recently published a general history of England, from the earliest times to the present. The direct cause was the complaint of students in Ghent that there was no modern textbook on the subject in their own Dutch language. The completion of this *Geschiedenis van Engeland* has inspired me to formulate a number of reflections, and in so doing we came to examine various current and popular notions and check them against the facts: not a few were found wanting.

Geographical Determinism:
Is an Island Bound to Become a Maritime Power?

I would like to start with some commonplace tenets relating to the insular position of Great Britain and stemming from a form of geographical determinism, which, in spite of Hegel's warning 'wo einst die Griechen waren sind jetzt die Türken', turns up regularly and irresistibly, receiving its classical expression in the 'Braudelian model'.[2] I am not thinking here of the influence of geography on history and the limitations imposed by the

---

[1] See, *inter alia*, my publications on *Royal Writs in England from the Conquest to Glanvill: Studies in the Early History of the Common Law* (London, 1959); *Les Iles Britanniques* (Brussels, 1963); *The Birth of the English Common Law* (Cambridge, 1973); 'Public Prosecution of Crime in Twelfth-Century England', *Church and Government in the Middle Ages. Essays Presented to C.R. Cheney* (Cambridge, 1976), pp. 41-70.

[2] This is not the place to discuss the impact of Braudel's *La Méditerranée et le monde méditerranéen à l'époque de Philippe II* (Orleans, 1949) and the author's distinction between the *histoire événémentielle* (striking, quick short-term movements), *conjoncturelle* (slow but observable rythm) and *structurale* (hardly visible movement), this last, the *longue durée*, being mainly determined by geography. It is also known that the French historian E. Le Roy Ladurie attaches considerable importance to the relation between social groups and their natural, i.e. essentially geographical environment; hence the name of 'eco-history', P. Burke, *Sociology and History* (London, 1980), p. 98.

geographical situation (which prevented Switzerland from becoming a maritime power, just as England could not have become the pioneer of heavy industry without her coal and iron ore), but of geographical determinism, which teaches that geography determines the course of history and conditions society. The first of these geographical clichés maintains that England has enjoyed exceptional security because of her insular position, with far-reaching consequences for her internal development, such as dispensing with a standing army, which was a necessity for insecure continental countries and led to absolutism. I shall not dwell for any length of time on this erroneous idea – although I am intrigued by the question who was responsible for it: world history shows that the sea has traditionally been the easiest way for travel and attack, and that maritime invasions have been innumerable. English history amply demonstrates that an insular situation in itself – for instance without an adequate navy and/or army – offers not the slightest guarantee of external security. The reader will recall the successful invasions of Caesar and Claudius in the first century B.C., the Vikings and Danes in the ninth and tenth centuries and the Normans in 1066, whereas the most famous failures, those of Harold Hardrada and of the 'Invincible Armada' were respectively beaten off in a battle on land and a naval encounter by a superior English army and navy.

Another stereotype assumes that England was bound to become a great seafaring and colonial nation because of her island position and the accessibility of her coastline and natural harbours. The facts, however, teach another lesson for, besides phases of impressive maritime deployment and colonial expansion, there were other, and longer, periods of neglect of the sea and concentration on land, either conquering it (as far as the knights were involved) or tilling it (as far as the peasants were concerned). As soon as the Angles and the Saxons in their search for better land had crossed the sea to ex-Roman Britain, they devoted themselves with marked preference to agriculture, and this pattern of the *adventus Saxonum* was exactly repeated six centuries afterwards with the *adventus Normannorum*: the new conquerors and landlords were interested in the domination and exploitation of the land and its inhabitants. They belonged to a social class, the continental feudal knighthood, which by its entire way of life was interested in the conquest and exploitation of land: crossing the Channel in the night of 27 to 28 September 1066 did not turn the Norman knights into seafarers. As far as we know, the one-night vessels of that crossing rotted away or were used as fuel, but whatever happened to them, the new Englishmen remained on their island exactly what they had been on the Continent: a military class which lived for the acquisition of more and bigger fiefs, in accordance with its fighting and land orientated way of life.[3] This same tradition of feudal hunger for land pushed England into the Hundred Years War, her kings

---

[3] Hence the study of both the English and the French feudal world in one work: C. Petit-Dutaillis, *La monarchie féodale en France et en Angleterre* (Paris, 1971).

dreaming of new crowns, the knights of new manors and the longbowmen of pay, treasure and other spoils of war.[4] The fleet and maritime trade in the meantime remained underdeveloped, the latter being for a long time in the hands of continental merchants – even the trade in English goods; the English fleet was in no way superior to that of other lands on the North Sea or the Channel.[5] It was only after the old feudal and knightly class had given way to the urban entrepreneurs, and the agrarian world had been overtaken by the urban economy, that the well-known modern orientation towards the sea and maritime trade took place. It was Henry VIII who put an end to the amazing long-term neglect of the navy (which had, for example, been strongly reduced a few years before the Norman invasion for reasons of economy) and laid the foundations for its modern success.[6] Traditions and social structures can be stronger than geography, and it was not because they crossed the Channel that continental peasants or warriors changed their way of life.

A third erroneous concept, which is continuously repeated as if it was evidence itself, maintains that living on an island necessarily leads to insularity, a closed and inward-looking social and cultural life. English history, however, again demonstrates that an island society – certainly when it is in proximity of a civilized and dynamic continent – is in no way condemned to lead a separate (let alone peculiar) existence and to undergo an odd, 'deviating' development: one can easily imagine an 'open society' on an island and a 'closed society' in the middle of a continental land mass. English history indeed shows that there have been phases in which the island consciously turned away from the rest of Europe, but that there were other, and longer, periods when it lived in complete symbiosis with the Continent and had its full share of European life; in any case, the journey from England to France or the Low Countries was not so long or dangerous as crossing the Alps from France or Germany to Italy. It is well known that the English and the Frankish church were in close relation in the Carolingian era – in the days of Willibrord, Boniface and Alcuin.[7] There was also interpenetration, supported by the personal union between England and Normandy of one homogeneous knightly class, which possessed land between 1066 and 1204 both in the old Norman country and in the English 'acquisition' on the other side of the Channel, where Norman French

---

[4] See the detailed study by J. Favier, *La guerre de cent ans* (Paris, 1980).

[5] Brief survey in A. Goodman, *A History of England from Edward II to James I* (London and New York, 1977), pp. 30ff. Classic analyses may be found in *The Cambridge Economic History of Europe*, iii, *Economic Organization and Policies in the Middle Ages* (Cambridge, 1965).

[6] England at the beginning of the Tudor Age was in no way a land of seafarers, of whom there were at the most some 20,000, i.e. 0.5 per cent of the total population. Henry VIII had a conscious navy policy and in 1514 already disposed of a fleet of twenty-seven ships, one of them being the *Great Harry*, a 1500 ton super-ship.

[7] See the classic work by W. Levison, *England and the Continent in the Eighth Century* (Oxford, 1946).

became the language of leading circles, the government and the central law courts. The Anglo-Norman and Angevin kings were constantly on the move in their domains on both sides of the Channel and ran them as one complex, feudal 'multinational'. The various parts of this 'Angevin Empire' were not separated but linked by the Channel: the crossings never stopped, although they were occasionally slowed down by gales.[8] Another striking aspect throughout the middle ages was the Roman orientation of the English nation and church; an uninterrupted stream of ecclesiastical and lay notables, but also of ordinary pilgrims, went to Rome, to the successor of St. Peter and Pope Gregory the Great, who had sent a mission to England. And the same is true of the 'Peter's Pence', a more material indication of the link with Rome, which was not even interrupted in the anxious years of the Danish invasion under Guthrum.[9] In modern times the ties with the Continent became more tenuous. The obsession with the French crown and French territory dwindled and the ties with Rome were cut (and only very partially replaced by those with Geneva), but true 'splendid isolation' did not arrive until the nineteenth century – strangely enough, at a moment when the technique of the means of communication reached unparalleled heights. In this perspective the accession of Great Britain to the European Community can be viewed as a return to the normal situation.

Social Determinism: Does Society Necessarily Produce the Leaders and the Science it Needs?

There are, of course, other determinisms than the geographical: there is, for example, a 'social determinism', which holds that in any given (social and economic) circumstances society necessarily produces the leaders or the science it needs. Whether in fact 'the need produces the organ' is a question which deserves to be examined in the light of the case of England. While reserving a more thorough analysis for another occasion, I limit myself here to a few provisional remarks. It is clear that England has in exceptionally critical phases of her existence produced exceptional leaders – Pitt against

---

[8] See the comprehensive analysis in J. Boussard, *Le gouvernement d'Henri II Plantagenêt* (Paris, 1956), and J. Le Patourel, *The Norman Empire* (Oxford, 1976); the expression 'Angevin Empire' used to be more current, but 'Norman Empire' is more correct, as the Normans were the leading element. Le Patourel does not hesitate to maintain that English history was throughout the middle ages no more than 'provincial history', as compared with the cultural centres on the Continent; see his article 'The Plantagenet Dominions', *History*, new series 50 (1965), pp. 298-308.

[9] In the so-called Anglo-Saxon Chronicle, ed. C. Plummer and J. Earle, *Two of the Saxon Chronicles Parallel*, 2 vols. (Oxford, 1892-99) the names of the dignitaries are carefully recorded who carried out the money transport to Rome in the years 887, 888 and 890.

Napoleon, Churchill against Hitler; and in a way the Tudors can be seen as the right monarchs for the kingdom at the transition from the middle ages to modern times. It is, however, not difficult to find other crises where much-needed leadership did not come forward. I am thinking of the miserable, rudderless government of Aethelred the Unready, possibly the nadir of English history. One may also wonder if England in the first half of the seventeenth century deserved no better leaders than the 'Scottish cousin', his son Charles I, Archbishop Laud (d. 1645) and the duke of Buckingham (d. 1628), who might conceivably have spared the country the Civil War.

The breakthrough of modern science, in that same century, is possibly a more interesting phenomenon. There is a school of historians who attribute this European phenomenon to the demands of existing social and economic circumstances: here again, the need is said to have produced the organ; others, the 'autonomists' (an expression used in contradistinction to 'reductionists'), maintain that scientific research ran its course according to lines of development of its own and an internal logic, which had little to do with the social context: far from making the discoveries which society and the economic milieus were waiting for, scholars often disclosed facts that were unpalatable and led to more or less brutal forms of persecution. What does the English experience teach us? I believe that I can, in a nutshell but without violating a very complex reality, give the following answer. It is obvious, on the one hand, that Newton and other physicists, astronomers and mathematicians produced scientific work of direct practical utility – in connection with the verification of weights and measures, coinage and navigation on the open seas, but on the other hand, several among them were more interested in abstract, semi-metaphysical speculation, which had religious or esoteric overtones and was far removed from practical and material needs and considerations. Further research will show whether this esoteric research into the secrets of nature and its laws played a greater role than the quest for practical results with immediate application.[10]

---

[10] This controversy deserves a separate study, and it must suffice here to refer to a few names. Thus J. Needham, the celebrated historian of Chinese science, can be considered as a reductionist. See his *Grand Titration* (London, 1969); his *Clerks and Craftsmen in China and the West* (Cambridge, 1970), and his *Within the Four Seas: The Dialogue of East and West* (London, 1969); (for a more complete bibliography: M. Teich and R. Young (eds.), *Changing Perspectives in the History of Science: Essays in Honour of Joseph Needham* (London, 1973)). In the other camp one may quote A.R. Hall and his *From Galileo to Newton, 1630-1720* (London, 1963) and R.K. Merton, author of *The Sociology of Science: Theoretical and Empirical Investigations* (Chicago, 1974). See also a recent survey in G.S. Rousseau and R. Porter (eds.), *The Ferment of Knowledge: Studies in the Historiography of Eighteenth-Century Science* (Cambridge, 1981); C. Webster, *The Great Instauration: Science, Medicine and Reform, 1626-1660* (London, 1975); R. Hooykaas, *Religion and the Rise of Modern Science* (London, 1971); and P. Mathias (ed.), *Science and Society, 1600-1900* (Cambridge, 1972).

Continuity or Discontinuity?

I would now like to approach a problem which can leave no student indifferent, that of the continuity of English history. Numerous traditional authors see no problem here at all, because they believe continuity is self-evident and even one of the fundamental characteristics of English life throughout the centuries – a conviction, or dogma, which is particularly widespread among historians of law and institutions. To them the history of English political institutions is merely an undisturbed progress towards modern parliamentary democracy, the crowning achievement and logical conclusion of an ingrained love of freedom which the English brought with them fifteen centuries ago from the Germanic past and which successive generations have preserved, cultivated, protected against tyranny and finally passed on to a grateful world.[11] This mythical representation, which was already demonstrably present in the sixteenth century,[12] is opposed to the discontinuous or catastrophic theory, which discerns in English history several highly dramatic and far-reaching reorientations and profound breaks with the past, and also pays attention to the role of chance in various turns and outcomes (I shall return to this later). The followers of the thesis of continuity agree that English history ran its course without jerks or upheavals and conserved the good old institutions – already present in an embryonic shape at the *adventus Saxonum* – or at least restored them after brief interruptions (such as the commonwealth of Cromwell). The stumbling block for this vision is the interpretation of 1066.

Most historians, however conservative or pro-continuity they are, find the dramatic events of that fateful year insurmountable: the discontinuity between Old English and Norman England is too great to be denied. Nevertheless, the idea of continuity can be saved by a truly amazing sleight of hand: one simply lets 'English' history start in 1066 and relegates the preceding centuries to another history, of other people, who are called the 'Anglo-Saxons'. This vision is so deep-rooted that some encyclopaedias start

---

[11] This is the fundamental tenet of W. Stubbs's *Constitutional History of England*, 3 vols. (1903-1906). This idea of continuity – with, for example, the denial of a Tudor despotism – may also be encountered in more recent literature. See the views of the well known theoretician and historian of the British constitution Sir Ivor Jennings, and his lecture *Die Umwandlung von Geschichte in Gesetz* (Cologne, 1965).

[12] No comprehensive work exists on the role of 'Germanism' in the development of European law, and especially that of the constitution, and the idea that freedom is of Germanic origin, and oppression a legacy of the Romans. See, however, some recent considerations in D.R. Kelley, *Foundations of Modern Historical Scholarship: Language, Law and History in the French Renaissance* (New York, 1970), and his article 'History, English Law and the Renaissance', *Past and Present*, 65 (1974), pp. 24-51, where he describes the toughness with which the English keep their myths alive.

the History of England in 1066 and refer for the preceding centuries to another entry, called 'Anglo-Saxons'.[13] Using this same perspective one understands why, for example, the English King Edward who reigned from 1272 to 1307 is counted as Edward I, without taking notice of the Anglo-Saxon kings of that name and as if Edward the Confessor, who reigned from 1043 to 1066, had been no king of England. Other historians, who could not swallow this, did in fact start the history of their people where in fact it began, at the 'coming of the English',[14] but even they wanted to save the continuity. They did so, however, by doing the exact opposite: by minimizing the caesura of 1066 to a mere change of dynasty without effect on the foundations of English society – an incident, a ripple that was soon smoothed over. One way of getting rid of the impact of 1066 consists of describing the Normans as barbarians who could not possibly have introduced anything constructive, particularly into the highly developed Old English kingdom.[15] But if so, what about the feudal system, which the Normans introduced and which played a considerable role in English history? As against this objection attempts are made to show 1.) that feudalism after 1066 was not at all as important as is often assumed;[16] and 2.) that already before 1066 there existed an embryonic feudalism, so that the importance of the year of Hastings is again denied or questioned.[17] It is clear that subjective insight and nationalist feelings have influenced English historians, but what is the judgment of the continental medievalist, who may be expected to take a cooler and more distant look at the problem? It is our feeling that, without representing English development as a whirlpool of ruptures, caesuras and revolutions, the majestic and continuous evolution, particularly of parliament and the common law, from Germanic antiquity to

---

[13] See, for example, in the 7th edition of the *Winkler Prins Encyclopedie*, vii, p. 145, the following expression of the traditional view: 'the history of the kingdom of England is deemed to start with the Norman Conquest under William the Conqueror in 1066'; for the history of the 'minor kingdoms of the Anglo-Saxons, who followed the Roman domination', the reader is referred to the entry 'Anglo-Saxons'.

[14] See the title of the work of K. Feiling, *A History of England: From the Coming of the English to 1918* (London, 1950).

[15] This may be considered the leading theme of the book by H.G. Richardson and G.O. Sayles, *The Governance of Mediaeval England from the Conquest to Magna Carta* (Edinburgh, 1963).

[16] This is the thesis of Richardson and Sayles, *The Governance of Mediaeval England*, pp. 62ff, where chapter iv, 'The Shadow of Feudalism', is devoted to fighting the 'myth' that feudalism was introduced by the Normans – in spite of the innumerable English documents from the period after 1066 where all the typical feudal rules and institutions are encountered with great regularity.

[17] This was the main thesis of E.A. Freeman's *History of the Norman Conquest*, 6 vols. (Oxford, 1867-79), who tried to demonstrate, against J.H. Round, his great adversary, that the events of 1066 had in no way had the impact usually ascribed to them. See the excellent *status quaestionis* and critical evaluation in R.A. Brown, *Origins of English Feudalism* (London and New York, 1973), pp. 84ff. The reader may find an excellent bibliography on this controversy in E.B. Graves (ed.), *A Bibliography of English History to 1485* (Oxford, 1975), nos. 4640-88, pp. 661-66.

the modern era belongs to the gallery of historical myths. There is indeed no lack of profound ruptures and abrupt changes of course.

It all started with the very *adventus Saxonum*: rarely has history known such a complete discontinuity as between the British-Celtic civilization of the Roman province and the Germanic society of the heptarchy that replaced it. In all respects – ethnic, religious, legal, linguistic and political – the rupture was complete: even as far as the form of habitation and the structure of agriculture were concerned British civilization had after a few generations totally disappeared. Although the Anglo-Saxons occupied the same soil (except for Wales), they had nothing in common with their Roman-British predecessors. The dramas of the fifth century were followed by a certain stabilization, which was rudely disturbed by the Danish invasions. It looked for a moment as if England might become the main component of a Viking state, stretching from Iceland and Ireland in the west to Sweden and Russia in the east. Alfred the Great frustrated this development and ensured the survival of a distinct Anglo-Saxon society, even though it absorbed a noticeable Scandinavian impact.[18] Not for long, however, since the arrival of the Normans caused a break whose depth and far-reaching consequences we can hardly fathom. The strong and powerful Old English monarchy, which just before the disaster of Hastings had crushed Harold Hardrada's army, became a conquered province. The country was occupied and exploited by an army of foreign adventurers who drove out the English leading class, seized the land, the state and the church, and turned the natives into a submissive mass of peasants, whose language – at the time the only written vernacular in Europe – was downgraded to the status of an unwritten peasant dialect.[19] Very slowly this military dictatorship gave way to a constitution with some democratic traits: the late medieval English monarchy had established control over the unruly nobility and had learnt to rule in collaboration with a parliament, the spokesman if not of the masses, at least of a broader spectrum of the population than the old feudal *curia*

---

[18] At the time of the battle of Edington, a considerable part of England was under Danish domination, and the result of the battle, which turned into an English victory, was no foregone conclusion; on the contrary, King Alfred's position was particularly critical. One sometimes comes across the opinion that King Guthrum's army consisted only of small bands, keen on quick and isolated plunder, whereas in fact he headed a mighty Danish army and was certainly capable of conquering and subjecting England. See in this sense the recent re-evaluation of the facts and the arguments by N.P. Brooks, 'England in the Ninth Century: The Crucible of Defeat', *Transactions of the Royal Historical Society*, 5th series, 29 (1979), p. 1-20. With Scandinavia and the British isles as their power bases and the North Sea as their inland sea the Vikings could have founded a powerful and extensive maritime empire. See on this H.R. Loyn, *The Vikings in Britain* (London, 1977); A.P. Smyth, *Scandinavian Kings in the British Isles, 850-880* (Oxford, 1977); and J. Graham-Campbell and D. Kidd, *The Vikings* (London, 1980).

[19] See D.M. Stenton, *English Society in the Early Middle Ages, 1066-1307* (Harmondsworth, 1952) pp. 268-74, who speaks of the survival of the English language, albeit 'English of a rustic sort'.

regis.[20] The Tudors put an end to this condominium of crown and parliament, especially Henry VIII, who – as is clear to the unprejudiced observer – established modern European absolutism in England (even though he respected various forms and trappings of the old order). The fact that his switch to absolutism went hand in hand with a radical break in the Roman orientation of the nationalized *ecclesia anglicana* makes the discontinuity all the more striking. Hardly had the English got used to the new situation, created by Henry VIII, when his daughter Mary attempted to undo everything and lead the English nation back to the Roman church – a policy which her successor immediately overturned. Elizabeth's long and popular reign seemed destined to give England a solid foundation for quiet times, based on a truly national church (free both from extreme calvinism and 'popery'), a strong monarchy and docile parliaments (comparable to the submissive assemblies of continental estates, with an administrative rather than a political role).[21] After a few years of Stuart rule little was left of this stability and continuity. The established church was challenged by the powerful Puritan opposition and the absolute monarchy by the parliamentary party (largely concomitant with the Puritan movement). The century which seemed destined to develop 'normally' (according to the common European pattern), i.e. into an absolutist state, in fact witnessed a total subversion, civil war, the execution of the king, the establishment of a (short-lived) republic, the recognition of the dissenters and ultimately the foundation of a parliamentary and constitutional monarchy without parallel anywhere in the world.

The eighteenth century carried on along the lines laid down in 1689, in a climate of great stability and continuity, for which classic oligarchy of the notables, mainly landowners, was responsible.[22] But again, this was not to last very long, as in this same century, when the gentry and the urban patriciate exuded peace and self-confidence and believed themselves to have scaled the heights of civilization, the First Industrial Nation was taking shape under their amazed eyes.[23] It was eventually to lead to the proletarian metropolis, the end of 'rural England' and, via a series of electoral reforms (each being represented as the last concession), to political democracy,

---

[20] See recent surveys or collections of articles, such as E.B. Fryde and E. Miller (eds.), *Historical Studies of the English Parliament*, 2 vols. (Cambridge, 1970); B. Wilkinson, *The Later Middle Ages in England, 1216-1485* (London, 1970); H.G. Richardson and G.O. Sayles, *The English Parliament in the Middle Ages* (London, 1981); R.G. Davies and J.H. Denton (eds.), *The English Parliament in the Middle Ages* (Manchester, 1981).

[21] Sir John Neale was right to speak of Elizabeth I and 'her' parliaments, J.E. Neale, *Queen Elizabeth I and her Parliaments*, 2 vols. (London, 1953-57). On the changes in the political significance of German representative institutions, see F.L. Carsten, *Princes and Parliaments in Germany from the Fifteenth to the Eighteenth Century* (Oxford, 1959).

[22] It is to that political class that Sir Lewis Namier devoted his: *The Structure of Politics at the accession of George III* (1929) and *England in the Age of the American Revolution* (1931).

[23] Thus the title of P. Mathias's *The First Industrial Nation: An Economic History of Britain, 1700-1914* (London, 1969).

symbolized by a parliament that had been reformed beyond recognition. Only the observer blinded by ceremonial pomp and concerned with folklore rather than political reality would deny that again a deep chasm was created between the past and the present. What is left of the political practice of Walpole's and Lord North's day, as described by Namier, in present-day England, which alternates between the mass appeal of nationalist Tory leaders and the mass appeal of Labour, the party of the trade unions?

The question may well be asked how the myth of English continuity ever took shape in the face of so much undeniable discontinuity, and what social role it has played. I believe that research into this theme might prove very revealing.

English and Continental Development: A Parallel Course?

However intriguing that question may be, I would now like to move on to another aspect of English history, to examine the comparative chronology of English and continental evolution. That England has passed through various phases of development in common with the Continent is well known; our question is whether this happened at the same time or whether there was a noticeable time-lag between the island and the Continent. And if the latter is the case and the similar continental and English stages were not coeval, was England (usually) ahead, as was manifestly the case in the rise of the 'Machine Age', or was this a singular accident, caused by an exceptional juncture of circumstances? In the Old English period we see no noticeable difference in timing. Christianity reached the Anglo-Saxons later than the Franks but earlier than the Frisians and the continental Saxons, and shortly after their conversion the English devoted themselves enthusiastically to the reorganization of the Frankish church.[24] The Old English political unification was roughly contemporary with that of the Franks, until the events of the second half of the ninth century pulled the two lines of development apart. France underwent disintegration and the collapse of central government (in fact, of any form of government), whereas in tenth-century England a centrally organized national state was founded. In France, feudalism, a Frankish inheritance, made constant progress, and played a centrifugal role. England experienced nothing of the sort: there was no question of royal vassals breaking away and dragging the vassals of their provinces with them, to found their own principalities; nor was there any question of feudal castellanies and law courts.

If one considers feudalism as a regressive development, an aspect of Carolingian decadence, then England was ahead of France; but if one considers it as a positive factor, a phase on the way to modern forms of

[24] See the recent survey in R. McKitterick, *The Frankish Church and the Carolingian Reforms, 789-895* (London, 1977).

organization, then France was ahead. Whatever the case, after 1066 continental feudalism was imported wholesale in England, and English society became thoroughly feudalized. Since there was no regional separatism, English feudalism became strong and centrally controlled, in fact realizing the original aim of the Carolingians, who had used the system to promote political cohesion and the creation of an army of horsemen. As the classic manorial system reached its zenith in England in the twelfth and thirteenth centuries, it appears that paradoxically the Carolingian paradigm was most fully realized in thirteenth-century England, a solid feudal monarchy and an agrarian society based on the manorial system. The latter was regressive, certainly in comparison with the Continent, where the dismemberment of the manor had already started.[25] If English and continental feudalism were coeval, England's unitary state and common national law were progressive elements when compared with France, Germany and Spain. English constitutionalism and parliamentarism were not exactly ahead, but were not slow to emerge, and the same can be said of the absolute monarchy which in the sixteenth century was making headway on both sides of the Channel.[26]

The seventeenth century, however, witnessed a remarkable parting of the ways. The significance of the parliamentarian party can be understood in two ways. To the contemporary continental observer, who saw absolute monarchy as a modern advance and charters of liberties and parliaments as medieval, feudal relics, the defeat of the Stuarts was a step backward. At present, however, we tend to see it as one of the great revolutions on the road to a modern democratic constitution and therefore a breakthrough full of promise for the future.[27] Seen in that perspective, seventeenth-century England made a great leap forward, although it all happened, paradoxically, in order to secure the return to the old constitution and the medieval common law: the cradle of our modern constitutions was in a country that was particularly attached to its feudal and medieval institutions. In the eighteenth century English society, dominated by trade and liberated from royal arbitrary rule, produced the Industrial Revolution, the economic counterpart of the political revolution of the preceding century.

---

[25] See the authoritative exposé by F.L. Ganshof and A. Verhulst, *The Cambridge Economic History of Europe*, i, *The Agrarian Life of the Middle Ages* (Cambridge, 1966), pp. 291-339.

[26] Amongst the most useful European surveys of the rise of parliamentarianism are A. Marongiu, *Medieval Parliaments: A Comparative Study* (London, 1968); A.R. Myers, *Parliaments and Estates in Europe to 1789*, London, 1975; G. Oestreich, *Geschichte der Menschenrechte und Grundfreiheiten im Umriss* (Berlin, 1968). See also the provisional conclusions in my textbook *De Instellingen van de middeleeuwen*, ii (Ghent, 1978), pp. 218-77.

[27] These 'great revolutions' are the English revolution of the seventeenth century, the American and French revolutions of the eighteenth, and the two Russian revolutions of the twentieth century, as studied in C. Brinton's famous analysis, *The Anatomy of Revolution* (New York, 1965). I would like to add to Brinton's series the revolt of the Low Countries against King Philip II, which can be considered the first national revolt against modern absolutism.

Together they produced the parliamentary industrial state, a model for progressive entrepreneurs and liberal innovators on the Continent.[28]

Aimless History and Long-Term Trends

I now propose to focus my attention on another group of problems: what the English past can teach us about the laws of history, recurrences and dialectic. Can we detect a pattern in fifteen centuries of English history? Can we distinguish a line, finality or guiding principle or do we find only a cyclical repetition of recurrent phenomena, determined by accidental circumstances, in other words by chance (if it is permitted to use this proscribed term, one of the worst skeletons in the historiographical cupboard and protected by a strict taboo)? Although I may seem to walk on the thin ice of ideology – Is this a scholarly question or mere meta-history inspired by subjective conviction? – I believe that it is possible to put forward a few considerations on the basis of well-established facts.

It is, to begin with, possible to detect certain main lines, directions and secular trends. I do not necessarily mean an uninterrupted rectilinear march forward, but a clearly discernible evolution, following easily defined stages, from one typical structure to another, in other words there was a movement from A to Z instead of an alternation on the spot between A and B. There is, for example, the transition from an agrarian to a commercial and industrial economy and the growing impact of the economy and of economic aims on the scale of values of English society. The replacement of the landowners by entrepreneurs and later by organized labour as a leading force was a parallel development. In the political field it is not difficult to discern a transition from royal monocracy to bourgeois oligarchy and labour orientated democracy. Nor are long-term trends lacking in intellectual life, such as the transition from *jenseits*-orientated thought and a worldview dominated by the supernatural to the present *diesseitige* outlook, based on rational criticism and the exact sciences.

The trend towards rationalism seems to have passed through the following stages. In the beginning human behaviour and thought were strongly influenced by an awareness of the supernatural world: it was the time of magical thought and a 'primitive mentality',[29] as expressed, *inter alia*, by the

---

[28] Recent research by economic historians has stressed the importance of the institutional framework and the legal conditions for the rise of modern industry, such as the protection of private investment and the calculable behaviour of the political authorities, who operate under the law. See D.S. Landes, *The Unbound Prometheus: Technological Change and Industrial Development in Western Europe from 1750 to the Present* (Cambridge, 1969), pp. 1-40; D.C. North and R.P. Thomas, *The Rise of the Western World: A New Economic History* (Cambridge, 1973), pp. 155ff.

[29] This appellation is borrowed from the famous book of L. Levy-Bruhl, *La mentalité primitive* (Paris, 1922); not everybody is happy with it, and some authors advocate using 'prerational' instead of 'primitive' thought, but so far no consensus has been reached on this point.

current recourse by the law courts to the ordeal.[30] This phase came to an end in the twelfth century, to give way in the later middle ages to a more scientific approach stimulated, in the scholarly world, by Aristotelian thought and the modest beginnings of experimental research,[31] and, for the public at large, by the crisis and eventual elimination of the supernatural means of proof in forensic practice.[32] The next phase followed in modern times, when traditional religion was 'demythologized' and freed from its supersensual dimension (no more miracles), while the reasonableness of Christianity was demonstrated and Holy Scripture subjected to historical criticism.

The breakthrough of seventeenth-century science coincided with the debunking as superstition of an immense folklore of magic, witchcraft and astrology. It reduced God's role to that of the *primus movens*, as the physical world He had created moved forever according to the unchangeable laws of nature.[33] It may seem appropriate in this context also to mention the secular transition from a monolithic to a pluralistic society, beginning with the seventeenth-century recognition of the dissenters and the abolition of censorship and continuing in the nineteenth century with Catholic Emancipation.

Recurrences and Constants

From lines to circles: what about cyclical movements, recurrences and permanences? It is not difficult to point out the permanent elements. The most obvious is the political structure of the country that preserved its unitary national monarchy throughout some eleven centuries. The non-English parts of Great Britain admittedly joined England, but that country

---

[30] The best general introduction can be found in H. Nottarp, *Gottesurteile: Eine Phase im Rechtsleben der Völker* (Bamberg, 1949). A considerable amount of information is gathered in vol. XVII of the *Recueils de la Société Jean Bodin: la preuve*, ii, *Moyen âge et temps modernes* (Brussels, 1965). For England the reader may consult P. Hyams, 'Trial by Ordeal: The Key to Proof', in M.S. Arnold et al. (eds.), *On the Laws and Customs of England: Essays in Honor of Samuel E. Thorne* (Chapel Hill, NC), 1981, pp. 90-126.

[31] To what extent scientific experiment was used in the middle ages is a much debated question. Among those who believe this to have been the case, notably in England, is A.C. Crombie, *Robert Grosseteste and the Origins of Experimental Science, 1100-1700* (Oxford, 1953). See, however, the criticism by A. Koyré, 'Les origines de la science moderne', *Diogène*, 16 (1956), pp. 13-42.

[32] See on the rationalization of evidence from the twelfth century onwards R.C. Van Caenegem, 'La preuve dans le droit du moyen âge occidental: Rapport de synthèse', *La preuve*, ii, pp. 709-48.

[33] On the decline of 'magic' and the progress of rational and scientific thought, even in broad popular circles, see the excellent work of Keith Thomas, *Religion and the Decline of Magic: Studies in Popular Beliefs in Sixteenth- and Seventeenth-Century England* (London, 1971).

never deviated from its precocious political unity: it ignored regional separatism, feudal or otherwise, as well as the urban autonomy that was so important on the Continent. English class structures also are a permanent characteristic. Disraeli's 'two nations' can, *mutatis mutandis*, be traced in Anglo-Saxon times, when slavery was widespread. After 1066 the social cleavage between landlords and subjected peasants was sharpened by the ethnic division between the *Franci* of the twelfth-century charters, who were the lords, and the *Anglici* – also called *nativi* or *rustici* – who were their inferiors.[34]

Even today, when the terrors of the workhouse are a thing of the past, England is deeply marked by class differences, in education (the public schools and the old universities still educating the elite) as well as in wealth: egalitarian policies have failed to produce the levelling of incomes and fortunes which some people had hoped for.[35] Besides these permanent elements I also discern some recurrences and a certain dialectic. Thus time and again the dominant class was driven from its position by one that was more (or more directly) economically productive: the medieval nobility and clergy by the entrepreneurs of modern times, who underwent in their turn the impact of organized labour. It is noteworthy that the Tudor monarchy was instrumental in the replacement of the warrior aristocracy and the clergy by the third estate. The Tudors indeed used the Star Chamber to tame the nobility, in so far as the latter had not eliminated itself in the Wars of the Roses, dissolved the monasteries and confiscated their immense landed wealth. By the Act of Supremacy the secular clergy was placed under the direct and exclusive control of the state. It would unfortunately carry us too far to examine who used whom: the Tudors the bourgeoisie or the other way round. In other words, were the submissive parliaments of Henry VIII and Elizabeth I so submissive precisely because the crown followed the anti-aristocratic and anti-clerical policy they desired? As soon as it became apparent that Stuart policy did not agree with that of the third estate (particularly the Calvinist middle class of the most urbanized areas), that submissiveness came to an end: it appeared that a powerful monocracy was no indispensable instrument for the political aims of the new notables, as parliament could do it equally well, if not better. However, before the hour of parliament and the third estate had arrived, during the century and a half when the barons had lost power and the bourgeoisie had not yet attained it,

---

[34] See the interesting survey of F. Joüon des Longrais, 'Le vilainage anglais et le servage réel et personnel: quelques remarques sur la période 1066-1485', *Recueils de la Société Jean Bodin*, ii, (Brussels, 1937), pp. 199-242. Amongst recent publications one may consult J.R. Maddicott, *The English Peasantry and the Demands of the Crown, 1294-1341* (n.p., 1975) and P. Hyams, *Kings, Lords and Peasants in Medieval England: The Common Law of Vileinage in the Twelfth and Thirteenth Centuries* (Oxford, 1980).

[35] See the figures in my *Geschiedenis van Engeland* (The Hague, 1982), p. 435.

the monarchy had an ideal opportunity of achieving the height of power. In the twentieth century, the fourth estate, organized labour, reduced in its turn the dominating position of the oligarchs, by using the same parliament which three centuries earlier had driven out absolutism and initiated the era of the bourgeois oligarchy.[36]

Another intriguing dialectic can be observed in the regularity (whether it is a 'law of history' is another matter) with which the instrument has come to play the role of master, or the product has dethroned its creator – it might be termed the 'law of the emancipation of the creature'. It is thus no exaggeration to maintain that the church in the time of the heptarchy produced the monarchy and turned temporary warlords, who had come over with their bands from Schleswig-Holstein, into permanent leaders and even anointed kings, invested with the prestige of Christianity. It was that monarchy which freed itself in the sixteenth century from the Roman church and turned the *ecclesia anglicana* into an institution of the state under the crown. Something similar happened with science, which in the middle ages was based on clerical initiatives and for many centuries was a product of religious institutions, until it freed itself not so long ago from its old substratum. The monarchy itself created parliament, conceived as an instrument of royal government and convened to listen to the chancellor, receive his message and vote the necessary aids. In the course of centuries parliament was emancipated and, at the cost of a civil war, established its supremacy. The parliamentarian oligarchy of the eighteenth and nineteenth centuries, first landlords and then entrepreneurs, in its turn brought forth a power that would eventually overtake it. We mean, of course, the industrial workers, the instrument *volens, nolens* of capitalist heavy industry and bourgeois finance, which eventually turned against the creators of modern industry. The latter were by legal means bereft of their control, and power came into the hands of a democratic parliament – a development still going on and whose denouement is still uncertain and therefore better left to futurologists.[37]

---

[36] Among the surveys of the events of the seventeenth century are C. Hill, *The Century of Revolution, 1603-1714* (London, 1980); L. Stone, *The Causes of the English Revolution, 1529-1642* (London, 1972) and G.E. Aylmer, *The Struggle for the Constitution, 1603-1689: England in the Seventeenth Century* (London, 1963).

[37] See among the best documented surveys of English twentieth-century developments E.E. Reynolds and N.H. Brasher, *Britain in the Twentieth Century, 1900-1964* (Cambridge, 1966); W.N. Medlicott, *Contemporary England, 1914-1964, with Epilogue, 1964-74* (London, 1976) and C.J. Bartlett, *A History of Postwar Britain, 1945-1974* (London, 1977). According to the famous economist and sociologist J.A. Schumpeter, one of the paradoxes of capitalism consists in the destructive role played by the intellectuals who had been produced and left at liberty by capitalism; see a recent analysis of his ideas in A. Heertje (ed.), *Schumpeter's Vision: Capitalism, Socialism and Democracy after 40 Years* (Eastbourne, 1981).

A History Full of Paradoxes

It is only natural that various situations can repeat themselves at various moments in history, as the number of possible solutions to the essential problems of man and society are finite. The aforementioned recurrences, constants and long-term trends should not, however, convince us that everything in the English past followed a rectilinear course, passing without a hitch from one 'ism' to the next (such as the succession of feudalism, capitalism and socialism). Nor should one imagine that everything happened according to the crystal-clear laws of logic: indeed, several phases and changes of course in England's past were anything but foreseeable, and I would now like to turn to some of the most striking of these paradoxes. The first is that eighteenth- and nineteenth-century England was saddled with the most feudal constitutional and private law of Europe, at the very moment when it produced the most modern economy and society in the world. The First Industrial Nation took root and grew up under the regime of an uncodified common law which, when compared to the codified law of the Continent, nurtured on Roman and natural law and the Enlightenment, was incredibly old-fashioned (at least until the Judicature Acts of 1873 and 1875).

The fundamental structure of the common law was quite simply medieval, its twelfth-century origin still clearly visible. Blackstone rightly – though without any intention of disparagement – called it a 'Gothic castle'. The paralysing dichotomy of common law and equity was still alive, the latter being followed in the court of Chancery where the chance was very slim that the initiator of a case could live to see its final denouement.[38] The medieval elements in the constitution were no less visible: parliament and charters of liberties – such as Magna Carta, the Petition of Right and the Bill of Rights – either were medieval or went back to medieval antecedents; the established church went back to the sixteenth century; the monarchy was attached in many ways to its medieval past; and the House of Lords, consisting of a few bishops and hereditary peers, was in fact an assembly of the hereditary aristocracy, wielding until the beginning of the twentieth century a right of veto over the bills voted by the House of Commons.

Another paradox lies in the fact that England, the pioneer industrialized and proletarian country, carrying the weight of an enormous and characteristic *Lumpenproletariat*, avoided a proletarian revolution, leaving this honour

---

[38] On the history of English law since the eighteenth century see B. Abel-Smith and R. Stevens, *Lawyers and the Courts: A Sociological Study of the English Legal System, 1750-1965* (London, 1967); G.J. Hand and D.J. Bentley (eds.), *Radcliffe and Cross: The English Legal System* (London, 1977); J.H. Baker, *An Introduction to English Legal History* (London, 1979) and A.H. Manchester, *A Modern Legal History of England and Wales, 1750-1950* (London, 1980).

or dishonour (according to everyone's political inclination) to the late comers – the latest recruit producing the biggest and most successful workers' revolution of all. The first industrial nation, destined according to all logical prognoses to become the first socialist people's republic, did not even produce the first workers' party; on the contrary, in comparison with German social democracy the Labour Party was an incredibly late and tame arrival on the political scene.[39]

A third paradox is, I believe, the remarkable, even spectacular, religious revival in the Victorian era. Again all reasonable prognoses were belied and all logical threads traversed. Can one, indeed, imagine a less fertile soil for religion and the churches than the eighteenth-century combination of the sceptical Enlightenment of the better classes and the proletarianization of the masses? Can one imagine a juncture more fatal to religion than that of an oppressed industrial proletariat combined with a philosophy averse to religious revelation and a science based on the laws of physics? Yet, in spite of all this, the Victorian revival took place, its well-known manifestations being religious enthusiasm, prudishness, obsession with Lord's Day Observance, large families, successful popular missions and world-wide efforts by English missionaries to convert the heathen. The consequences for scientific research, which never stood still, were amazing: Darwin's work would in the eighteenth century not have caused the scandal which it created in 1850 and the following years.[40]

A fourth and last paradox which I would like to mention concerns the English, or rather the British constitution, and incidentally judicial review of the constitutionality of laws. It is prima facie strange that the cradle of constitutional monarchy and liberties manages to live without a written constitution: it is, incidentally, one of the few examples in the present world of the purely medieval notion of the sources of the law, that custom is the essential matrix, only occasionally complemented by statutes.[41] It is possible to go even further and to maintain that English law in reality ignores the very notion of a fundamental law, since this is based on a hierarchy of laws, in which constitutional rules cannot be changed or abolished by an ordinary

---

[39] Whereas the German social-democratic party was already before the First World War the largest in the Reichstag, the Labour Party was still a very minor formation in parliament, operating in the shadow of the two important parties. Its first 'success' came in 1906, with the election of twenty-nine of its candidates: even if one adds twenty-four other members from the workers' movements, the total of fifty-three was very modest in a House with more than 600 seats. The powerful Chartist Movement (c. 1830 – c. 1850) had been a failure and made no impression on Westminster.

[40] See G. De Beer, *Charles Darwin: A Scientific Biography* (London, 1965); J. Huxley, *Charles Darwin and his World* (London, 1965); G. Kitson Clark, *The Making of Victorian England* (London, 1966).

[41] Thus, for example, Sir Edward Coke (1634) in Bonham's Case (1610) defended the thesis that the common law, as interpreted by the judges was a touchstone for Acts of Parliament, which were not supposed to go 'against common right and reason' on pain of nullity. This position was expressly abandoned in 1871 in *Lee v. Bude* (L.R.6, C.P., 576, 582).

parliamentary majority. All English laws are equal and they can all be changed, suspended or abolished by the normal process and an ordinary majority in parliament. One consequence is that judicial review of the constitutionality of laws is unknown in England (in contrast, *inter alia*, to the United States) and is hardly imaginable there. Lord Hailsham admittedly launched an appeal in that sense a few years ago and advocated the promulgation of a written constitution and the recognition of the aforementioned judicial review, but it looks as if he was a *vox clamantis in deserto*. As a consequence, in strictly juridical terms, the protection of fundamental freedoms is poorly guaranteed in Great Britain, as parliament has the unlimited power to suspend, for example, such freedoms as Habeas Corpus, and consequently to allow arbitrary imprisonment in certain parts of the United Kingdom. One might say that the *parliamentum legibus absolutum* has taken the place of the old *princeps legibus absolutus*, so that terms such as 'democratic' or 'collective dictatorship' are not so far fetched as one might at first be inclined to believe.

One final point, which goes beyond the scope of English history, may be allowed here. It concerns the role of historical research in general, and can be formulated as follows. Beside such scholarly disciplines (retrospective or otherwise) as sociology, economics and jurisprudence, which are concerned with laws, paradigms and schemes, historical research conserves a purpose of its own in showing what unexpected roads humanity has sometimes followed and how unpredictable the ultimate results have been of certain important turns in human development. That is why the study of history remains an indispensable part of the study of man and society.

5

Parliament: A European Deviation?

The parliamentary system is a great bone of contention of the twentieth century. To some people parliamentary democracy is a superior form of government, well adapted to developed societies with traditions of freedom and cultural sophistication. They consider that the establishment of a military regime or of one-party rule, and the abolition or emasculation of parliament, are always disastrous developments. They believe that parliament is the *nec plus ultra* and its origin and rise is the leitmotif that gives sense to the history of a nation. The Oxford medievalist William Stubbs, for example, saw the Victorian parliament as the majestic outcome of a continuous evolution which had started in the Germanic forests, whence the Angles and Saxons had crossed to Britain: such an outcome gave sense to English history and was, as it were, pre-ordained.

Not everyone, however, adores the parliamentary form of government. In the eyes of many political movements it is the great enemy, blocking the way to national greatness, and no more than a *féodalité des partis*, a conspiracy of sectional interests against the *bonum commune* and the state. To them parliament is a 'talking shop', the 'palladium of the bourgeoisie', and the first measure taken by dictatorships of the right and of the left has been to castrate parliament by turning it into a powerless mass-meeting where rulers were frequently and frenetically acclaimed. A Russian bourgeois parliament on the western pattern knew only a very brief honeymoon before being swept away by the October Revolution.[1] The parliament of the Weimar Republic abolished itself as a political entity in 1933: it continued to play a modest role as the recipient of speeches by the Führer and – in an

---

[1] See the *status quaestionis* for old Russia in M. Szeftel, 'La participation des assemblées populaires dans le gouvernement central de la Russie depuis l'époque kiévienne jusqu'à la fin du XVIIIe siècle', *Recueils de la Société Jean Bodin*, xxv (Brussels, 1965), pp. 339-65. Except for a certain amount of popular participation in the preparation of a – never-published – codification in the day of Catherine II the people played no role in the exercise of governmental power between the old Zemskii Sobor (which culminated in the mid seventeenth century) and 1905, when the Tsar, on 30 October, announced the convocation of an elected Duma and the recognition of fundamental liberties.

interesting show of legal formalism – dutifully renewed the 1933 transfer of full power every four years. It was proclaimed that the one-party regime would give the country an efficient government and prove that the Nazis' sarcastic comments about parliament and the rule of the political parties were fully justified.

In practically every European country defenders and enemies of parliament virulently fought each other. An observer who ignored the past might have believed that the parliamentary regime was a recent invention, a modern innovation, which for various reasons had met with resistance and dividing the modern world. Nothing is further from the truth: parliamentarianism is a product of the late medieval phase of European history and our present-day parliaments go back – more or less directly – to the parliaments, estates, estates general, cortes and diets of the thirteenth and fourteenth centuries.[2] It is nevertheless clear that even in cases of the most direct continuity – parliament in Westminster, for example – the composition, function and aims of parliament have changed considerably in the course of the centuries. European parliaments did not originate as national, democratically elected assemblies, where parties debated and decided matters of policy and legislation and voted the budgets required by governments. On the contrary, they were created as elements of the royal administration, cogs in the machinery of the monarchy. They were deemed to represent the country – although their members were drawn (in so far as they were not heriditarily elected) only from a small ruling class of leading clergymen, nobles and urban notables – and were supposed to listen to communications on the king's policy. They were also expected to grant the necessary taxes and to take the collection of the moneys upon themselves, as state bureaucracies were not yet capable of carrying out such cumbersome chores.

It is therefore understandable that the earliest parliaments appear in the stronger monarchies – England, Spain – but not in Germany, where the monarchy was fast losing ground, or in northern Italy, where the city-state filled the void left by the bitter struggle between pope and emperor. Gradually parliaments have become a European phenomenon, either as

---

[2] See the *status quaestionis* in A. Marongiu, *Medieval Parliaments: A Comparative Study* (London, 1968); rev. transl. of *Il Parlamento in Italia nel medio evo e nell' eta moderna* (Milan, 1962), itself a complete revision of the author's *Istituto parlamentare in Italia dalle origini al 1500* (Rome, 1949). Numerous articles on the subject can be found in the series of *Studies Presented to the International Commission for the History of Representative and Parliamentary Institutions*, and for Belgium in *Standen en landen*, (Leuven, from 1950). Among older works the following are of particular significance: H. Spangenberg, *Vom Lehnstat zum Ständestaat: Ein Beitrag zur Entstehung der landständischen Verfassung* (Munich and Berlin, 1912) and E. Lousse, *La société d'ancien régime: organisation et représentation corporatives* (Leuven, 1943). The Société Jean Bodin which specialises in the comparative history of institutions, devoted one of its congresses to the theme *Gouvernés et gouvernants en Europe occidentale durant le bas moyen âge et les temps modernes*, xxiv (1966), pp. 7-48.

national (*états généraux*) or as regional assemblies. They have outgrown their original humble task and have come to play an important role in legislation and in politics *stricto sensu*, particularly by winning control of the use of the taxes they granted. In the late middle ages the Spanish cortes and the English parliament were powerful institutions, with which the monarchy had to come to terms. The question was whether this system of power sharing could last: was it conceivable that a country would forever be ruled by the crown and parliament? Could it go on serving two masters? Or was this impossible, so that a moment would inevitably arrive when either the monarchy or parliament would become the real master, in whose sphere no other political gods would be tolerated.

In modern times the medieval condominium came to an end. In most countries the monarchy rid itself of parliament, whose services could be dispensed with and whose activities interfered with royal government. This was the case of the absolute monarchies, particularly in France, where the glory of Louis XIV 'le Roi Soleil' and his policy of territorial expansion could manage without the Estates General: the monarchy had dropped the latter as a healed cripple throws away his crutches. There were, however, exceptions to the rule. The English parliament resisted royal attempts to govern without a national assembly and its grants. The Civil War between the parliamentary and the royalist camps led to the defeat of the crown and to the execution of King Charles I in 1649. The medieval parliament had vanquished the absolutism of the state, which to many observers, mainly on the Continent, was the form of government of the future. In most countries the seventeenth and eighteenth centuries witnessed the nadir of parliament. But there has been a reaction. In the late eighteenth and particularly in the nineteenth century parliament became popular in anti-absolutist, liberal circles. Under the banner of the illustrious English example, the self-confident bourgeoisie sought the introduction and empowerment of parliament as its most powerful tool. When, before the First World War, Europe stood at the pinnacle of its power, parliament enjoyed an enormous prestige, in constitutional monarchies as well as republics, and was widely regarded as the civilized form of government par excellence, just as western civilization was considered as the undisputed model, whose universal expansion was only a question of time.[3] However, the First World War and the subsequent difficult years were critical for parliamentarianism. At present only a limited number of states – including very powerful and prosperous ones – are governed by parliaments made up of freely elected politicians of various parties.

One of the countries to show the greatest enthusiasm for parliamentarianism at the end of the eighteenth century was France, and the country that was most highly praised in that anglophile century was, of course, England.

---

[3] See R.C. Van Caenegem, *De plaats van de westerse middeleeuwen in de universele geschiedenis* (Bruges, 1964) (inaugural lecture University of Ghent).

France had previously been familiar with parliamentarianism, but had abandoned it after 1614.

Why was the parliamentary system victorious in England while it floundered in France? This question has intrigued many historians; it does not only concern France, but also other countries which went the same way. One often hears the explanation that France was so much larger than England and the convocation of a national assembly was too cumbersome because of the long distances to Paris and the very large population of the country.[4] This argument is not entirely convincing. Distances within France certainly were considerable, but they were not longer than those travelled by the numerous clerics and laymen who went to Rome from remote parts of Latin Christendom to obtain privileges and appointments or to conduct their lawsuits. Nor did huge distances discourage the hundreds of participants from every corner of Europe who took part in the great ecumenical councils in Switzerland and Italy in the late fourteenth and the first half of the fifteenth century. I am inclined to look for an explanation in another direction, in the great difference in the political development of France and England in the centuries preceding parliamentarianism: what Helen Cam called the 'role of chronology'.[5] Indeed, England was more strongly unified than France, where in the late middle ages political life on the regional level was still very important. France was rich in provincial assemblies of estates (just as numerous provincial great Charters were proclaimed), but there was no national 'fundamental law', as existed in England in 1215.[6] England had only one parliament, which sat at Westminster and spoke for the whole country – an enormous strength.

This difference in national unity and cohesion was a direct consequence of the very divergent political history of the two countries from the ninth to the twelfth century. It was exactly at the time of French feudal dismemberment and the establishment of regional dynasties combined with the collapse of central government, that England finally overcame the divisions of the 'heptarchy' and was turned into a unified and well-organized kingdom. From the twelfth century onwards the French monarchy attempted to turn the feudal leaf, but it had a lot of leeway to make up. Consequently the financial organization of the crown and the establishment of central admin-

---

[4] R. Fawtier, 'Parlement d'Angleterre et états généraux de France au moyen âge', *Académie des Inscriptions et Belles Lettres: Comptes rendus* (1953), pp. 275-84.

[5] H. Cam, 'The Theory and Practice of Representation in Medieval England', *History*, 1 (1953), pp. 11-36; repr. in her *Law-Finders and Law-Makers in Medieval England: Collected Studies in Legal and Constitutional History* (London, 1962), pp. 163ff. See also B. Lyon, 'Medieval Constitutionalism: A Balance of Power', *Album H.M. Cam*, ii (Leuven, 1963), pp. 172ff.; A.R. Myers, 'The English Parliament and the French Estates-General in the Middle Ages', ibidem, pp. 139-53 and P.S. Lewis, 'The Failure of the French Medieval Estates', *Past and Present*, 23 (1962), pp. 3-24.

[6] See F. Lot and R. Fawtier, 'Institutions royales', Lot and Fawtier, *Histoire des institutions françaises au moyen âge*, ii (Paris, 1958), pp. 537ff.; B. Lyon, 'Medieval Constitution'.

istrative and judicial institutions lagged about a century behind England. The political unification of the two countries was in no way comparable either. Regional separatism and urban autonomy – the 'communal movement' – of the twelfth and thirteenth centuries retarded the construction of a centralized state, tempered by a national parliament; urban autonomy was also a very different way of giving the burgesses a say in national affairs from the English solution of sending urban representatives to a central parliament. England has never known such a communal movement, in spite of the remarkable privileges obtained by the city of London. This was for the same reason the strength of the communal movement: it stood in inverse proportion to that of the crown.

Although there were differences from country to country, the popularity of parliament was a European phenomenon. Even the strongly centralized church, with the papal *plenitudo potestatis* leaving little room for lay participation (the 'sheep' entrusted to their 'shepherds'), was influenced by parliamentary ideas and went through the great experiment of the conciliar movement, after the example of the royal parliaments. This constituted a brief but interesting episode characterized by a participation in the affairs of the church by all its parts, through the hundreds of representatives intent on demolishing the centralism of the Roman curia at the ecumenical councils of Basle, Constance and Ferrara-Pisa.[7]

Parliamentarianism gained in popularity because it was seen to combine two elements which at first sight were mutually exclusive: political centralization and the association of the country in the exercise of power. Europe had previously oscillated between royal centralization on the one hand and revolt against royal oppression and feudal anarchy on the other. Now a solution was found capable of reconciling those two extremes. Parliamentarianism accepted the central government but at the same time provided the people with an institutional forum for playing a political role and exerting pressure on the government within the limits of the law. Political and legal notions of popular sovereignty (Marsilius of Padua)[8] and the role of the 'representative institutions' (Bartolus: 'concilium representat mentem

---

[7] See among recent works: A. Black, *Monarchy and Community: Political Ideas in the Later Conciliar Controversy, 1430-1450* (Cambridge, 1970); B. Tierney, 'The Prince is Not Bound by the Laws: Accursius and the Origins of the Modern State', *Atti Accursiani*, Milan (1968), pp. 1245-74 also in *Comparative Studies in Society and History*, 5 (1963), pp. 378-400; P. De Vooght, *Les pouvoirs du concile et l'autorité du pape au concile de Constance* (Paris, 1965); G. Post, *Studies in Medieval Legal Thought: Public Law and the State, 1100-1322* (Princeton, 1964) (containing, *inter alia*, 'Plena Potestas and Consent in Medieval Assemblies: A Study in Roman Canonical Procedure and the Rise of Representation', *Traditio*, 1 (1943)); E. Cortese, *La norma giuridica: spunti teorici nel diritto comune classico*, 2 vols. (Milan, 1962-64); B. Tierney, *Foundations of the Conciliar Theory: The Contribution of the Medieval Canonists from Gratian to the Great Schism* (Cambridge, 1955).

[8] W. Ullmann, 'De Bartoli sententia: "Concilium repraesentat mentem populi"', *Bartolo da Sassoferrato*, ii (Milan, 1962), pp. 726ff.

populi') played an important role.[9] There is no doubt that parliamentary monarchy was a felicitous formula, combining the advantages of centralism and political unity (concentration of power, riches and talent) with those of a considerable degree of popular freedom and association in the exercise of power. The aforementioned problem of the dichotomy at the top was solved by entrusting government to the executive power, which was distinct from parliament but could not govern without it, so that in the last analysis the fundamental political options were left to parliament.

For practical reasons the direct democracy of some medieval cities and of the Swiss cantons was hard to realize in the confines of a kingdom: indirect democracy, via national representatives, was a satisfactory substitute. It should, however, be clear that whereas parliaments came to play that role in course of time, they were not created for that purpose. They were neither invented by theoretical thinkers, wanting to solve the problem of how to reconcile centralism with popular consensus, nor by political interests inventing and convening parliament in order to limit royal power. This happened in later centuries, whenever a revolution broke out and 'national assemblies' or 'estates general', keen on toppling despots and fired on by great orators, blossomed. The early parliaments, as we have seen, were products of the royal administration, convened because of the shortcomings of existing institutions and the treasury, during the transition from a primitive, patrimonial monarchy to a modern bureaucratic state. They involved therefore a good deal of ambiguity: parliaments were, in the eyes of the monarchy, destined for very different ends from those the notables later gave them. It was therefore quite natural that this ambiguity was eventually eliminated and a moment arrived, in the sixteenth and especially the seventeenth century, when the situation was finally clarified. Three options seemed open then: the triumph of the national parliament (as in England); its disappearance (as with the French *états généraux*); or its continued existence as a purely administrative organ in the ruler's service (the normal course in the German principalities).[10]

It may seem a paradox that, as we will see, this excellent institution has been – and still is – so exceptional in the world at large. It may also seem paradoxical that this form of government, created in an underdeveloped agricultural Europe, which believed in witches and devils and attributed the plague to 'bad air', has been adopted and retained by several important countries in our own sophisticated and industrialized age. The reason lies in its intrinsic value and its usefulness in various functions and circumstances (rather like biology's polyvalent cells that can develop in all directions). Parliament has not only gone through remarkable ups and downs, it has also shown great flexibility, in the transition, for example, from an exclusive club

---

[9] Ibid.
[10] See F.L. Carsten, *Princes and Parliaments in Germany from the Fifteenth to the Eighteenth Century* (Oxford, 1959).

of notables to a democratic assembly, elected by universal suffrage. Parliament has demonstrated its excellence not only in the field of political theory, but also in terms of practical usefulness.

One might therefore be inclined to consider it as a very common, universally known form of government, comparable to such omnipresent institutions as the monarchy, the family, religion, the city state, the republic and the army. Nothing is further from the truth. The historic European parliament is neither a universal form of government nor a survival from Antiquity, 'resurrected' in the middle ages like the Roman empire; on the contrary, it is an original creation of the West and unique in world history. Even today truly parliamentary regimes are 'rari nantes in gurgite vasto', notwithstanding the undoubted prestige of parliament and its paraphernalia, which are so diligently copied in ex-British colonies in Africa by a chancellor on the 'woolsack' and a speaker with a mace. The Romans and the Greeks, who gave us so much in the field of legal practice and political theory are irrelevant here, for they did not know the institution of parliament.[11] This means that no compelling universal factors have been at play but rather concrete circumstances in the West. Which circumstances?

The German historian Otto Hintze went deeply into this comparative-historical question.[12] Hintze, who died in 1940, had started as a traditional historian, by editing documents and publishing solid studies on Prussian constitutional history. When increasing blindness prevented him from continuing in that vein, he devoted himself to research into various aspects of universal history, in which he betrayed uncommon knowledge and remarkable insight. The manuscript of his main work, the *Allgemeine vergleichende Verfassungsgeschichte*, completed before 1933 but never published, was lost during the war,[13] but one of his published studies concerned the 'universal-historical conditions for the representative form of government'. The author noted that parliamentarianism 'is no invention common to humanity, but originated as an autochthonous institution in the Christian West', and only there, initially in the *Vorform* of the estates; this evolution 'does not warrant us to speak of a general sociological law, but rather of a singular historical development, albeit common to all of Western Europe,

[11] See the *status quaestionis* by J. Gaudemet, 'Gouvernés et gouvernants dans le monde grec et romain: rapport de synthèse', *Recueils de la Société Jean Bodin*, xxiii (Brussels, 1968), pp. 21-44. R. Van Compernolle, 'Gouvernés et gouvernants dans la Grèce classique', ibid., pp. 139-80, and J. Gaudemet, 'Le peuple et le gouvernement de la république romaine', ibid., pp. 189-252; J.A.O. Larsen, *Representative Government in Greek and Roman History* (Berkeley, 1966). It should not be forgotten that the Roman senate, which managed to conserve part of its original importance, was no emanation of the people, but an assembly of aristocrats under tight imperial control.

[12] O. Hintze, 'Weltgeschichtliche Bedingungen der Repräsentativverfassung', *Historische Zeitschrift*, 143 (1931), pp. 1-47; repr., *Gesamm. Abh.*, i (Göttingen, 1962), pp. 140-85. See also his 'Typologie der ständischen Verfassungen des Abendlandes', ibid., 141 (1930), pp. 229-48; repr., *Gesamm. Abh.*, i, pp. 120-39.

[13] M.C. Brands, *Tijdschrift voor geschiedenis*, 79 (1966), p. 220, and the introd., 'Otto Hintzes Lebenswerk', by F. Hartung in vol. I of the *Gesamm. Abh.*, pp. 7-33.

whose products were later transferred to other countries'. Hintze wondered, of course, what factors were responsible for this exceptional development. His explanation, full of nuances, is that parliamentarianism was essentially a by-product of the late medieval state. As the western state contained strong feudal elements, feudalism also played a role. In another essay Hintze also pointed out that feudalism was 'no general phase of transition, common to humanity in its social and political development'.[14] He mentioned the opposition between church and state, which in the West prevented the establishment of a universal empire and led to the triumph of the national monarchies, whose rulers depended on the notables *inter alia*, for financing their numerous wars.

When one encounters important institutions or attitudes which occur in Europe but not in other civilizations, one is naturally reminded of Jan Romein's 'European deviation from the common human pattern'. Parliament appears as a specific example of such a European 'anomaly', which did not originate in modern, but in late-medieval Europe.[15] The common human practice seems indeed to vary between oligarchy or direct democracy in the towns, city-states or small republics on the one hand, and imperial omnipotence in centralized superstates on the other. The reader will be familiar with Romein's vision of modern European development as the great exception in the universal-historical pattern. Among the factors that explain Europe's exceptional lustre and power, the author rightly mentioned modern parliamentarianism as the political instrument par excellence for the concentration of the national effort. For him the modern state was the essential factor, while parliamentarianism was one of the elements which helped it to gain the loyal adherence of the people at large, *inter alia*, by associating them in the prosperity of the state. This is of course a recent development, but historically speaking it is no more than a new phase in the fluctuating story of representative institutions. The question of how and why parliamentary deviation occurred arises.

Such an exceptional form of government must either be the work of an exceptional inventor, a political thinker of genius, or the product of an exceptional conjunction of circumstances. I shall try to demonstrate that the latter is the case. It is obvious that a minimal intellectual level, a minimal degree of freedom and a minimal sense of law and order are necessary prerequisites for a parliamentary regime. Where reasonable discussion is unknown, the population is largely servile and the exercise of power consists of arbitrary violence (and its consequences, violent revolts and tyrannicide),

[14] O. Hintze, 'Wesen und Verbreitung des Feudalismus', *Sitzungsberichte der Preussischen Akademie der Wissenschaften, Philologisch-Historische Klasse* (Berlin, 1929), pp. 321-47; repr., *Gesamm. Abh.*, i, pp. 84-119.
[15] J. Romein, *Aera van Europa: De Europese geschiedenis als afwijking van het algemeen menselijk patroon* (Leiden, 1954); idem, *In de ban van Prambanan* (Amsterdam, 1954), pp. 21-58; idem, 'Het algemeen manselijk patroon: ontstaan, belang en draagkracht van historische theorieën', *Eender en anders: twaalf nagelaten Essays* (Amsterdam, 1964), pp. 65-83.

no parliament can flourish. However, more specific circumstances were required for the rise of parliamentarianism in the West. They are of such variety that their concurrence in western Europe from *c*. 1200 can be called a remarkable coincidence.

The first condition was the rise of semi-bureaucratic monarchies in England, Spain, France, Sweden, Denmark, Hungary, Bohemia and Poland. Parliament is only conceivable in kingdoms or principalities (many of the latter in the Low Countries and Germany) with a monarchic form of government, where the ruler really governs instead of exercising a purely ceremonial or external role.[16] The Germanic tribes which conquered the *Pars occidentis* of the Roman empire had weak political structures, even though their rulers tried to imitate the imperial model and to behave as heads of state – with debatable success.

Initially they were tribal kings. The most successful among them, the kings of the Franks, eventually ruled over such a vast territory and acquired such international importance as protectors of the Latin church, that the Roman empire was resuscitated on their behalf. They had, however, over-rated their strength – or rather that of their society – and their neo-Roman empire collapsed. One of the victims was the administration of the Frankish state, which had previously made considerable progress; the regression was most acute in West Francia or France, where royal power became nominal and remained so for a long time. England had not taken part in the reckless imperial ambitions of the Continent, so her monarchy did not suffer the relapse of the continental states: unification progressed slowly but surely, and in the tenth century England was a single monarchy with one central government. Her internal organization kept pace with this political evolution. When the Conqueror was crowned king on Christmas Day 1066, he combined the fighting spirit and ambition of the Normans with the stable infrastructure of the old English monarchy, so that England became one of the most solid national monarchies of Europe. Feudalism, which William and his continental followers introduced, was given no chance of playing a centrifugal role, being turned into an instrument of royal policy. The French monarchy was revived in the twelfth century and launched a two-fold development of political unification and efficient centralized administration.[17] In Spain arose various kingdoms, which were well organized and governed by powerful rulers – a necessity in the struggle against Islam.

The nation states were not only a political reality, they were also supported intellectually by two great currents, the revival of Roman law and of

---

[16] See the excellent work by a scholar who devoted his career to the study of the rise of the modern state: J.R. Strayer, *On the Medieval origins of the Modern State* (Princeton, 1970) (devoted essentially to England and France from the twelfth century, as the starting point of modern political development).

[17] See the classic survey by R. Fawtier, *Les Capétiens et la France* (Paris, 1942), and Lot and Fawtier, *Histoire des institutions françaises au moyen âge*, ii, *Institutions royales* (Paris, 1958).

Aristotelian thought. The former produced the notion of the sovereign state and an arsenal of terms and concepts about the power and the role of central authority, every king being considered 'emperor in his kingdom' and therefore enjoying the prestige of the Roman *princeps*. The latter contributed the idea of the state as the normal form of human society and sharpened the ability to reflect on political problems in a systematic way. Finally, economic development was also favourable: a money economy made progress, enabling the state to finance an expanding bureaucracy. As long as there was land in abundance and little money around, a feudal class of dignitaries of the crown was the best that could be achieved; as soon as more money was available, a body of salaried officials became realizable, with all this entailed in the way of bureaucratization. The revival of the towns as social and economic centres and essential motors of a money economy put qualified personnel, among whom numerous clerics who were university graduates, at their rulers' disposal.

This development was the direct origin of the modern European state. It did not automatically lead to a government with the estates (*Ständestaat*). Neither Roman imperial law nor royal ambition pointed in that direction. On the contrary, the rise of various miniature sovereign empires, each with its own bureaucracy after late-Roman and Byzantine models – seemed to be the normal outcome. It is typical that Glanvill, in his *Tractatus de legibus et consuetudinibus Angliae* (1187-89), expressly quotes the great principle of late-Roman public law: 'what pleases the prince has force of law';[18] and shortly before, Richard fitz Neal, in his *Dialogus de scaccario* (1177-79), had defended the idea that the king was responsible to God alone, in other words, that he stood above human laws.[19] This notion was launched in the middle ages under the famous phrase 'Princeps non est sub lege fori, est tamen sub lege poli', i.e. the ruler does not stand under the law of the courts, but under the law of heaven. Yet, history has moved in another direction. The western kingdoms became no miniature replicas of the Roman empire, and their kings no Roman emperors within national frontiers.

The path of the common human pattern has not been taken, because various factors have interfered with that evolution. There was, to begin with, the traditional representation of the king as the guarantor of the law and himself bound by it, in other words no creator of law, but at most its

---

[18] Ed. G.D.G. Hall, *The Treatise on the Laws and Customs of the Realm of England Commonly Called Glanvill* (London, 1965) p. 2: 'Cum hoc ipsum lex sit "quod principi placet, legis habet vigorem"'.

[19] C. Johnson, *The Course of the Exchequer by Richard, Son of Nigel* (London, 1950) p. 1. There is ample evidence for King John's behaviour as one placed above the law and acting as a prince *legibus solutus*. The examples of royal interference with the normal course of justice can be found in the royal archives themselves, see R.V. Turner, *The King and his Courts* (Ithaca, NY, 1967), pp. 56-120.

interpreter.[20] The king, who reigned rather than ruled, was a military leader and spoke for his people to foreigners. He was not seen as a lawgiver and even less as the head of a centralized bureaucratic machine. The conviction that the king was under the law was deeply held and a king who was *legibus solutus* after the Roman fashion was widely rejected: a monarch whose will was law was no king but a tyrant, and some thinkers authorized tyrannicide.[21] Could this traditional way of thinking be overcome? Another cherished tradition was that the *consensus*, the agreement of the spiritual and temporal aristocracy, was needed for governmental decisions.[22] One constantly reads of royal decisions taken *cum consilio magnatum*. The king was certainly not empowered to raise taxes without the people's consent. Great landowners could freely tax their servile peasants, but freemen could not be treated in such a way. A king who tried this would be treating his people as serfs, an unheard-of scandal and an act of downright robbery in medieval society: it was very dubious whether a 'modern' ruler could set aside these ancient feelings.

Another obstacle was the feudal character of society. Kings were indeed the anointed rulers of the people whom God put in their care, but they were also feudal suzerains from whom the notables directly or indirectly held fiefs. The relationship between king and subject went hand in hand with that between lord and vassal, but the latter was of a very different complexion. Feudal authority was not imposed from above and built on mere subjection, but was based on a contract, freely engaged in, involving mutual rights and duties and, as in every contract, the possibility for one party to terminate it whenever the other party did not fulfil its obligations. The vassal had the right to put an end to his obligations (*diffidatio*) whenever the lord infringed his rights (for example by demanding unreasonable feudal aids); that this feudal lord might be the king himself did not, to the feudal mind, make any difference. We find here the basis of the right of resistance of the *fideles*, who were not mere *subjecti*.[23] Here again rulers who attempted to enlarge their power met with an obstacle which could not easily be overcome.

It is clear that ambitious kings in the twelfth century were bound to encounter stiff resistance, for the political structures they had in mind were

---

[20] See H. Krause, 'Königtum und Rechtsordnung in der Zeit der sächsischen und salischen Herrscher', *Zeitschrift der Savigny Stiftung für Rechtsgeschichte, Germanistische Abteilung*, 82 (1965), pp. 1-98.

[21] See Turner, *The King and his Courts*, pp. 102ff. On the doctrine of the justifiable tyrannicide, see R.H. and M.A. Rouse, 'John of Salisbury and the Doctrine of Tyrannicide', *Speculum*, 42 (1967), pp. 693-709.

[22] *Consensus* has of old played an important role, *inter alia*, in connection with legislation. See, for example, the necessary *consensus* of the magnates speaking for the nation in Frankish times; F.L. Ganshof, *Recherches sur les capitulaires* (Paris, 1958), pp. 30-36.

[23] See the classic analysis by F. Kern, *Gottesgnadentum und Widerstandsrecht*, 2nd ed. by R. Buchner (Munich and Cologne, 1954).

of a different type than the 'primitive' middle ages of Frankish and post-Frankish times. Their attempts to obtain freedom of action and financial contributions, outside and even against current laws and usage, went against existing feeling and came into conflict with powerful vested interests. The ensuing power struggle – of which the revolt against King John is the most famous example – could have led to the liquidation of the monarchy,[24] as happened in ancient Rome with the tyrannical kings; alternatively, it could have led to a victorious monarchy and the establishment of absolute power, as happened in Rome with the regime of Caesar. In fact neither of these paths was taken: the monarchy was preserved, but limited by constitutionalism and parliamentarianism. It became a kingship that gave the country an efficient, but non-tyrannical, central government, which had to operate in consultation with the country.

The church played a role in this compromise. It anointed the kings and supported the monarchy with the prestige of religion; we know that bellicose vassals sometimes refrained from attacking the Anointed of the Lord.[25] However, the Investiture Struggle had shown that certain sectors of public life escaped the control of the kings, who had to share their authority with the church and to accept certain limitations and forms of interference – a contrast with the Christian emperors of Antiquity and Byzantium. This same notion of real, but limited, royal authority was rooted in feudalism, where the obligation of respect and reverence for the lord went hand in hand with a limitation of his position, the feudal nexus being based on a free contract between free people. The clash of all those factors – royal ambitions, the search for modern forms of government, the church as an autonomous and supranational organization, and flourishing feudalism – led to a result which was as extraordinary as the constellation of factors which we have analysed: a centralized but not absolute monarchy. Financially speaking this required the country's consent to any request for taxes, and the convocation of national representative assemblies to grant them.

The form of the assemblies was determined by the existing social structure. The peasant masses were deemed to be represented by their landlords. The burgesses usually did not depend on lords and spoke for themselves, and so, of course, did the clerical and lay landowners. In the old Carolingian lands the tricameral system prevailed and the three estates of clergy, nobility and burgesses (the 'third estate') sat separately. A number of peripheral

---

[24] J.C. Holt, *The Northerners* (Oxford, 1961); idem, *Magna Carta* (Cambridge, 1965).

[25] In 1185 at Boves the army of the count of Flanders, Philip of Alsace, faced that of his suzerain, King Philip Augustus of France and a decisive battle seemed imminent. Nevertheless the count suddenly agreed to a treaty, by which he lost the county of Vermandois, without putting up a fight. See H. Van Werveke, 'Het beeld van Filips van de Elzas', *Weerklank op het werk van Jan Romein* (Amsterdam, 1953), p. 222, and H. Van Werveke, *Filips van de Elzas als biografisch probleem* (Brussels, 1969), p. 14 – but with a different interpretation of the count's motives. Taking up arms against one's feudal lord, who happened to be an anointed king, was a Rubicon which was not lightly crossed.

areas – England, Scandinavia, Poland, Hungary – knew the bicameral system. Here the Upper House continued the old *curia regis*, with the tenants in chief of the crown, clerical and lay, who were summoned personally, whereas in the Lower House knights and burgesses sat together: they were consulted at a later stage and they consisted of a limited number of elected spokesmen who represented their shires or towns.

It is generally known that the control of the royal finances, through the conditional grant of taxes and the check on expenses, was the strongest weapon of parliaments. Their economic basis was the impossibility of the kings covering their growing expenses with the traditional proceeds from their own domains. Economic progress made the new states possible, by urban revival and monetary expansion, indispensable for a centrally conducted bureaucracy. The riches of kings consisted of land and the latter's rising productivity could not offset the enormous growth in crown expenditure. While the monetary stock increased, the new wealth created by higher agricultural prices and expanding trade and industry favoured enterprising landowners and burgesses. They had the money the state needed and from them the state had to get it, in one way or another. Hence the never-ending royal attempts to tap such sources without the intervention of parliament – for example, by the imposition of permanent indirect taxes – and the eternal resistance of parliament, which insisted that the required money should on every occasion be asked for. The king of France eventually succeeded, but the king of England (where the problem was crucial in the seventeenth century) failed.

It was a weakness of the monarchy that it dated back to a purely agrarian period and that its agrarian income was not in step with the expansion of commerce and industry. The crown's income was adequate as long as the role of the state was small, but when the monarchy developed into a modern bureaucracy it needed adequate modern financial means. Certain ingrained notions, however, hindered this solution: kings could not simply take whatever money they needed, they had to ask for it, and the conquest and plunder of whole provinces, which had fed the Roman fisc, was no realistic solution in thirteenth-century Europe. Hence kings were forced to accept restrictions, at least as long there was no other way. The line 'Polonorum comitia sunt regum martyria' applied not only to Poland, but to all monarchs whose national assemblies were, if not martyrdom, at least a great nuisance.

The rise of parliamentarianism would have been impossible without the fulfilment of certain intellectual preconditions. Various essential conceptions derived from the great scholarly currents of the time – Roman law and Aristotle: ideas on representation, popular sovereignty and the *bonum commune*. Representation made it juridically possible for a limited number of bearers of full powers to listen, speak and enter into obligations on behalf of their class or region. Medieval lawyers elaborated this concept, which in canon law was widely used for the representation of bishoprics and orders in general councils. The phrase 'quod omnes tangit ab omnibus approbari debet', derived from Roman private law, was widely quoted to justify the participation of the whole community in the running of government, even in the church: as 'the general council represents the whole Catholic Church' (as was claimed at the council of Constance), the council, and not the curia, was the highest ecclesiastical authority. Similarly Marsilius of Padua said that, in temporal matters, legislative power was in the hands of the community or of 'the best part, representing the whole community'.[26]

Important political theories and technical legal rules for all these aspects were formulated and analysed. Simple notions, as of a village-chief representing the whole village, were of course familiar without Roman law, but the theoretical elaboration of the aforementioned ideas and techniques on the basis of Roman and Aristotelian science was useful for the practical organization of parliaments and gave them intellectual prestige. The other, royal, camp, however, did not lack their own theoretical and Roman-law weapons: the pope was the *haeres beati Petri*, the king was 'emperor in his kingdom' and the emperor was *dominus* and *legibus solutus*. This is not to say that theoretical arguments have been decisive when, from the late fifteenth century onwards, autocracy prevailed over councils and parliaments. In fact, it was normal that the modern *Fürstenstaat* outgrew the restrictions of its infancy and, in modern times, reached its full maturity and disposed directly and freely of the necessary means of action, a standing army and permanent taxation. Europe had, after all, accepted the modern state and had to admit the consequences. People could argue that the parliamentary phase had been a consequence of temporary imperfections, caused by economic circumstances and old-fashioned ideas.

The remarkable thing is that in a few countries parliaments and estates-general not only continued to exist, but even became the main political power. Several local circumstances played a role here. The Northern Netherlands in 1581 renounced their allegiance to Philip II and created a void which had to be filled by the Estates General, for they and the monarchy were the only supraprovincial institutions. In contemporary England there was nothing like a political vacuum, Tudors and Stuarts being all too ready to rule and govern, but religious conflict sharpened the opposition of parliament to the crown, while the numerous jurists in the Commons strongly defended traditional English law, which was not influenced by Roman rules and followed the medieval principle that the king was under the law.[27] The defeat of absolutism in a country with such a strong and old monarchical tradition was amazing and went against the

---

[26] Ullmann, 'De Bartoli sententia', p. 729.

[27] See C. Robbins, 'Why the English Parliament Survived the Age of Absolutism: Some Explanations Offered by Writers of the 17th and 18th centuries', *Studies Presented to the International Commission for the History of Representative and Parliamentary Institutions*, 18 (Leuven, 1958), pp. 199-213.

trend of the time; it was determined by specific, English circumstances, but its consequences were widely felt abroad.

It may have struck the reader that the parliamentary regime originated and survived thanks to the concurrence of various heterogeneous factors and chance circumstances (to the dismay of historians for whom chance is taboo and everything happens logically and according to the laws of history), but it explains why parliamentarianism can be considered one of the European deviations of the common human pattern. Germanic tradition produced the necessity of popular consent and some feudal ideas; Roman tradition produced arguments for a centralized state and legal notions on representation and mandate: European civilization has borrowed unashamedly from various treasure-houses and the interaction of Germanic and Mediterranean elements is one of its characteristics. While the nation states were being organized, the Gregorian Reform founded the independence of the Church. *Libertas ecclesiae* and papal centralism deprived the kings to a considerable extent of their traditional control of the national churches. This allowed the clergy to act vis-à-vis the monarchy as an estate, instead of forming just a group of royal officials: a deviation from the ordinary caesaro-papist pattern.

The rise of the modern state was preceded by a feudal phase, and we have seen the consequences of this contingent phenomenon. Some feudal elements were of Germanic origin, such as the cult of personal loyalty between the war lord and his *Gefolgschaft*, but the system as a whole was an original medieval creation especially through its joining the personal (homage) and the material element (the fief) and the feudalization of public life. However, feudalism was not essential, and England, for example, was well on the way to becoming a modern nation-state without passing through it, while on the Continent certain internal factors in the overambitious empire of the Carolingians resulted *inter alia*, by such fortuitous circumstances as Edward the Confessor dying childless, to the introduction of continental feudalism, just in time to push the monarchy during the two following centuries in a specific direction and causing it to accept certain limitations, contained in the very feudal Magna Carta of 1215.

Another important factor was the far from preordained coincidence in several important countries of the rise of the centralized state with that of an urban money economy. Without the latter the modern state could not live, even if a modern economy could very well live without the former, as appears from the history of northern Italy from the eleventh century onwards: where, because of political, religious or other local circumstances, economic expansion coincided with a crisis of the state, no parliamentary regime could develop. Yet, where, as in England, economic and urban expansion coincided precisely with the rise of a modern state administration, the economic conditions (beside the other aforementioned ones) were ripe for the 'corporate state' and a parliamentary form of government.

At the outset of this essay I posed a question. I have not endeavoured to answer it with a straightforward yea or nay. It would be premature and would create the illusion of a certainty that does not yet exist. The reader, however, may decide for himself how to answer it, unless he prefers to wait and undertake further research: if I have encouraged him to do this, I shall have accomplished my aim.

6
The Sources of Flemish History in the *Liber Floridus*

When Professor Strubbe, president of the *Liber Floridus* committee, invited me to prepare a paper on the sources of Flemish history in Lambert of Saint-Omer's *Liber Floridus*, I envisaged the compilation of a simple and straightforward *status quaestionis*, a summary of common knowledge. So many learned historians have studied the early sources of Flemish history and so famous is the autograph of the *Liber Floridus*, conserved in the university library of Ghent, that I was not expecting discoveries or new data of any importance. I felt rather like Lambert of Saint-Omer, who explained that he made his famous digest because his contemporaries were frightened by the voluminous learned works of the past and thankful for brief information and short extracts. It was therefore with real surprise that I came upon several important passages in Lambert which had been overlooked. It is no doubt because of the miscellaneous nature of the *Liber Floridus*, which is bewildering on first contact, that these important data, although plainly there for everyone to see and even partly printed by Léopold Delisle, have not received the attention they deserve. The symposium on the *Liber Floridus* held in Ghent in 1967 provided the opportunity not only to recall and bring together what is commonly known on the Flemish historical sources in Lambert's venerable work, but also to draw attention to some important material that has hitherto been neglected.

There is, however, one text, which was not so clear as the rest: a brief but unmistakable fragment of an account of revenues in kind of a count of Flanders. These lines only came to light recently, when the eighteenth-century binding was removed for purposes of photography.[1] The tantalizing words and figures of this palimpsest are at least twenty years older than

---

[1] The fragment occurs between fo. 147 v, p. 298 and fo. 153, p. 309 under the heading: *Ratio de curtibus comitis*. See the footnote on p. 298 of the Derolez edition of the *Liber Floridus*. Throughout this essay I refer to the foliation of the autograph MS (except for the fragments missing there and supplied by the copies) and to the pagination of the 1968 edition: *Lamberti S. Audomari canonici Liber Floridus*, edited by A. Derolez, with a preface by E.I. Strubbe and A. Derolez, in folio (Ghent, 1968).

the oldest – and much larger – fragment of an account of a Flemish count hitherto known (A.D. 1140)[2] and must be the oldest fragment of its kind in Europe.[3] The fragment was first noticed by Dr. Albert Derolez, who kindly allowed me to make his discovery known.

The *Liber Floridus* has long been famous for its annals and chronicles. Lambert had a deep historical sense and a pronounced preference for historical material, particularly of a genealogical, annalistic type, and for various forms of chronological lists and series. His book is full of calendars, annals and genealogies – not forgetting his own genealogy; even the hagiographical sections are often presented in annalistic form. Altogether about one quarter of his encyclopaedia deals with history, biblical and profane, in which he gives pride of place to the county of Flanders, and to the town of Saint-Omer in the south of the county, where both the older abbey of Saint-Bertin and Lambert's own younger collegiate church of Saint-Omer were situated.[4] Some of these Flemish sources are well known complete texts of some size, others are entries of a few lines, scattered extracts, selected from some unknown source because of their topicality.

Amongst the former, the *Genealogia comitum Flandriae* is the most famous (fo. 104-105 bis, pp. 211-13 bis, Delisle, no. 177).[5] It is probably Lambert's own work and constitutes a brief history of Flanders, based on the deeds of its remarkable dynasty of rulers. It is in prose, starts with the beginning of the reign of count Lidric in 792 and reaches events of the year 1120 – there is a brief continuation on the dramatic events of 1127-28.[6] The *Genealogia comitum Flandriae* is based on the *Genealogia Bertiniana* and to a lesser extent on the *Annales Bertiniani*, the ninth-century West-Frankish annals, called *Bertiniani* because the oldest manuscript comes from Saint-Bertin; for the rest it is original. It served in its turn as a basis for the *Flandria Generosa* of 1164 or shortly after. Lambert's work is a link in the well-known chain of Flemish historiography that started in the tenth century with a short genealogical list, the *Genealogia Arnulfi comitis Flandrensis* of the priest Witger

---

[2] E.I. Strubbe, *Het fragment van een grafelijke rekening van Vlaanderen uit 1140* (Brussels, 1950).

[3] On the oldest accounts of kings and territorial princes, see R.C. Van Caenegem, *Kurze Quellenkunde des westeuropäischen Mittelalters* (Göttingen, 1964) [with the collab. of F.L. Ganshof], pp. 99ff. In England the oldest Pipe Roll is from 1130; on the advanced financial organization of the English monarchy in the twelfth century, see B. Lyon and A. Verhulst, *Medieval Finance: A Comparison of Financial Institutions in Northwestern Europe* (Bruges, 1967).

[4] Later generations showed their interest in Lambert's historical data by continuations and interpolations such as the one in the calendar on fo. 29 v, p. 60, p. [22] under the date 11 July, which reads 'Hec fuit dies bona Curtracensis', referring to the Flemish victory of the Golden Spurs, near Courtrai on 11 July 1302.

[5] L. Delisle, *Notice sur les manuscrits du 'Liber Floridus' de Lambert, chanoine de Saint-Omer* (Notices et extraits des MSS. de la Bibliothèque Nationale, xxxviii, Paris, 1906), pp. 93-94 [669-70]; ed. L.C. Bethmann, *MGH, SS*, ix (1851), pp. 308-12.

[6] Ibid., pp. 312-13.

who wrote between 951 and 959, possibly at Saint-Bertin;[7] was continued in the eleventh century with the *De Arnulfo comite*, probably written by a monk of St. Peter's abbey in Ghent,[8] with the *Genealogia Bertiniana* in the eleventh and twelfth centuries, probably a product of Saint-Bertin's and St. Peter's,[9] with Lambert's own genealogy of the counts of Flanders and the *Flandria Generosa*, written in or shortly after 1164 by a monk of Saint-Bertin and continued in the thirteenth and fourteenth centuries.[10] The tradition was carried on in the vernacular by such works as the *Ancienne chronique de Flandre* and the *Rijmkroniek van Vlaenderen*,[11] down to the *Excellente Kronike van Vlaenderen*, the first printed history of Flanders (Vorsterman, Antwerp, 1531).

Lambert's *Genealogia* is more than a mere genealogy or list of names; it is a narrative and constitutes in fact a short political history of the county, in which the rulers are always conspicuous. It is no coincidence that he wrote this work in the town of Saint-Omer and in the neighbourhood of the abbey of Saint-Bertin. The abbeys in the south of the county played an important intellectual role and Saint-Bertin was the great centre of Flemish historiography. Its role can be compared with that of Saint-Denis in French historical writing, for, as Bethmann put it: 'Genealogiae comitum Flandrensium quas novimus omnes ortae sunt apud Sanctum Bertinum atque in eius viciniis.' Nor were the monks of Saint-Bertin only interested in Flemish history; they produced the *Annales Sithienses* and the lost Annals of Saint-Bertin, which were used in the *Annales Blandinienses* of the abbey of St. Peter

---

[7] Ibid., pp. 302-4. The work, the autograph of which was in Saint-Bertin and is now MS 776 of the Municipal Library of Saint-Omer, consists in fact of two parts, differing in style, a Carolingian and a Flemish genealogy; only the latter mentions the author, the priest Witger. Whether Witger himself was at Saint-Bertin is not certain; there are indications, both in the Frankish and in the Flemish genealogy, connecting him with Compiègne. The data 959-60 was suggested by P. Grierson in *Revue du Nord*, xxv (1939), p. 137, as against the traditionally accepted date of 951-59.

[8] Ed. Bethmann, p. 304.

[9] Ed. with continuations, ibid., pp. 305-308; the archetype was written under Baldwin V (1035-67) or Baldwin VI (1067-70) and continued in Ghent down to Robert II (d. 1111); there are later continuations, written *inter alia* at Marchiennes, down to 1280, and Cîteaux, down to 1279; cf. O. Oppermann, *Die älteren Urkunden des Klosters Blandinium und die Anfänge der Stadt Gent* (Utrecht, 1928), i, pp. 210-11; P. Grierson, *Les annales de Saint-Pierre de Gand et de Saint-Amand* (Brussels, 1937), p. xlix.

[10] Ed. Bethmann, pp. 313-34.

[11] Both works ed. in J.J. De Smet, *Corpus chronicorum Flandriae*, ii and iv (Brussels, 1841 and 1865). De Smet printed the text of E. Kausler, *Denkmäler der altniederländischen Literatur* (Tübingen, 1840), cf. H. Pirenne, *La Rijmkronijk van Vlaenderen et ses sources* (Brussels, 1888), pp. 346-64; see also H. Pirenne, 'Les sources de l'histoire de Flandre au moyen-âge', *Annales du cercle historique et archéologique de Gand*, i (Ghent, 1895), pp. 1-8. The introductions of Bethmann are most important; much of the material was gathered in his *Lettre à M. l'abbé Carton sur les généalogies des comtes de Flandres* (Bruges, 1849).

in Ghent (and should of course not be confused with the *Annales regni Francorum*).[12] Nor is it remarkable that the oldest Flemish historical writing occurs in genealogical form. Genealogies are one of the primitive forms of historical writing in monarchical and aristocratic societies.[13] The Frankish kings had had their genealogies – and Witger's genealogy of Count Arnulf came after a Carolingian royal genealogy. After the empire of the Franks had broken up into principalities, the new regional rulers found their genealogists – the counts of Flanders in the abbey of Saint-Bertin, the dukes of Brabant in the abbey of Affligem – who naturally traced the respective dynasties back to Frankish royal ancestors. The Capetians themselves were the object of a similar effort, the theme of the *reditus regni Francorum ad stirpem Karoli*.[14]

What is remarkable, however, is first of all the extremely precocious appearance of these Flemish genealogies and other Flemish historical writing, much ahead of their counterparts in Brabant and Holland,[15] and also the very strong accent which they placed on the role of the dynasty in the history and even in the very creation of the county of Flanders. The belief expressed by Lambert in the famous opening line of the *Genealogia*, that Flanders was created by its counts, is remarkable and far from unfounded, for only a remarkable dynasty can explain the rise of that incongruous, bilingual and artificial state and its development into a real *patria*, the Flemish fatherland, which inspired even in Lambert's day the lyrical *Laus Flandriae* of Petrus Pictor.[16] The opening line of the Genealogy runs as follows: 'Anno ab Incarnatione Domini septingentesimo nonagesimo secundo, Karolo Magno regnante in Francia, Lidricus Harlebeccensis comes videns Flandriam vacuam et incultam ac nemorosam occupavit eam' (*L.F.*, fo. 104, p. 211), which became later in the attractive, archaic French of the

---

[12] *Annales regni Francorum*, ed. F. Kurze, 1895 (*MGH, SS in usum scholarum*); *Annales Bertiniani*, ed. G. Waitz, 1883 (*MGH, SS*) and ed. F. Grat, J. Vielliard, S. Clemencet (Paris, 1964). On the lost Annals of Saint-Bertin, see Grierson, *Les Annales de Saint-Pierre de Gand*, p. xv.

[13] See the remarks of G. Duby, 'Structures de parenté et noblesse: France du nord, XIe-XIIe siècles', *Miscellanea mediaevalia J.F. Niermeyer* (Groningen, 1967), pp. 149-65, and of F. Vercauteren, 'Une parentèle dans la France du Nord aux XIe et XIIe siècles', *Le Moyen Age*, lxix (1963), pp. 223-45.

[14] K.F. Werner, 'Die Legitimität der Kapetinger und die Entstehung des "Reditus regni Francorum ad stirpem Karoli"', *Die Welt als Geschichte* (1952), pp. 203-25.

[15] H. Patze, 'Adel und Stifterchronik: Frühformen territorialer Geschichtsschreibung im hochmittelalterlichen Reich', *Blätter für deutsche Landesgeschichte*, 100 (Wiesbaden, 1964), pp. 8-79.

[16] Ed. L. Delisle, *Littérature latine et histoire du moyen âge* (Paris, 1890), pp. 29-31; W. Wattenbach, 'Beschreibung einer Handschrift der Stadtbibliothek zu Reims', *Neues Archiv*, xviii, pp. 508-10; A. Boutemy, *Recueil de textes historiques latins du moyen âge écrits en Belgique ou s'y rapportant* (Brussels, 1943), pp. 53-55; J. Van Mierlo, *De laude Flandriae* (Brussels, 1944). The *Laus Flandriae* is not included in the *Liber Floridus*.

Ancienne chronique de Flandre: 'Lidris de Harlebeke vit Flandres vuide, nient ahanée et plaine de bos est prist et aquist Flandres.'[17] However faulty their chronology may be, these lines are the poetic expression of the historical fact that Flanders was created by its counts.[18] After the *Genealogia comitum Flandriae* we find a numbered list of Flemish counts, beginning with 'Anno Domini DCCXCI comites Flandriȩ regnare ceperunt' and running from Lidric of Harelbeke to Charles the Good (fo. 105 bis, p. 213 bis).[19]

Lambert's Flemish Genealogy is followed by a *Genealogia regum Francorum comitumque Flandrie* (fo. 105 bis v, p. 213 ter, Delisle, no. 178). It is a short genealogy in verse of the Frankish kings and of the Flemish counts (down to Charles the Good), whose link with the Carolingian dynasty was real, since Baldwin I married Judith, the daughter of Charles the Bald. The work is probably Lambert's own, and is a straightforward genealogical list.[20]

Two other well-known historical works with some bearing on Flemish history are the so-called Annals of Saint-Omer and the so-called *Chronicon de gestis Normannorum in Francia*. Both are annals and almost exclusively compilations without much originality or value of their own.

The Annals of Saint-Omer, as Delisle called them, or *Lamberti Audomariensis chronica*, as Pertz called them, appear in the *Liber Floridus* under the title *Anni Domini* (fo. 36 v-46, pp. 74-93, pp. [27]-[50], Delisle, no. 43).[21] They consist of a list of years (with the dominical letter, the date of Easter and computistic notes), which starts with the year 1 and goes on well beyond 1120 (it stops in fact at 1291), and of short notes on historical events, which stop after 1120.[22] They concern general history and are pure compilation until the middle of the eleventh century; thereafter they become original and we may assume that this latter part is Lambert's own work – it is here that he records the death of his father in 1077. The sources of the compilation are the Frankish annals, lists of popes and bishops and the lost

---

[17] Ed. J.J. De Smet, *Corpus chronicorum Flandriae*, ii (Brussels, 1841), p. 31.

[18] Bethmann's reaction to this passage is noteworthy: 'Ineptum, ni fingas Karolum Magnum tunc temporis in utramque aurem dormiisse' (*MGH, SS*, ix, p. 309, n. 26), i.e. 'This is inept, unless one is to believe that Charlemagne was sound asleep while Lidric occupied Flanders.' The remark, which is taken verbatim from J.N. Paquot, *Historiae Flandriae synopsis* (Brussels, 1781), p. 2, n. (g), misses the point by taking literally what was meant to convey in a striking image the historical truth that Flanders was a creation of its counts. If not at the time of Lidric, then certainly at the time of Baldwin II, after the great Norman invasion, the county must have looked pretty desolate and ready to be taken over by a powerful line of rulers.

[19] Ed. Bethmann, p. 336.

[20] Ibid., p. 308; Bethmann omitted numerous interlinear data on regnal years etc.

[21] Ed. G.H. Pertz, *MGH, SS*, v, (1844), pp. 65-66, only the years 919-1120. Pertz added in footnotes on p. 66 a certain amount of historical material which Lambert inserted in his calendar, fo 26 v, p. 54, Delisle, no. 38.

[22] The last entries are 'Balduinus comes obiit' under 1129, recording the death of Baldwin VII in that year, and 'Ab Adam usque hic sunt anni VI CCCLXXX' under the year 1120.

Annals of Saint-Bertin; there is some similarity to the *Annales Sithienses*[23] and to the *Annales Fuldenses*.[24] Although the work is important only for the later years, there are some entries in the earlier part which do not occur in any known Frankish annals and concern Flemish history. There is, for example, the interesting entry on fo. 41 v, p. 84, p. [37] under the year 792: 'Lidricus comes Flandr' I regnavit'.[25]

The other work, which André Duchesne published under the title *Gesta Normannorum in Francia* or *Chronicon de gestis Normannorum in Francia*, and which the *Liber Floridus* calls *Gesta Francorum de Nortmanis*, does not deserve all the attention it has received (fo. 212-215 v, pp. 423-30, Delisle, nos. 241, 242).[26] It is a compilation, not always accurate, made at Saint-Omer,[27] of extracts from the *Annales Bertiniani* and the *Annales Vedastini*. The only passage which (apart from two lines at the beginning, and the final phrase) was supposed to be original and of historical importance (Pertz prints it in italics) concerns the alleged sheltering of various saints' relics in the fortified town of Sithiu, alias Saint-Omer, in 846.[28] However, as we shall see later, the passage in question has nothing to do with this chronicle and was inserted without any justification, apparently in the *editio princeps* of A. Duchesne in 1619. As historical source-material the *Chronicon de gestis Normannorum in Francia* is a worthless compilation.

The minor items of Flemish historical material in the *Liber Floridus* deserve our attention no less than the major texts. They are numerous, heterogeneous and scattered throughout the book.

There are valuable lists of bishops (fo. 230 v, p. 460, pp. [101-2] and fo. 240 v, p. 480, Delisle, nos. 265, 285), *inter alia* for Noyon, for Cambrai and for Thérouanne, whose first bishop, St. Audomarus or St. Omer, gave his name to the town of Sithiu and to the collegiate church of Lambert.[29] There are lists of abbots of Saint-Bertin (fos. 13, p. 27, p. [5] and 270 v-271, pp. 542-43, Delisle, nos. 13, 319, 320 and 323). This valuable material is the work of Lambert himself.[30]

Lambert has included the calendar of his own church of Saint-Omer, which is the subject of a separate essay. It contains a few notes on Flemish

---

[23] Ed. G. Waitz, *MGH, SS*, xiii (1881), pp. 34-38, annis 548-823.
[24] Ed. F. Kurze, 1891, *MGH, SS in usum scholarum*, annis 714-901.
[25] The passage has escaped notice because it is not included in Pertz's edition; I shall come back to 'Lidric first count of Flanders' later.
[26] Ed. G.H. Pertz, *MGH, SS*, i (1826), pp. 532-36. Neither Pertz nor the older editors used the *Liber Floridus*.
[27] The author changes the *monasterium nostrum* of the *Annales Vedastini* into *Sithiu oppidum*.
[28] *MGH, SS*, i, p. 533, l. 22-23.
[29] The lists are very well edited in *MGH, SS*, xiii, pp. 382 and 389 and reprinted by Mgr. L. Duchesne in his *Fastes épiscopaux*, iii (Paris, 1915), pp. 130-31, for Thérouanne.
[30] Ed. *MGH, SS*, xiii, pp. 390-91.

events of the eleventh and early twelfth centuries, entered amidst the liturgical material (fos. 26 v-32, pp. 54-65, pp. [14]-[27], Delisle, no. 38).[31]

There naturally is also some hagiographical material concerning the life and cult of St. Audomarus himself (fo. 6 v, p. 26, p. [4]; fos. 259 v, p. 538, p. [112] and 260 v and 270 r and v, pp. 540-42, Delisle, nos. 12 and 316-18).

On fo. 6 v we find some *Versus de Sancto Audomaro* and a few notes on his life, in annalistic form.[32]

On fos. 259 v, 260 v and 270 r-v there is some chronological information on the saint, such as names of contemporary popes, emperors and kings and the principal dates of his episcopal career. The chronological notes on fo. 259 v (Delisle, no. 316) have been printed in the Appendix to Delisle's study (pp. 200-1 [776-77]).

There is some historical material here not strictly related to St. Audomarus or the town of Saint-Omer, to which we shall return.

The short chronological notes concerning St. Audomarus on fo. 270 v (Delisle, no. 318) had not been printed before the recent edition of the *Liber Floridus*.[33]

On fo. 260 v, pp. 540 and 270, p. 541 respectively we find a short *Vita* of St. Audomarus and six miracles (Delisle, no. 317). Although hitherto unedited (and not listed in the *Bibliotheca hagiographica latina*), these materials are not new, except for certain dates which are added in the *Liber Floridus*. The *Vita*, which is neither in the *AA.SS.*, 3 September 1750, nor in the *M.G.H., S.R.M.*, v (1910), where Levison edited other texts on the saint, is clearly based on well-known material, but in a much shortened form.[34]

There is also an extract from the text of the Peace of God of Soissons of 1092, which was introduced in Flanders, namely from part of canon 10 to the end (fo. 84 v, p. 172, p. [58], Delisle, no. 106).[35]

Finally there are brief entries, mainly in annalistic form scattered

---

[31] Ed. G.H. Pertz, *MGH, SS*, v (1844), p. 66, in the footnotes to the edition of the Annals of Saint-Omer, marked *Martyr*. This edition is incomplete, thus the date of 1071 has been omitted from the entry on the storming of Saint-Omer by the French king (*L.F.*, fo. 27 v, p. 56, p. [16], *MGH, SS*, v, p. 66, n. 1), which reads: 'Rex Phili*ppus* c*e*pit castrum s*ancti* Aud*omari* anno domini MLXXI'.

[32] Printed in Delisle, *Notice sur les manuscrits du 'Liber Floridus' de Lambert, chanoine de Saint-Omer*, p. 39 [615]; not in *AA.SS*.

[33] They are not mentioned in the *Bibliotheca hagiographica latina*.

[34] See *AA.SS.*, 3 September, 1750, pp. 384-85. This is not the place for a systematic analysis of the hagiographical sources on St. Audomarus and his cult, but a first analysis of the material in the *Liber Floridus* convinced me that it deserves further study. I was thus struck by the fact that certain themes are found in Lambert's book which only appear in the *Vita tertia*, which the Bollandists place in the twelfth or thirteenth century.

[35] This text is well known and can be found in the editions of M. Sdralek, *Wolfenbüttler Fragmente* (Münster, 1891), pp. 140-42 and F. Wasserschleben, 'Zur Geschichte der Gottesfrieden', *Zeitschrift der Savigny Stiftung für Rechtsgeschichte, Germanistische Abteilung*, 12 (1891), pp. 113-15. It has recently been studied again by H. Hoffmann, *Gottesfriede und Treuga Dei* (Stuttgart, 1964), passim, especially pp. 186-88.

throughout the book, relating to the history of Lambert's own country and his native town.[36] Some of these texts are highly interesting.[37] Not all are original or important of course: thus there are some extracts from the well-known *Annales Vedastini* and the famous *Annales Bertiniani*, concerning Norman invasions of Flanders, a miracle in Thérouanne,[38] the attack of Baldwin II on Péronne in 898 or 899, the occupation of Saint-Omer by King Philip I of France in 1071, and such like. Two entries or groups of entries, however, cannot be traced to any extant sources, one relating to the fortification of Saint-Omer in 846, the other to the enigmatic first count of Flanders, Lidric of Harelbeke. I shall deal with them separately later, but first a few words should be said about the Flemish material in the *Liber Floridus* which is at present missing in the Ghent autograph, but conserved in its copies.[39]

The three first items, which appear together in the copies, and are edited in the appendix to this essay, concern the political and religious geography of Flanders and the succession of the counts. Delisle places them between the Geometrical Sphere (no. 173) and the *Genealogia comitum Flandrie* (no. 177). There is first a list of *Comitatus et urbes et abbatie Flandrensis provincie* (Delisle, no. 174), there is also a list of *Sanctorum reliquie in comitatibus Flandrie* (Delisle, no. 175);[40] and finally a list of *Nomina comitum Flandrie* (Delisle, no. 176), explaining that from Lidric in 792 to 1119, when Charles the Good became count, fifteen counts had ruled in a span of 327 years, and giving their names. The fragment ends with a list of names of Flemish rivers. The fourth of these fragments is only partially missing in Ghent: it is a *Computatio annorum ab Adam usque ad tempora Roberti comitis Flandrie* (Delisle, no. 302). Flanders appears for the first time where the death of Count Robert II is mentioned 'sixteen years after the council of Clermont' and again at the very end, where after the capture of Jerusalem the death of Count Robert II (d.

---

[36] Some are in the form of a computation, e.g. on fo. 257 v, p. 516 (Delisle, no. 301), starting with: 'From Adam to Noah 2242 years' down to 'from the council of Clermont [1095] to the death of Count Robert [1111] sixteen years'; some are in the form of a miscellaneous collection of noteworthy events, e.g. on fo. 1 v, p. 4, p. [3] (Delisle, no. 2) starting with 'Chaim the son of Adam founded the first city' down to 'Lidric of Harelbeke, the first count of Flanders, started to reign in 792' and some further data on Flemish counts.

[37] The passages we have in mind are on fo. 1 v, p. 4, p. [3]; fo. 102, p. 207; fo. 208, p. 415; fo. 211 v, p. 422; fo. 216, p. 431; fo. 257 v, p. 516 and fo. 259 v, p. 538, p. [112] (Delisle nos. 2, 168, 224, 240, 244, 301 and 316).

[38] The miracle involved a garment dripping with blood and was connected with the introduction of the feast of the Assumption in Thérouanne; the populace obviously needed some impressive encouragement to celebrate this feast which was being introduced in Western Europe about that time.

[39] They are Delisle nos. 174-76 and 302; I publish nos. 174-76 at the end of this essay.

[40] Here we find e.g. the three saints from the abbey of Saint-Wandrille, who were claimed to rest in St. Peter's in Ghent, Wandregisilus, Ansbert and Wulfram, of whom we shall hear more later on.

1111) is mentioned again and a final remark made that 6369 years separate the death of the count from Adam. This computation appears in the autograph on fo. 257 v, p. 516, but only down to the council of Clermont and the death of Robert II sixteen years later. The rest is supplied by various copies.[41]

With most of these sources medievalists have long been familiar. There are, however, three historical problems on which the *Liber Floridus* contains material which has been overlooked so far. These are the date of the fortification of Saint-Omer, the whereabouts of the relics of the saints of Saint-Wandrille and the role of Lidric in the foundation of the county of Flanders. To them we must now turn our attention.

The Date of the Fortification of Saint-Omer

When was the town of Saint-Omer fortified against the incursions of the Normans? The question has occupied numerous medievalists and was the subject of an excellent critical study in 1963, when the conclusion was reached that there were no fortifications at Saint-Omer before 878-881.[42] One of the crucial elements in the debate is a paragraph in the *Chronicon de gestis Normannorum*, which I have already mentioned. The paragraph says that Saint-Omer was a fortified town in 846, for in that year numerous saints' relics were taken to safety there within the existing fortifications. The 1963 article made clear that this passage on Saint-Omer in 846 was not an original part of the *Chronicon*, being absent from the text of the *Chronicon* in the Ghent *Liber Floridus*; hence the conclusion that the paragraph had been inserted 'in one of the copies known to André Duchesne', some time 'in the twelfth or thirteenth century'.[43]

Although the incriminated passage is indeed absent from the *Chronicon* in the Ghent *Liber Floridus*, it occurs elsewhere in the same manuscript.[44] This fact, which has been overlooked, deserves to be pointed out and forces me to enter into this old and complicated question. One thing is certain: the

---

[41] From 'A mundi exordio usque ad diluvium . . .' to 'a Roma condita impletur'.
[42] H. Van Werveke, 'A-t-il existé des fortifications à Saint-Omer antérieurement à 878-881?', *Revue belge de philologie et d'histoire*, xli (1963), pp. 1065-90.
[43] Ibid., pp. 1073, 1074.
[44] On fo. 102, p. 207 we read under the title *De pyratis Danorum Fresiam adeuntes* (sic) 'Anno Domini DCCCXLVI pyratę Danorum Fresiam adeuntes provintias et ęcclesias vastaverunt et populum in eis occiderunt. Quod audientes Flandrenses vicinarumque urbium pontifices et abbates cum sanctorum suorum reliquiis ad sanctum venerunt Audomarum, quia muro valido et turribus atrium eius divina providentia munitum erat. Isti sunt sancti qui propter persecutionem illam convenerunt: sanctus Wandregisilus et sancti Wlframnus, Ansbertus, Bavo, Wasnulfus, Piatus, Bainus, Winnochus et sancta Austraberta et XL annis ibi fuerunt.' The text was published by Delisle, *Notice*, pp. 89-90. The entry is repeated in the Ghent *Liber Floridus* on fo. 240, p. 479 by a later hand, with slight variants.

paragraph on the fortifications of Saint-Omer in 846 can no longer be treated as a late and negligible insertion, since it occurs in Lambert's autograph of 1120, as one of the scattered pieces of information on Flanders and on the town of Saint-Omer. Considering Lambert's great interest in the history of his fatherland and his native town, and the great care with which he collected his information, a detailed and precisely dated entry like the paragraph on 846 in his book deserves close attention.

But first a few words about the external history of this paragraph. It occurs in the *Liber Floridus* in the hand of 1120 on fo. 102; it does not occur in the *Chronicon de gestis Normannorum* (fo. 212-215 v, pp. 423-30), but it occurs again, this time as an addition by a thirteenth-century hand, on fo. 240, p. 479. This addition must have been made (in a blank space) by a monk of the abbey of St. Bavo in Ghent, where the autograph arrived before the end of the thirteenth century (and whence it eventually came to the university library of that city), because it mentions St. Bavo amongst the saints whose relics found refuge in Saint-Omer in 846. The thirteenth-century writer took care to place the name of St. Bavo first in the list, whereas he was only fourth in the enumeration in Lambert's hand on fo. 102 (the nine names in the two lists are the same).[45] The first editor, André Duchesne, must have thought that this loose entry belonged in fact to the *Chronicon* under the year 846 (on fo. 212 v, p. 424), where an incursion of Danes in that year is mentioned; hence the insertion of the fragment into the *Chronicon*.[46]

What is the historical importance, in other words the credibility of Lambert's note on the events of 846? His annalistic entries, precisely dated and formulated, cannot easily be overlooked, even though there are some demonstrable errors in his dating.[47] There is no intrinsic impossibility in

---

[45] A fourteenth-century hand also added 'et de Sancto Bavone' to the title De ęcclesia Sancti Audomari on fo. 4 v, p. 10. It is clear that this fragment, in their own copy of the *Liber Floridus*, has been the source of the passage on Saint-Omer in 846 in the *Annales Sancti Bavonis*, written by the monks of St. Bavo in the fourteenth century; see the question raised in Van Werveke, 'A-t-il existé des fortifications à Saint-Omer?', pp. 1074ff.

[46] In his *Historiae a Normannorum scriptores* of 1619, p. 2, the passage on Saint-Omer is given outside the text proper of the *Chronicon*, between brackets beside the year 846, and with the warning that it is taken *ex fine codicis*. The codex used by Duchesne is the famous copy of the *Liber Floridus* from the Chartreuse of Montdieu, now Paris, lat. 8865 (Delisle's MS P1) – here St. Bavo occurs in the fourth place. In the edition of 1636, ii, p. 525, however, (for which Duchesne used the MS from Montdieu and also a MS from Rooklooster or Rouge-Cloître near Brussels, which is now lost) the passage on Saint-Omer is simply inserted into the text of the *Chronicon* – and here St. Bavo occurs first, cf. Delisle, *Notice*, p. 89, n. 2. Although the passage occurs separated from the *Chronicon* in the Montdieu ms., it is not, as Duchesne mistakenly writes, to be found at the end of the codex, but on fo. 115.

[47] He misdates the accession and the death of Edward the Confessor on fo. 43, p. 87, p. [40]: 'MLXIII Eduardus rex Anglorum obiit'; on fo. 75 bis, p. 153 we read: 'Anno Domini Mmo XXmo Vto electione populi Ęduardus regum piissimus sublevatur in regno regnavitque annis XL feliciter. Quo mortuo quidam comes Herroldus nomine valde perfidus regnum invasit. Quo audito Willelmus Nothus comes Normannię transfretavit in Angliam, id est Britanniam et expugnavit eam et Herroldum occidit anno Domini Mmo LXmo Vto regnumque optinuit . . .'

admitting some fortification of Saint-Omer at this early date. The place was very much exposed because of its closeness to the sea at that time. Compared with the rest of the west Frankish lands, fortifications at this date would be very early,[48] but not impossibly so. Nor would they be the oldest on record, since we know that in 830 the abbot of Saint-Philibert in Noirmoutiers built a *castrum* near the monastery to repel any Norsemen who tried to attack the island.[49] The invasion of Frisia in 846, which meant the whole of the Frisian, Dutch and Flemish North Sea border, is well-known from such sources as the *Annales Bertiniani*.[50] But there is more: in an entry on fo. 259 v, p. 538, p. [112] (Delisle, no. 316), Lambert mentions the interesting fact that in the year 840 the Danish King Rorik came to Sithiu, but was kept away *iudicio Dei* and withdrew; the entry is in the usual annalistic style: 'Anno Domini DCCCXL Orichus rex Danorum ad Sithiu venit, sed iudicio Dei timore perterritus, fugam arripuit et recessit.' The text occurs in a miscellaneous collection of short annalistic fragments on Flanders and Saint-Omer, under a beautiful picture of the town. This piece of information tallies well with what we know of the movement of Rorik and his Danes. We know that the Danes attacked the English east and south coast in 840-41 and that they penetrated up the Seine in 841; it is probable that they ravaged southern Frisia in 834-39 under Harald and Rorik.[51] The following sequence emerges: the Danish threat to the town of Sithiu, desirable because of its churches and exposed because of its position close to the coast, had been averted in 840,[52] but the citizens had had a fright, defences were built around the church of Saint-Omer on the hill and when the Danish threat reappeared in 846 the town was an obvious shelter to which people fled with their valuables.[53] Amongst them were clerics with saints' relics. It is here that a difficulty arises, for amongst the latter we find Wandregisilus, Ansbert and Wulfram, three illustrious saints from the abbey of Saint-Wandrille on the

---

[48] F. Vercauteren, 'Comment s'est-on défendu au IXe siècle dans l'Empire franc contre les invasions normandes?', *XXXe Congrès de la fédération archéologique et historique de Belgique 1935* (Brussels, 1936), pp. 117-32.

[49] Ibid., p. 121.

[50] Ed. G. Waitz (1883), p. 33, ed. Grat *et al.* (1964), pp. 51-52: '846. Pyratae Danorum Fresiam adeuntes, recepto pro libitu censu, pugnando quoque victores effecti, tota pene provincia potiuntur'; cf. *Annales Xantenses* under the year 846, ed. B. Von Simson (Hanover and Leipzig, 1909), p. 15, and W. Vogel, *Die Normannen und das Fränkische Reich bis zur Gründung der Normandie (799-911)* (Heidelberg, 1906), pp. 117-18.

[51] Ibid., pp. 75, 84-85, who makes no use of the fragment.

[52] I cannot follow A. D'Haenens, *Les invasions normandes en Belgique au IXe siècle* (Louvain, 1967), p. 261, who believes that in this fragment Lambert has summarized and situated at Saint-Omer a passage of the *Annales Bertiniani* (anno 845, ed. Waitz, p. 33; Grat *et al.*, pp. 50-51) narrating the pillage by the Normans of an unnamed monastery in the Seine region (believed to be Saint-Germain-des-Prés by F. Lot). The course of events is quite different and so are the dates.

[53] We cannot follow D'Haenens, *Les invasions normandes*, p. 117, n. 127, who sees a contradiction between Lambert's data on the fortifications in 846 and 879: the former concern Saint-Omer on the hill, the latter, undertaken by Abbot Fulco, concern Saint-Bertin by the river.

Lower Seine who, according to reliable sources, were still quietly in their original abbey at the time of King Rorik's attacks. We must therefore turn to the problem of the saints of Saint-Wandrille and particularly one of them, St. Wulfram.[54]

The Relics of the Saints of Saint-Wandrille

The relics of the three saints, which eventually turned up in St. Peter's abbey in Ghent,[55] were the subject of monkish strife in the middle ages and of critical study in modern times. The two scholars who have gone into the problem most deeply in this century, Oppermann and Van Werveke, made no use of the fragment on fo. 102, p. 207 of the *Liber Floridus*, which has some bearing on the subject.[56] The problem is as follows. In the ninth century the monks of Saint-Wandrille, dangerously close to the sea and under the Viking threat, left their abbey for safer places. They took their valuables with them, saints' relics naturally being amongst them. The evacuation took place after 853/4, since a charter of Charles the Bald, dating from one of those two years, mentions the bodies of the three confessors of Christ as resting in the abbey;[57] the detailed account of the *Miracula Sancti Wandregisili* places it in the year 858 (*MGH, SS*, xv, i, p. 408). After much travelling, some of it obscure, the monks and their relics found refuge at Chartres in 885-86, whence they left for the north, finally settling at Boulogne for a long time.[58] When we next hear of the saints of Saint-Wandrille, in 944, they are being transferred from Boulogne to Ghent, where a *congregatio sancti Wandregisili* had been formed in the abbey of St. Peter.[59] This congregation had taken over certain goods of the extinct Norman abbey.[60] It is at this point that the problems begin. The story of the

---

[54] Saint-Wandrille or Fontanella was founded in the middle of the seventh century. Wandregisilus (d. 667) was the founder and first abbot, Ansbert (d. 695), the third abbot, was archbishop of Rouen and Wulfram became archbishop of Sens in the last decade of the seventh century and died before 704, Duchesne, *Fastes épiscopaux*, ii, p. 417; F. Lohier and J. Laporte, *Gesta sanctorum patrum Fontanellensis coenobii* (Rouen and Paris, 1936), pp. 20-21, n. 48.

[55] They are listed together as *Sanctorum reliquie . . . in Gandavo* in the *Liber Floridus* (Delisle, no. 175), in one of the fragments missing in the autograph, see appendix ii.

[56] O. Oppermann, *Die älteren Urkunden des Klosters Blandinium und die Anfängen der Stadt Gent*, i (Utrecht, 1928), pp. 184-219; H. Van Werveke, 'Saint-Wandrille et Saint-Pierre de Gand (IXe et Xe siècles)', *Miscellanea mediaevalia Niermeyer* (Groningen, 1967), pp. 79-92.

[57] G. Tessier, *Recueil des actes de Charles II le Chauve*, i (Paris, 1943), no. 160, p. 424.

[58] Boulogne's fortifications were rebuilt at the end of the ninth or the beginning of the tenth century by Count Erkenger, after whose death (after 923) the Boulonnais fell into the hands of Arnulf I of Flanders.

[59] First mentioned in a document of 945-59 in A. Fayen, *Liber Traditionum Sancti Petri Blandiniensis* (Ghent, 1906), pp. 87ff; for the date see A.C.F. Koch, 'De dateringen in het "Liber Traditionum" . . . ', *Bul. Com. roy. Hist.*, 123 (1958), pp. 172-73.

[60] For all this see Van Werveke, 'A-t-il existé des fortifications à Saint-Omer?'

flight from Saint-Wandrille has reached us through the contemporary *Miracula Sancti Wandregisili*,[61] where two of the three saints of the abbey are mentioned, Wandregisilus and Ansbert. Some indications from other sources confirm the impression of a journey with two saints' bodies, as if St. Wulfram's relic had been left behind.[62] It is on this point that conflict arose, for the monks of the Blandinium in Ghent claimed to possess the three bodies, after their transfer from Boulogne in 944 on the orders of Count Arnulf I and in agreement with the monastic reformer Gerard of Brogne. Yet, the monks of the restored abbey of Saint-Wandrille claimed in the eleventh century that Ghent had only Saints Wandregisilus and Ansbert, whereas they had St. Wulfram, who had never left their abbey and had, so they said, been discovered there in 1027, in his original tomb beside the empty tombs of the two other saints.

In 1928 Oppermann subjected the hagiographical material from the Blandinium, together with the charters, to thorough criticism, rejecting *inter alia* the presence of St. Wulfram in Ghent. In 1967 Van Werveke presented a hypothesis to explain all the known facts. He believes that the monks of Saint-Wandrille fled with only two of the three saints and that these two relics ended up in Boulogne in the late ninth century. When they were transferred to Ghent in 944, it was believed, owing to confusion, that three saints were there. Research in the restored abbey of Saint-Wandrille brought to light the fact that St. Wulfram had always remained there. The consequence – and here Oppermann's criticism comes in – was a series of falsifications and interpolations in Ghent, the monks being unwilling to give up even one of their claims to fame.

The theory of Van Werveke, which is the theory of Saint-Wandrille,[63] sounds plausible enough on the whole but leaves some questions unanswered. It is based on the assumption that when the monks of Saint-Wandrille evacuated their abbey and took understandable care to take their saints with them, they left behind St. Wulfram. No explanation for this improbable step is offered.[64] It seems to me therefore that another hypothesis deserves to be formulated, based on the natural assumption that, when the monks reluctantly left their abbey under the Viking threat, they did not leave one of their treasured saints behind; and that when the monks of Ghent were granted the saints of Saint-Wandrille in 944, the three saints,

---

[61] Ed. *AA.SS.*, 5 July, 1727, pp. 281-91; partial ed. O. Holder-Egger, *MGH, SS*, xv, 1, 1887, pp. 406-9; cf. F. Lot, *Études critiques sur l'abbaye de Saint-Wandrille* (Paris, 1913).

[62] Van Werveke, 'A-t-il existé des fortifications à Saint-Omer?', p. 89, n. 47.

[63] This agrees with the Bollandists, who rejected the story of the translation of St. Wulfram to Ghent, *AA.SS.*, 3 March, 1668, pp. 161-62.

[64] A. D'Haenens, *Invasions normandes*, p. 131-33 rightly insists that the monks took their saints with them before anything else. The relics were a heritage 'omni auro arabico pretiosior' as the monk of Saint-Vaast, quoted by D'Haenens, put it; they were of particular importance for fleeing monks since 'elles valaient à leurs porteurs un accueil bienveillant dans les localités traversées, assurant dons et largesses'.

who had always been together at the Norman abbey,[65] were together in Boulogne and were taken together to Ghent – in spite of the resistance of such local clerics as Notger, the provost, and Helger, the sacristan of the church of Saint-Vulmar in Boulogne, and of Bishop Wicfrid of Thérouanne and Boulogne.

Against the fact that the Ghent *Sermo de adventu SS. Wandregisili, Ansberti et Vulframni* is only of the late eleventh or even early twelfth century,[66] and that the martyrologies of St. Peter's mentioning the *Adventus sanctorum corporum Wandregisili abbatis, Ansberti et Vulframni archipraesulum* may well be of a late date,[67] I should point out that the *Vita Dunstani* of Adalard, written in Ghent in 1006-1011, i.e. before the *inventio* in Saint-Wandrille of 1027, mentions the three relics,[68] a point which Oppermann discards by declaring the offending words to be an interpolation ('Eingriffe in den Text der vita Dunstani').[69] The three saints are also expressly mentioned as being in Ghent in an authentic charter of Otto II of 977, long before Saint-Wandrille made its claim and Abbot Gerard his discovery.[70] Oppermann tried to eliminate this annoying text also by declaring it an interpolation,[71] but as we now have the original, containing the suspect phrase, this thesis is untenable.[72]

It seems to me that it would be more fruitful to have a critical look at events at Saint-Wandrille. Indeed, when in the first half of the eleventh century the abbey was being restored, the need for saints' relics must have

---

[65] The three saints had been buried together at Saint-Wandrille in 704, by Abbot Bainus, formerly bishop of Thérouanne (d. 710), according to F. Lohier and J. Laporte, *Gesta sanctorum patrum Fontanellensis coenobii* (Rouen and Paris, 1936), pp. 14-15, n. 30.

[66] Ed. *AA.SS.*, 5 July 1727, pp. 291-302; partial ed. *MGH, SS*, xv, 2, 1888, pp. 624-31. The inventory of the objects belonging to the saints, which were taken to Ghent is, however, contemporary with the translation. Here we find objects belongiong to all three saints; see Van Werveke, 'A-t-il existé des fortifications à Saint-Omer?', p. 88, n. 46 and p. 92, n. 60.

[67] Oppermann, *Die älteren Urkunden des Klosters Blandinium*, i (Ghent, 1928), pp. 193ff, most of the relevant ms. material is lost.

[68] Ed. W. Stubbs, *Memorials of St. Dunstan, Archbishop of Canterbury* (London, 1874) (Rolls Series), pp. 59-60: 'Wandregisilum cum sociis archipraesulibus'.

[69] O. Oppermann, *Die älteren Urkunden des Klosters Blandinium*, i (Ghent, 1928), p. 193. Why, one wonders, if a monk of St. Peter's took the trouble to make this interpolation around 1070, did he not expressly mention the name of Wulfram?

[70] M. Gysseling and A.C.F. Koch, *Diplomata Belgica ante annum millesimum centesimum scripta*, i (Brussels, 1950), no. 66, pp. 166-68; this ed. is based on the original, which was unknown to Th. Sickel in *MGH, Diplomata*, ii, 1, *Ottonis II diplomata*, 1888, no. 149, pp. 167-68.

[71] One of his arguments is the adjective *gloriosi* given to the saints, which the author finds 'recht verdächtig', pp. 198-99.

[72] The fact that the *Translatio SS. Wandregisili et Ansberti* (*MGH, SS*, xxx, 2, 1926, pp. 814-20) mentions only the transfer from Boulogne of Wandregisilus and Ansbert and leaves Wulfram out is of little weight. The text is only known through a fifteenth-century version made at Saint-Wandrille, which explicitly claimed to have had Wulfram all along; for further criticism of this late compilation of little or no value, see J. Laporte, 'Que vaut le texte bref de la *Translatio Wandregisili et Ansberti in Blandinium?*', *Revue Mabillon*, xxviii, (1938), pp. 153-58.

been great and the loss in Frankish times of the three great holy men bitterly regretted. But were they really all lost and gone for ever? A look at the available information, the *Miracula Sancti Wandregisili*, brought a real ray of hope. The work, which the monks knew through Saint-Bertin, mentioned only two saints on the journey that finally led to Boulogne, leaving the possibility open and even suggesting that at least one of the saints had never left Saint-Wandrille and might very well still be there, to be found with the necessary effort and luck.[73] The *Historia inventionis Sancti Vulframni* points out the fact that the *Miracula Wandregisili* only mentions two saints and never Wulfram. Hence the hope and even the conviction of abbot Gerard (c. 1008-31) and his monks at Saint-Wandrille that the relic was still there and should be found. The search was made and the hope fulfilled: Saint Wulfram, so the story goes, was duly unearthed, in the original place beside the empty tomb of the other two. But was he really?[74] Let us not be naive: medieval monks had a knack of finding a relic when they hoped and wanted to find it. This even happened with relics of saints who had never existed; nor must bones and other suitable remains have been far to seek in old church ground. The least one can say is that it would be imprudent and unwarranted, in the circumstances described, to take the story of the *inventio* of St. Wulfram in 1027 at its face value: it looks too much like a case of self-fulfilling prophecy. That some relics were found is plausible enough, but that they were St. Wulfram's, which they supposed had been left behind in the ninth century, seems very doubtful.[75] So to my alternative hypothesis. It

---

[73] Van Werveke, 'A-t-il existé des fortifications à Saint-Omer?', pp. 90ff has made this important point: the oldest extant copy of the *Miracula Wandregisili*, of the tenth century, belonged to Saint-Bertin; Saint-Wandrille had a copy (of the eleventh century, now at Le Havre), which the author of the *Historia inventionis* has apparently used; it seems that when the relics left Boulogne for Ghent, the writings went to Saint-Bertin, where Wicfrid, bishop of Thérouanne-Boulogne, had been provost. Van Werveke writes (pp. 90ff): 'Il semble bien, en tout cas, que les moines de Saint-Wandrille, au XIe siècle, voulant se renseigner sur l'histoire des reliques de leur premier et de leur troisième abbé, n'ont eu d'autre ressource que de recourir aux manuscrits reposant dans les abbayes de l'"espace flamand", et notamment à Saint-Bertin'.

[74] F. Lot, *Études critiques sur l'abbaye de Saint-Wandrille* (Paris, 1913), p. xlv narrates the happy event of 1027 as follows: 'Gérard . . . eut la chance de trouver ce qui lui faisait toujours défaut, les reliques d'un saint renommé, élément indispensable pour produire des miracles, [et faire] affluer les dons des malades et des gens pieux'; and Lot concludes: 'l'avenir du monastère était désormais assuré'.

[75] One of the best-known examples of tricked discoveries of relics is provided by the abbey of St. Bavo in Ghent, and was studied by O. Holder-Egger, 'Zu den Heiligengeschichten des Genter Sankt Bavoklosters', *Historische Aufsätze G. Waitz* (Hanover, 1886), pp. 622-65; another is the discovery of the body of King Arthur in Glastonbury in 1191 'in circumstances which proclaim to find a most ingenious but blatant fraud for a most praiseworthy purpose, the rebuilding of Glastonbury Abbey', R.F. Treharne, *The Glastonbury Legends* (London, 1967).

matches the known facts, though it leaves some questions open, e.g. why, if the monks had left with the three relics, were only two of them mentioned in the *Miracula*? The answer may be that the monks did not travel all in one group and with everything of value which they had, but split up for practical reasons and in order not to burden their hosts or manors.[76] Thus the monks and the relics would have been divided until, much later, they all ended up together, the three saints and the surviving monks, at Boulogne, where the saints remained until the translation to Ghent.[77]

Lambert's contribution to the problem, although slight, deserves to be mentioned. It indicates a tradition at Saint-Omer that at one stage of the Norman danger the saints of Saint-Wandrille found refuge in that town and that the three were taken there together.[78] What shall we conclude from it? I find it difficult to reject off-hand the precise annalistic fragments entered by Lambert of Saint-Omer in the *Liber Floridus* on the first invasion of Rorik in 840 and on the subsequent fortification of Saint-Omer or rather the hill of the collegiate church of Saint-Omer, which made the place an obvious refuge when the Danes returned to the region in 846. The facts and the dates have nothing improbable, let alone impossible, in them, and they tally with other data on the whereabouts of the Norsemen at the time. That a certain number of saints' relics found refuge in Saint-Omer in 846, as

---

[76] Two remarks in this context. Where the *Miracula Wandregisili* describes how the monks from Saint-Wandrille reached their manor of Bloville with SS. Wandregisilus and Ansbert, we read that they were welcomed there by the *custodes* of the local church, the whole local population and by part of the monks who had already gone there; this seems to point towards the monks leaving their abbey in more than one group and possibly in more than one direction. The text says (*AA.SS.*, O.S.B., ii. p. 549 and *AA.SS.*, 5 July 1727 p. 283 C): 'cumque iam eidem cum ipsis sanctissimis propinquaretur corporibus, venerunt eis obviam custodes ecclesiae ac aliqua pars [here Holder-Egger, *MGH, SS*, xv, 1, p. 408, has *reliqua pars*] fratrum et reliquus populus omnis'. The version *reliqua*, of Holder-Egger, should be retained, since it occurs in MS Saint-Omer, 764 (tenth century) and MS Douai, 837 (twelfth century); on the whereabouts of the MSS from Saint-Wandrille, see Van Werveke, 'A-t-il existé des fortifications à Saint-Omer?', pp. 90-91. That the author omits what happened at that stage to St. Wulfram may also be due to the fact that he was expressly narrating the miracles of St. Wandregisilus – as we see in the title and the proemium – and not of all the saints of Fontanella.

[77] The *Miracula Wandregisili* consists really of three parts, a first *libellus* on the miracles of the saint (dating from the first half of the ninth century), a second *libellus* on the travels of St. Wandregisilus and his companion Ansbert that led them from Fontanella in 858 to Chartres and finally Boulogne, and a third part, the 'seventh miracle' which took place in Boulogne (after 886 and before 944) and was added there to the *Miracula* by one of the local clergy; in this last section the three saints are expressly mentioned (cf. on this point Van Werveke, 'A-t-il existé des fortifications à Saint-Omer?', p. 89): the conclusion that at that stage the three saints were united again is obvious. It is noteworthy that the Bollandists and F. Lot, who refused to believe in the presence of Wulfram with the other two, declared the offending name to be an interpolation; Van Werveke's opinion, that this last miracle is an addition, is much more satisfactory.

[78] When can this have been? Not in 846, considering the charter of Charles the Bald of 853-54; maybe during the long years before and after 885-86, when there are gaps in our information about the saints' whereabouts.

Lambert proudly points out, is quite plausible, but the actual list of names which he gives does not stand up to criticism. Some of the saints he names are known from other sources to have been at Saint-Omer,[79] some may have found shelter there,[80] but some were not there in 846 and some may never have been there at all.[81] It is probable that Lambert has added to his list a few saints who never were at Saint-Omer, to the greater glory of his native town, and/or has antedated the arrival of some saints who in later years did find refuge at Saint-Omer (e.g. during the great crisis of A.D. 879 and following).[82]

Count Lidric and the Origins of Flanders

The following point to be reconsidered in the light of Lambert's work is even more important, since it concerns the very origins of the county of Flanders. Did the line of Flemish counts start with Baldwin I or with some less well-known figures, such as Audacer and Ingelram or the enigmatic Lidric of Harelbeke, linked with the legendary 'foresters of Flanders'? Were these lesser figures real or are they no more than Longfellow's 'visions of the days departed, shadowy phantoms', who 'filled the poet's brain'? The *Liber Floridus* contains some precise information on this question which, though it may be dubious, certainly should not have been overlooked. Yet this has been the case. A well-known critical assessment of the problem, which appeared in 1940 in the *Bulletin de la Commission Royale d'Histoire* and contains the extant fragments of information on Lidric and the foresters down to the end of the twelfth century, omits the data in the *Liber Floridus* (except those printed in the *Monumenta Germaniae Historica*);[83] it maintains that Lambert of Saint-Omer does not yet go so far as to call Lidric the first count of Flanders and credits an anonymous author of the end of the

---

[79] St. Winnoc, who was buried at Wormhoudt, was taken to safety in Saint-Omer following the Norman invasions under Charles the Bald, Van Werveke, 'A-t-il existé des fortifications à Saint-Omer?', pp. 1070-71. It is also known that the relics of St. Austreberta have later been the object of veneration at Saint-Omer and at Montreuil, ibid., p. 1071.

[80] St. Bavo was taken in the ninth century to a 'safe place' and afterwards to Laon; there is no indication where this first place was, ibid., pp. 1076ff.

[81] The three saints of Saint-Wandrille did not leave their abbey until 858. No other text than the *Liber Floridus* mentions a transfer of St. Bainus; nothing is known on the whereabouts of the relics of St. Piatus in the ninth century; we only know that his body was originally conserved at Seclin and turned up at Chartres at some later date. St. Wasnulfus was conserved at Condé before and after the ninth century, ibid., pp. 1070-72.

[82] See the remarks in P. Grierson, 'The Early Abbots of St. Bavo's of Ghent', *Revue bénédictine*, 49 (1937), pp. 52ff.

[83] J. Dhondt, 'De forestiers van Vlaanderen', *Bulletin de la Commission royale d'histoire*, cv (Brussels, 1940), pp. 282-305; pp. 304ff contain the appendix of texts; the article is a critical examination of A. De Saint-Leger, 'La légende de Lydéric et des forestiers de Flandre', *Bulletin de la Commission historique du département du Nord*, xxvi (1904), pp. 115-37.

twelfth century with having been the first to say so in so many words.[84] Yet Lambert of Saint-Omer said expressly, and on numerous occasions, that Lidric was the first count of Flanders and that he started to reign in 792. Even though it is probably the statement that occurs most frequently in the *Liber Floridus* and was clearly very important to Lambert, but it has been overlooked by modern historians, just as the statement about his own identity has been overlooked and his book repeatedly attributed to a namesake who was abbot of Saint-Bertin.

Ever since Louis the Pious, the practice of uniting the administration of several *pagi* in the hands of one count or *comes* was known. By the middle of the ninth century groupings of this sort were known in Flemish lands. Baldwin (d. 879), the first count of Flanders of whom we are well informed, was such a royal official at the head of a number of Frankish *pagi* or counties. This son-in-law of King Charles the Bald administered the *pagi* of Ghent and Waas, Ternois, probably also the *pagus Flandrensis* and the *pagus Rodanensis* and possibly the large *pagus Mempiscus*. With Baldwin II, his son (879-918), begins the real history of the county of Flanders as an autonomous principality. Baldwin II was not a royal administrator but an independent regional ruler.[85] All this is well known, but what do we know of the ancestors and predecessors of these remarkable people? We know that Baldwin I's father was called Audacer. We also hear of one Ingelram, a man of some importance in the kingdom of Charles the Bald, who administered a number of *pagi* in the Flemish area, as we learn from a capitulary of 853.[86] We finally hear of one Lidric of Harelbeke. The *Annales Blandinienses* call him count and mention his death in 836;[87] he must have been ordinary *Gaugraf* in one of the *pagi* of the Flemish area. In the *Liber Floridus* this 'first count of Flanders' is just called Lidric of Harelbeke, and it is only in a missing part of the autograph that Harelbeke is called a *county*. At some stage, expressed for the first time in the *Genealogia Bertiniana*, a genealogical

---

[84] J. Dhondt, 'De forestiers van Vlaanderen', p. 299: this anonymous chronicler, writing after the *Flandria generosa* and before 1194, is called an 'enfant terrible' by Dhondt, because he 'spoke up clearly and said what the tradition of Harelbeke wanted, without daring to speak openly, i.e. that Lidric was the first count of Flanders'; we shall see that in 1120 Lambert had already repeatedly said so in so many words. See further J. Dhondt, 'Het ontstaan van het vorstendom Vlaanderen', *Revue belge de philologie et d'histoire*, 20 (1941), p. 535, n. 2. For criticism of certain points made by Dhondt, see J.M. De Smet, 'Robrecht de Fries, "Dominus de Silva" en de forestiers van Vlaanderen', *Miscellanea J. Gessler*, ii (s.l. 1948), pp. 1135-44.

[85] F.L. Ganshof, *La Flandre sous les premiers comtes* (Brussels, 1949); J. Dhondt, 'Het ontstaan van het vorstendom Vlaanderen', *Revue belge de philologie et d'histoire*, 20 (1941) and 21 (1942), H. Sproemberg, *Die Entstehung der Grafschaft Flandern: Die ursprüngliche Grafschaft Flandern (864-892)* (Berlin, 1935).

[86] A Boretius and V. Krause, *Capitularia regum Francorum*, ii (Hanover, 1897), p. 275; cf. Dhondt, 'De forestiers van Vlaanderen', pp. 284, 304.

[87] Ed. Grierson, p. 11: 'Lidricus comes obiit', a later hand has added 'et Arlabeka sepelitur'. The *Annales Blandinienses* are of the eleventh century, but based on older Saint-Bertin material; cf. *Annales Formoselenses* (c. 1087); 'et Harlabecce sepelitur', ibid., p. 124.

link was made between these figures: *Lidricus Harlebeccensis comes* was said to be the father of Ingelram, said to be the father of Audacer, whose son was, as we have seen, Baldwin I.[88] Thus Lidric became the ancestor of the great line of Baldwins. Was he also their predecessor, and can he be considered the first Flemish ruler? A positive answer to this question can be found in Lambert's work, confirming the date 792 of the *Genealogia comitum Flandrie* (*MGH, SS*, ix, p. 309). The importance of these neglected passages is twofold: they show that the idea of Lidric as first count was already clearly expressed by 1120; and they expressly give the date of the beginning of his administration. The texts in the *Liber Floridus* are the following:

On fo. 1 v, p. 4, p. [3] we read, amongst a series of chronological data on Flemish and other princes and on other famous people: 'Lidricus Harlebeccensis primus comes Flandrię anno D[omini] DCCXCII regnare cepit.'

On fo. 41 v, p. 84, p. [37] we read, in a part of the Annals of Saint-Omer that was omitted from Pertz's edition: 'Lidcric*us* com*es* Flandr*ie* I regn*avit*.'

On fo. 105 bis, p. 213 bis we read, in a list of the counts of Flanders: 'Anno Domini DCCXCI comites Flandrie regnare ceperunt: I Lidricus Harlebeccensis, II Ingelramnus, III Audacer, IIII Balduinus Ferreus . . .'

On fo. 259 v, p. 538, p. [112], amongst miscellaneous notes under a picture of the town of Saint-Omer, we read: 'Anno Domini DCC et XCII Lidricus comes regnavit in Flandriam.'

Finally we find in one of the parts missing in the original, under the title *Comitatus et urbes et abbatie Flandrensis provincie*, the following line: 'comitatus Harlebeccensis de quo primus comes Flandrensis Lidricus nomine regnare cepit anno Domini DCCXC secundo' (Delisle, no. 174; see appendix i, p. 93).

It is clear that these items constitute an important addition to the body of texts on Lidric and the 'foresters of Flanders': Lambert clearly and expressly mentions Lidric of Harelbeke – and not Baldwin I – as first count of Flanders and places the beginning of his rule in 792 (saying explicitly what could anyway be read into the opening phrase of the *Genealogia* on fo. 104, p. 211). It is impossible to try and solve the riddle of the 'foresters of Flanders' in an essay on the Flemish source-material in the *Liber Floridus*. The problem is much too complex and wide. The hard kernel of historical fact which is probably hidden in the layers of legend is not easy to discover. That there was a Carolingian *Gaugraf* called Lidric who made his mark on Flemish history between 792 and 836 is acceptable enough; he may have even become count of several *pagi* and thus acquired exceptional importance. The seat of his power may have been in the region of Saint-Omer. In this case the connection with Harelbeke must be based on the eleventh-century legend that the Lidric buried at the collegiate church of St. Salvator

---

[88] Ed. Bethmann, *MGH, SS*, ix, p. 305: 'Lidricus Harlebeccensis comes genuit Ingelrannum. Ingelrannus genuit Audacrum. Audacer genuit Balduinum Ferreum qui duxit filiam Karoli Calvi nomine Iudith.'

of Harelbeke was the *comes Lidricus* who died in 836. The name *comitatus Harlebeccensis* in the list of *Comitatus et urbes* is known elsewhere: it clearly stands for the *pagus Curtracensis*, just as in the same list the name of *comitatus Blandiniensis* stands for the *pagus* of Ghent (see appendix I).[89] That Lidric had genealogical links with Audacer and Baldwin I is a late and very dubious assertion; that he was count of the Flemish principality and in a proper sense the first count of Flanders is clearly anachronistic and untenable. The desire to stretch the comital house of Flanders as far back as possible has played a role. The patent impossibility of counts of a Flemish principality as early as the end of the eighth century led Andrew of Marchiennes at the end of the twelfth century to consider that Lidric and the other two were royal foresters, not counts.[90]

Lost Sources of Lambert

It is, of course, intriguing to know where Lambert found his information, on Lidric, the Norman invasions, the town of Saint-Omer and its churches and saints. These 'Flemish' fragments, scattered throughout the book, are in the purest annalistic style. They begin with the indication of the year of the Lord and are brief, precise and devoid of literary ambition. It is tempting to assume that, when they do not come from well-known sources such as the *Annales Bertiniani* or the *Annales Vedastini*, they are extracts copied by Lambert from one set of annals and inserted in various places in the *Liber Floridus*, as he saw fit. Naturally the name of the lost Annals of Saint-Bertin comes to mind, local annals which were compiled at the abbey of Saint-Bertin and used by the *Annales Blandinienses*,[91] and possibly by Folcuin in the 'annalistic' parts of his *Gesta abbatum Sithiensium*.[92] The consultation of such a

---

[89] Cf. the works of Dhondt, Ganshof, De Saint-Leger, De Smet and Sproemberg, quoted above nn. 83-85, and also L. Vanderkindere, *La formation territoriale des principautés belges*, i (Brussels, 1902).

[90] See on him K.F. Werner, 'Andreas von Marchiennes und die Geschichtsschreibung von Anchin und Marchiennes in der zweiten Hälfte des 12. Jahrhunderts', *Deutsches Archiv*, 9 (1952), pp. 402-463.

[91] Grierson, *Annales de Saint-Pierre*, pp. xivff.

[92] O. Holder-Egger, 'Zu Folcwin von St. Bertin', *Neues Archiv*, vi (1880), pp. 428-38. The author points out that in Folcuin's *Gesta* there are, for the ninth century, annalistic entries which excel through the precision of their chronological indications. He compares them with the *Annales Blandinienses* without deciding what their relationship is (one copying from the other or both following a common source), but he does maintain that Folcuin doubtless had before him a set of annals for those passages; he further quotes arguments against the possibility that the *Annales Blandinienses* were based on Folcuin for those entries; cf. Oppermann, *Die ältesten Urkunden*, p. 167. Folcuin's *Gesta* of the abbots of Saint-Bertin, written in 961-62 at Saint-Bertin, where the author was a monk, is available in an edition made on the basis of one ms. by B. Guerard in 1840, the narrative parts are available in a critical edition by O. Holder-Egger, *MGH, SS*, xiii (1881), pp. 600-35 and the charters in M. Gysseling and A.C.F. Koch, *Diplomata Belgica*, i, 1950, nos. 1-48, pp. 5-83.

manuscript would have been easy for Lambert who lived so close to the famous abbey. Those lost annals must have been an immense source of information on all things Frankish, French and Flemish. However, the possibility that Lambert collected his bits of information from several sources is equally to be reckoned with, so that the problem of the source or sources of the Flemish annalistic fragments in the *Liber Floridus* is still unsolved.

Not enough is known yet of Lambert's basic ideas and concepts to make a final assessment of the importance and the proper role of Flemish history in his *Liber Floridus*. It is clear, however, that he attaches quite naturally great importance to his native country, its ruling house and its history. There is not so much on the geography of the county, its towns, rivers, saints' relics and churches,[93] but a good deal on the past of the ruling house. This is traced back to old native rulers, but also shown to be linked with the Carolingians.[94] Lambert makes an effort to situate Flanders firmly in the universal time-scale. He knows how many years passed between Adam and the death of Count Robert II: exactly 6369.[95] He states that between the death of Charlemagne and the 'council of Clermont on Jerusalem' there were 283 years and that sixteen years separate the latter council from the death of Count Robert II.[96] The first Crusade to Jerusalem, which was decided at the council of Clermont and in which the Flemish contingent was conspicuous, clearly made a great impression on Lambert, as his iconography shows. The Flemish participation in the First Crusade, so fresh in everyone's memory and celebrated in the *Laus Flandriae* of Petrus Pictor, must have seemed a culminating achievement.[97] We find Lambert's view, put in a nutshell, in the succinct notes right at the beginning of the Book (fo. 1 v, p. 4, p. [3]), where he enumerates the following main steps of Flemish history: Lidric of Harelbeke was the first count of Flanders and his rule

[93] *Flandria* is duly marked on the map of fo. 241, p. 481, p. [105].
[94] 'Lidricus Harlebeccensis, primus comes Flandrię, anno D*omini* DCCXCII regnare cępit. Balduinus Ferreus, quartus comes Flandrię, anno D*omini* DCCCLXII Iudith, filiam regis Calvi Karoli, [cepit], fo. 1 v, p. 4, p. [3].
[95] MS Leyden, Univ. Library, MS Vossius 31, fo. 62 v-63: 'Ab excidio Rome usque ad captam Iherusalem sub Godefrido rege anni DCLXXXX. Summa annorum ab Adam usque ad captam Iherusalem VICCCLVIII, anno videlicet ab Incarnacione Domini MXCIX indictione XIIII . . . A Christo usque ad captam Iherusalem sub Godefrido rege anno presulatus Paschalis pape tercio anni MXCIX. Iherusalem capta, Rotbertus comes Flandrie Chelis obiit anno post XII. Summa annorum Domini ab Adam usque ad obitum Rotberti VICCCLXIX et annus MusDCCC LXusIIus a Roma condita inpletur.'
[96] Autograph, fo. 257 v, p. 516.
[97] A few years after Lambert wrote, in 1123, the royal crown of Jerusalem was offered to the count of Flanders, Charles the Good, according to Galbert of Bruges, c. 5, ed. Pirenne, *Histoire du meurtre de Charles le Bon* (Paris, 1891), pp. 9ff.

began in 792; Baldwin Iron Arm was the fourth count and he took Judith, daughter of Charles the Bald, as his wife in 862; Godfrey, son of Eustace count of Boulogne, conquered Jerusalem in 1099; Robert, fourteenth count of Flanders, then made Godfrey king in Jerusalem.[98]

---

[98] The entry on Lidric is preceded by notes going back to Adam. As part of the kingdom of the Franks (linked with Antiquity through Pharamund and Priam of Troy), Flanders is given its proper niche in world history.

Appendix

Unedited *Liber Floridus* fragments on the county of Flanders, missing from the autograph manuscript in Ghent.

Texts based on MS L, Leyden, University Library, Vossius 31, fo. 176 v, with variants from
MS W, Wolfenbüttel, Ducal Library, Cod. Gud. lat. I, fo. 70 v
MS H, The Hague, Royal Library, Y 392 (72 A 23), fo. 83 v
MS P, Paris, Bibliothèque Nationale, lat. 8865, fo. 124 v.[99]

I: Comitatus et urbes et abbatie Flandrensis provincie

(Delisle, no. 174)

Comitatus et urbes et abbatie[a] Flandrensis[b] provincie[c]

Sunt in Flandria comitatus X[d]: comitatus Tervanensis, comitatus Atrebatensis,[e] comitatus Tornacensis, comitatus Boloniensis, comitatus Gisnensis, comitatus Hesdinensis,[f] comitatus Castri Sancti Pauli, comitatus Blandinensis[g] id est Gandavum,[h] comitatus Brugensis, comitatus Harlebeccensis[i] de quo primus comes Flandrensis Lidricus nomine regnare cepit, anno Domini DCCXC secundo.[j]

[a]abbatie] abatie *H*. – [b]Flandrensis] Flandrie *H*. – [c]provincie] provincie *W*// Flandrensis provincie] *om.P*. – [d]X] decem *P*. – [e]Atrebatensis] Attrebatensis *HP*. – [f]comitatus Hesdinensis] [c]omitatus Hisdinensis *post* Brugensis *script. P*. – [g]Blandinensis] Blandiniensis *P*. – [h]id est Gandavum] *supra lin. LWH; om. P*. – [i]Harlebeccensis] Harlebecensis *P*. – [j]secundo] II *P*.

Civitates, castella et abbatie Flandrie[a]

Sunt in Flandria IIII civitates Tervenna, Atreba,[b] Nervia[c] id est Tornacum[d] et Bolonia;[e] castella et abbatie[f] Sithiu, id est Sancti Audomari castrum, Watanis, Arda, Gisnes, Broiborch,[g] Bergas, Furnas,[h] Dicasmud,[i] Roslar,[j] Ypra, Torhout,[k] Brugis,[l] Formassella,[m] Oudenard,[n] Geroldimons,[o] Oudenborch,[p] Rodenborch,[q] Blandinum,[r] id est Gandavum, Harlebeca,[s] Tenramunda, Doacus, Alost, Cortracus,[t] id est Curia Traiani, Insula, Elnona, Lens, Mecinas, Baliolus, Casletum, Aria,[u] Lilers, Ham, Bituna,[v] Soccas,[w] Batpalma, Albegni,[x] Alchi, Falchanberga,[y] Hesdin, Castrum Sancti Pauli, Pernas, Motania,[z] Aurivilla,[aa] Brai,[bb] Orchia,[cc] Hasnon, Ouvecin,[dd] Affligahem,[ee] Marcenas.[ff]

---

[99] This edition is based on transcripts made by L. Milis.

ᵃCivitates . . .] *om.LWH*; *in marg. add. man. XVI s.*: Flandrie civitates *L*. – ᵇAtreba] Attreba *H*; Attrebas *P*. – ᶜNervia] Nenria *P*. – ᵈid est Tornacum] *supra lin. L*; id est Tornacus *supra lin. WH*; *om. P*. – ᵉet Bolonia] Colonia *P*. – ᶠabbatie] abbatię *W*. – ᵍBroiborch] Borborch *P*. – ʰFurnas] Furna *H*. – ⁱDicasmud] *corr. ex* Discamud *L*, Dicasmud *WH*; Discamud *P*. –ʲRoslar] *in ras. man. XIII s. W*. – ᵏTorhout] Torhut *H*; Morhout *P*. – ˡBrugis] Burgis *P*. – ᵐFormassella] Formasella *W*; Formasela *HP* (*l expunct.*). – ⁿOudenard] *cor. ex* Oudemard *L*. – ᵒGeroldimons] *om. P*. – ᵖOudenborch] Oudenburch *P*. – ᑫRodenborch] *om. H*. – ʳBlandinum] Blandinium *WHP*. – ˢHarlebeca] Halebecca *post* Tenramunda *P*. – ᵗCortracus] Rorderacus *P*. – ᵘAria] Fria *P*. – ᵛBituna] Libitunia *P*. – ʷSoccas] Scoccas *WHP*. – ˣAlbegni] Albengni *WH*. – ʸFalchanberga] Falcamberga *WHP*. – ᶻMotania] Mortania *WHP*. – ᵃᵃAurivilla] Arinvilla *P*. – ᵇᵇBrai] Bray *WH*. – ᶜᶜOrchia] Lichia *P*. – ᵈᵈOuvecin] Owencin *P*. – ᵉᵉAffligahem] Afflingahem *P*. – ᶠᶠMarcenas] Marchenas *P*.

II: Sanctorum reliquie in comitatibus Flandrie

(Delisle, no. 175)

*Sanctorum reliquie in comitatibus*ᵃ *Flandrie*

Requiescunt sancti in Flandria. In Urbe Tervennaᵇ Sanctus Maximus Regensis episcopus Sanctusque Bainus atque Hunfridusᶜ Morinorum episcopi. In Atrebaᵈ Sanctus Vedastus. In Tornaco Sanctus martyr Piatus. In Bolonia Sanctus confessor Wlmarus. In castello Sithiuᵉ tres Morinorum episcopi, Sancti Audomarus, Erkenbodo,ᶠ Folquinus Sanctusque Silvinus Tolosaneᵍ urbis episcopus atque Bertinus et Sancta Austraberta.ʰ In Furnis Sancta Walburga. In Bergis Sanctus confessor Winocusⁱ. In Brugisʲ Sanctus Donacianus,ᵏ Remensis archiepiscopus. In Gandavo Sanctus Bavo et Sancti Wandregisilus, Ausbertus,ˡ Wulframnus,ᵐ Macharius, Livinus, Landoaldus,ⁿ Gutwalo,ᵒ Bertulfus et Sancte virgines Amelberga,ᵖ Fairaildis,ᑫ Venciana.ʳ In Albinioˢ Sanctus Kilianus.ᵗ In Lens Sanctus Wlgannus.ᵘ In Elmonaᵛ Sanctus Amandus. In Doaco Sanctus Amatus. In Hasnonʷ pars media reliquiarum Sanctorum martyrum Marcellini et Petri.ˣ In Ostkerka requiescit Sanctus Guthagonus.ʸ

ᵃcomitatibus] commitatibus *H*. – ᵇTervenna] Tavenna *P*. – ᶜHunfridus] Gunfridus *P*. – ᵈAtreba] Attrebas *P*. – ᵉSithiu] Sythiu *H*. – ᶠErkenbodo] *corr. ex* Ercenbodo *W*; Erkembodo *P*. – ᵍTolosane] Tholosane *P*. – ʰAustraberta] Austreberta *P*. – ⁱWinocus] Winnocus *WH*; Winnochus *P*. – ʲBrugis] Burgis *P*. – ᵏDonacianus] *corr. ex* Danatianus *W*. – ˡAusbertus] Ansbertus *WHP*. – ᵐWlframnus] Wlfranus *H*; Wlfrannus *P*. – ⁿLandoaldus] Mandoaldus *P*. – ᵒGutwalo] Gutrwalo *P*. – ᵖAmelberga] Amalberga *P*. – ᑫFaraildis] Pharaildis *P*. – ʳVenciana] Ventiana *P*. – ˢAlbinio] Albino *H*. – ᵗKilianus] Kylianus *P*. – ᵘWlgannus] Wlganus *P*. – ᵛElmona] Elnona *WHP*. – ʷHasnon] h – *add. supra lin. W*; has non *P*. – ˣmartyrum Marcellini et Petri] Marcellini et Petri martyrum *P*. – ʸIn Ostkerka . . .] *om. LWH*.

III: Nomina comitum Flandrie

(Delisle, no. 176)

Nomina comitum Flandrie xvi[a]

Regnaverunt in Flandria ab anno Incarnationis dominice DCC.XC. secundo per annos CCC.XX.VII. usque ad Karolum comites XV videlicet Lidricus, Ingelramnus, Audacer, Balduinus[b] Ferreus, Bald*uinus* Calvus, Arnulfus Magnus, Bald*uinus*[c] Iuvenis, Arnulfus secundus, Balduinus[d] Barbatus, B*alduinus* Insulanus, Bald*uinus* Montensis, Arnulfus, Robertus, Robertus, Bald*uinus*,[e] Karolus.[f] Iste regnare cepit anno dominice Nativitatis M° C° nono[g] X°. Sunt in Flandria VI[h] fluviola: Ysarra,[i] Scalda, Leia, Agniona, Scarpia, Tenera.[j]

[a]XVI] CXVI *H.* – [b]Balduinus] Bald' *W.* – [c]Bald*uinus*] Balduinus *H.* – [d]Balduinus] Bald' *WH.* – [e]Bald*uinus*] *om.H.* – [f]M°] millesimo *WH.* – [g]nono] IX *H.* – [h]VI] sex *P.* – [i]Ysarra] Ysara *WH*; scilicet Sara *P.* – [j]Tenera]Tenra *P.*

7

Considerations on the Customary Law of Twelfth-Century Flanders

Historians have known for a long time that the twelfth century was an important dividing line in western history. New faces and new ideas, many going back to the eleventh century, caused deep social changes, while the old, archaic world of Carolingian and post-Carolingian times gave way to a richer, more differentiated, confident and strikingly dynamic society. Whereas previously the west had been static and on the defensive, it now entered upon an offensive phase, whose impact was felt in northern, eastern and western directions. It is, however, not my aim to study those external movements, but rather the internal desire for renovation that then dominated the West. It was one of those optimistic periods when man felt capable of everything, including that most difficult of all ambitions, the construction of a new and better world on the ruins of an antiquated and outmoded order. Whoever undertakes such renewal and the uprooting of existing abuse is obliged to introduce new structures, new institutions and new law. His weapon is called legislation; his enemy is called tradition. During the 'First Middle Ages' law and institutions were rooted in custom. The predominant feudalism was shaped by custom, as legislation had played a minimal role in its creation and development. The famous capitularies were to a large extent administrative instructions rather than legislative texts; even that source of the law had dried up by the late ninth century. A society dominated by custom tends to be static: things are done the way they have always been done and 'because it had always been so'. Custom is conservative. It serves to defend existing privileges or liberties against modernizing governments. Not surprisingly late medieval customs were deemed to be the best guarantee of freedom against ambitious rulers.[1]

---

[1] Our ancestors were quick to invoke their ancient customs against various initiatives of the Burgundian dukes, *inter alia*, against the introduction of the learned law, R.C. Van Caenegem, 'Boekenrecht en Gewoonterecht: het Romeinse recht in de Zuidelijke Nederlanden op het einde der middeleeuwen', *Bijdragen en mededelingen van het historisch genootschap*, 80 (1966), pp. 12-37, in this volume: 'Bookish Law and Customary Law: Roman Law in the Southern Netherlands in the late Middle Ages', below, pp. 119-33. Elsewhere also, in the English parliament, for example, we find a striking opposition between liberties and customs on the one

continued

From the second half of the eleventh, but mainly in the course of the twelfth century, a mighty organizational ambition took hold of Europe and bold plans were made for new structures and a more rational order, as well as for a new artistic style and way of life. The old social order was one of shapeless and endless proliferation and vegetation of local and regional customs,[2] forming an opaque mass of social relations and a confusion of divine and human, spiritual and temporal elements. To confront it there arose the principle of a conscious ordering of society and creation of new law, supposed to realize the ambitions and ideas of various new social groups and of progressive, mainly intellectual circles. The acceptance of what existed had to give way for the deliberate creation of new law: organization replacing vegetation.

It is well known that the first impetus for this renewal was given by the Gregorian Reform. An attack was directed against the Roman emperor and German king, the leader of the imperial church (*Reichskirche*), the symbol of the old order that went back to the Carolingians. Gregory VII inveighed against customary law, upon which his enemy's position was founded. With characteristic vehemence the pope decried custom, which could not by itself create law: injustice always remained injustice, no matter how long it went on.[3] Gregory VII put it with his usual sharpness: 'Christ did not say: "I am custom", he said "I am truth."'[4] The onslaught of the new on the old world was an onslaught on custom. Law was no longer inviolable simply because it existed and had been in existence for a more or less long time: henceforth it could be examined critically, and abolished, improved or replaced. The 'old world' was the world of the feudal aristocracy, the imperial church and the universal Roman empire. The new forces were the reformed and reforming

---

continued
hand, and governmental initiatives on the other. Thus, when the Commons asked in Henry IV's first parliament (1397) for the annulment of the condemnation of Thomas Haxey, who had introduced a bill protesting against the extravagant expenditure of the court, they maintained they were acting 'pur salvation des Libertees de lez ditz Communes' and because the judgment had been pronounced 'en anientisment des Custumes de lez Communes'. See the justified comment in J.S. Roskell, *The Commons and their Speakers in English Parliaments, 1376-1523* (Manchester, 1965), p. 40 that 'it is important to observe how the Commons' liberties are here equated with their customs'.

[2] The expression *végétation coutumière* occurs in G. Le Bras, Ch. Lefebvre and J. Rambaud, *L'âge classique, 1140-1378: sources et théorie du droit* (Paris, 1965), p. 207.

[3] Le Bras, Lefebvre and Rambaud, *L'âge classique*, pp. 205ff., 'Coutumes et usages', particularly p. 215 on the centralizing policy which had dominated since Gregory VII and 'supporte mal les tentatives d'indépendance que toute coutume de par la nature même entraîne', cf. pp. 422ff. an interesting analysis of the role of legislation, and pp. 533ff. of the role of custom. Cf. the pages devoted to the conflict between law and custom in P. Legendre, *La pénétration du droit romain dans le droit canonique classique de Gratien à Innocent IV* (Paris, 1964), pp. 54ff.

[4] J.F. Lemarignier, in F. Lot and R. Fawtier, *Histoire des institutions françaises au moyen âge*, iii, *Institutions ecclésiastiques* (Paris, 1962), p. 87. Flemings were familiarized with this conception ever since the bull of Pope Urban II to Count Robert the Frisian of 2 Dec. 1092 (J.-L. 5471, *MGH, SS*, ix, p. 310): 'Scire debes creatorem suum dixisse "Ego sum veritas", non autem usus vel consuetudo'.

papacy, modern kings, dukes and counts – particularly in Anglo-Norman, Flemish, Capetian and Norman-Sicilian lands – and rising towns and their ambitious patricians. It is my aim to examine in the following pages what happened to the ancient customary law in twelfth-century Flanders, an area where some profound innovation was taking place.[5]

Leading clerical circles felt suspicious or sometimes inimical towards customary law. Stephen of Tournai even assumed that Gratian had written his *Decretum* in order to fight the impact of custom on ecclesiastical law.[6] Some interesting echoes of this view could be heard in Flanders: legislation and written law were preferable to custom. When Abbot John of Saint-Amand granted a village charter, called *lex*, to Déchy and Férin (both in the arrondissement of Douai) in 1205, he justified his initiative as follows:

> The inhabitants of Déchy and Férin, who live under our jurisdiction, have no written law, but live according to usage and custom instead of legislation, and therefore they are more inclined to evil doing, such as the killing of men and women and other enormous crimes, which it is better to correct than to describe.[7]

There is not much left here of the old venerable splendour of customary law: the abbot does not place his trust in *usus et consuetudo* but in *lex*. This early thirteenth-century text betrays the reversal that had taken place in the preceding century, at least in the ecclesiastical world. We sense here not only how the new doctrine had inspired a negative attitude towards customary law, but that it was also responsible for a sharp distinction and even contrast being made between *consuetudo* and *lex*. This was in line with canon law teaching but not with the old notions which ignored the distinction between custom and legislation, but considered custom as the universal source of the law, so that all law was evidently customary. Even the term *lex*, which appeared frequently, was used for the customary law.[8] In one and the same

---

[5] I have based my remarks to a large extent on J. Gilissen, 'Loi et Coutume: Quelques aspects de l'interpénétration des sources du droit dans l'ancien droit belge', *Revue d'histoire du droit*, 21 (1953), pp. 257-96.

[6] Le Bras, Lefebvre and Rambaud, *L'âge classique*, p. 207, n. 6; Stephen and Sicard of Cremona underline Gratian's idea that every concession to custom ought to be as restricted as possible; they deem particular customs dangerous and find it preferable that the church be ruled by legislation (ibid., p. 215). Later canonists developed the theory that customs were only valid because of the presumption of legislative approval.

[7] A. Wauters, *De l'origine des libertés communales: preuves* (Brussels, 1869), pp. 61-3.

[8] The Great Borough Charter of Arras of 1157-1163, art. 1: the usage of destroying the house of a contumacious criminal is called the *lex* of the *viri Atrebatenses* ('quoniam talis est lex eorum'). It is well known that this *Wüstung* was no new law of the twelfth century but an ancient Germanic institution. Learned circles on the contrary were familiar with the precise distinction between *lex* and *consuetudo*. See, for example, Lambert of Saint-Omer's *Liber Floridus* (1120): 'Lex autem juris est species. Lex est constitucio scripta. Mos est vetustate probata consuetudo' (Ghent, University Library, MS 92, fo. 229). Cf. F.L. Ganshof, 'Note sur deux textes de droit canonique dans le Liber Floridus', *Études d'histoire du droit canonique dédiées à G. Le Bras*, i (Paris, 1965), p. 100. It is probable that Lambert here follows Anselm of Laon.

document one finds either *lex et consuetudo* or *lex vel consuetudo*,[9] while Galbert of Bruges, a cleric specializing in legal and administrative business, talks without inhibition of *leges consuetudinariae*.[10] There are several Flemish texts where an echo of the canonistic doctrine can be captured, for example in the notion of *consuetudo approbata*, which we find in a borough charter of Philip of Alsace for the town of Aire from 1188,[11] and in that of *consuetudo rationabilis* which we find in the borough charter of Matilda for Ghent from 1191.[12]

The attitude of the church was not purely negative – fighting custom – but positive as well – creating or inspiring new law and institutions. Thus the Peace of God movement clearly played a role in the maintenance of law and order in Flanders, both through the proclamation of the Peace of God itself and by the promulgation of a worldly peace – by the count – under the obvious influence of the church. The introduction of a *pax* in a number of villages and the proclamation of a special peace situation (with special law courts) in various West-Flemish territories are clear indications of this trend, even though their importance was restricted.[13] This ecclesiastical influence has possibly led to the authority granted expressly by the count of Flanders, Thierry of Alsace, to the abbot of St. Peter's Abbey in Ghent to issue legislation. It is probably that here also we catch an echo of the learned law, when it was clearly stipulated that the *leges* proclaimed by the abbot could not be undone by an ordinance or custom.[14]

---

[9] Charter of Aire of 1188, ed. G. Espinas, *Recueil de documents relatifs à l'histoire du droit municipal, Artois*, no. 20, i (Paris, 1943), p. 56. Cf. the *lagas seu consuetudines* of Saint-Omer, granted in 1127 by the new count ('concedo et ratas permanere precipio'), ed. Espinas, ibid., no. 622, iii (Paris, 1943), p. 296. This, to my mind terminological confusion, goes back a long way. See, for example, the passage in Gregory of Tours' *Historia Francorum* where King Charibert promises, in 589, not to introduce *leges consuetudinesque novas*, (ed. W. Levinson and B. Krusch, *MGH, SRM*, i (Hanover, 1951), pp. 448-49).

[10] Ed. H. Pirenne (Paris, 1891), c. 55, p. 87. H. Krause, 'Königtum und Rechtsordnung in der Zeit der sächsischen und salischen Herrscher', *Zeitschrift der Savigny Stiftung für Rechtsgeschichte, Germanistische Abteilung*, 82 (1965), pp. 1-98, has shown that in Germany also the law at that time was essentially customary. See also the interesting remarks in H. Hattenhauer, *Die Bedeutung der Gottes-und Landfrieden für die Gesetzgebung in Deutschland* (Marburg, 1958), who talks of the almost religious immobility of ancient customary law.

[11] Espinas, *Recueil*.

[12] In the arenga. Ed. W. Prevenier, *De oorkonden der graven van Vlaanderen (1191-aanvang 1206)*, ii, *Uitgave* (Brussels, 1964), no. 1, p. 12.

[13] For example, in Poperinge in 1147, ed. L. Gilliodts-Van Severen, *Coutumes de Lombardside, Loo et Poperinghe* (Brussels, 1902), no. iii, p. 298; and Saint-Amand in 1164, ed. H. Platelle, *La Justice seigneuriale de l'abbaye de Saint-Amand du XIIe au XVIe siècle* (Louvain and Paris, 1965), no. vi, pp. 431-33.

[14] D. Berten, *Coutumes de la seigneurie de Saint-Pierre-lez-Gand* (Brussels, 1905), p. xxx; text in A. Van Lokeren, *Chartes et Documents de l'abbaye de Saint Pierre*, no. 250, i (Ghent, 1868), p. 148. Cf. art. 19 of the charter of Philip of Alsace for Saint-Armand (1164): 'Verum huic paci quicquid ad meliorationem visum fuerit proficere, licebit abbati adicere, detrahere et mutare', ed. Platelle, *La justice seigneuriale de l'abbaye de Saint-Armand*, no. vi, p. 433.

The counts of Flanders were builders of states and legislators, in the twelfth century laid the foundations of a modern principality, disposing of adequate institutions, officials and legal rules. At first they restricted themselves to confirming in writing existing urban organizations or to granting certain liberties and privileges of an economic or juridical nature.[15] From Philip of Alsace onwards they became legislators. He introduced in numerous towns similar borough charters which formed a coherent and written synopsis of new principles of criminal law and procedure. He himself and his successors occasionally amplified them with additional ordinances which were clearly of a legislative character. The history of criminal law shows that we are confronted by new laws and not a registration of ancient customs. When these borough charters mention and conserve old institutions, they say so expressly. This applies, for example, to the destruction of houses of criminals, which remained in force 'because the law of the town happens to provide this'.[16] It is nevertheless interesting to note that these charters are represented as a registration of existing customary law – at least initially. This camouflage was later dropped. We can follow an interesting shift here, from 'This is the customary law of the citizens of Arras',[17] via 'This is the customary law which Count Philip ordered the citizens of Ghent to observe',[18] to the peremptory, 'These are the precepts which the lord count promulgated' or 'These are the points which the count ordained to be observed throughout the county'.[19] This was the voice of a lawgiver who introduced new rules and ordered their observance, whereas previously the suggestion was rather that of a sealed recording of existing customs. The reason was probably that legislation as a juridical category had not yet really revived, or at least had not yet reached practical application by the political authorities, and also that law and custom were still seen as synonyms:

---

[15] Krause, 'Königtum und Rechtsordnung', rightly stresses the importance of the grant of privileges as a legislative technique in his period. An interesting Flemish example is afforded by the charter of Ypres of 1116, by which Count Baldwin VII granted the town a *libertas* excluding *infra jus Iprense* ordeals of judicial combat, hot iron or water, ed. F. Vercauteren, *Actes des comtes de Flandre, 1107-1128* (Brussels, 1938), no. 79, p. 178.

[16] Espinas, *Recueil*, no. 107, i (Paris, 1934), p. 270, art. 1. (charter of Philip of Alsace of 1157-63, probably 1163), cf. n. 8.

[17] Ibidem, 'Talis est lex et consuetudo quam cives Attrebatenses tenent' (1157-1163).

[18] A.E. Gheldolf, *Coutumes de la ville de Gand*, i (Brussels, 1868), no. 1, p. 385: 'Haec est lex et consuetudo quam Philippus, illustris Flandriae et Viromandiae comes, Gandensibus observandam instituit'; cf. A.C.F. Koch, *Vroegmiddelnederlands ambtelijk proza* (Groningen, 1960), no. i, p. 2 (Great Borough Charter of Philip for Ghent 1177 at the latest).

[19] Gheldolf, *Coutumes de la ville de Gand*, no. vi, p. 396: 'Haec sunt edicta quae Philippus, marchio Namurcensis tempore suo ad destruendam discordiam in Gandavo constituit, consilio scabinorum' (charter of Philip of Namur, c. 1205); Prevenier, *Oorkonden der graven*, ii (Brussels, 1964), no. 214, p. 445: 'Hec sunt puncta que per universam terram suam comes observari precepit' (the so-called 'Ordinance for the bailiffs' of 1191-1202); cf. n. 32.

whoever introduced new law and put it in writing had at least to do lip service to the old gods.[20]

The question may well be asked why the initiative was taken in the twelfth century to proceed to the registration of real or apparent *consuetudines*. The general *Verschriftlichung*, of course, played a role: it became usual to demand written documents where an oral attestation or promulgation had previously been deemed sufficient (the increase of *spuria* in that period is a well-known phenomenon); and naturally the desire of a greater certainty of the law was also instrumental. There were also some less general motives which explain why at a given moment some customs and not others were selected to be fixed in writing. The normal situation for juridical as well as other customs is that they are so evident and ordinary that they naturally are, and remain, unwritten. One could go even further and maintain that as soon as it becomes necessary or useful to define customs and put them in writing, they in fact stop being 'customary' or 'ordinary', as the unconscious, natural and self-evident character of real custom is lost. Hence twelfth-century registration of customs was either no more than a seeming *record de coutumes*, which in fact introduced new law, or was caused by some crisis, because customary law was changing and some people felt menaced, who hoped to save their threatened position or even to regain lost rights or privileges. This means that the 'registration of customary law' could be a way of creating new law, but could also be used to turn the clock back and to prevent the development of a more modern custom by fixing the old and making it binding forever.

A striking, but not unique example in twelfth-century Europe is afforded by Henry II's Constitutions of Clarendon of 1164, the written record of the English *consuetudines* concerning the relations between church and state, as they had existed in the time of his grandfather, Henry I (1100-35).[21] Those old customs had in fact been overtaken by the evolution of canon law and the events at the time of the Anarchy, and their registration was an attempt to go against the tide of the new legal consciousness of the period. The worst aspect was that the king was not content with the agreement of the bishops to recognize those rules, but demanded that they be fixed in writing and conformed with the bishops' seals. This met with dramatic resistance.[22] It

---

[20] See the aforementioned study of Krause, 'Königtum und Rechtsordnung', who demonstrates with abundant source material what as essential, almost exclusive role was played by custom in the pre-Hohenstaufen period. J.C. Holt, *Magna Carta* (Cambridge, 1965), p. 206, rightly points out that the draftsmen of Magna Carta could not invent a completely new form for that innovative document, which nobody would recognize, and that therefore they had to represent their programme as the ancient customary law which the Angevin kings had broken; they thus avoided the reproach of *novitas*, which was anathema to the traditional mind of the time.

[21] W. Stubbs, *Select Charters*, 9th ed. by H.W.C Davis, (Oxford, 1913), p. 163-67.

[22] A.L. Poole, *From Domesday Book to Magna Carta* (Oxford, 1951), p. 207: 'Yet it was one thing to promise obedience to vague customs, quite another to written law.' According to Henry II the customs that arose during the Anarchy to the detriment of the rights of the crown, as they

thus appeared that the recording of customary law could be a hindrance to its evolution.

If that is so, customary law cannot have been so immobile as first suggested. Could the aversion of the rulers, and in the first place the popes, have been based on different grounds? The question deserves attention. Customary law could certainly remain unchanged for centuries and become a serious obstacle to the reformer by the sheer weight of tradition. But not all parts of the customary law remained necessarily and always the same. On the contrary, it is noteworthy how quickly new customs originated and became compulsory law: medieval doctrine is unambiguous on this point.[23] What irked the rulers in customary law was not so much its immobility and inertia, but its uncontrollable character and unforeseeable development. Just like language, customary law could be a flexible instrument which could evolve fast, but outside the grip of the authorities. It could also change so unobtrusively that it was hard to tell when the change had occurred: customary law changed without anyone ever having expressly introduced a change. Custom adapted itself so naturally to new situations and needs that it escaped the grip of the ruler – and his attempts at modernization and unification – by its elusive and many-headed proliferation. A period in which the sovereign heads of church and state had the ambition to introduce new social structures and to modernize the administrative and judicial apparatus could not be favourable to a customary law that tended to go its own way.

The leaders of church and state were not the only ones to be confronted with the problem of customs. The growing towns also had the ambition to conquer a place in feudal society and to enjoy a position appropriate to their specific needs and ideas. They wanted a law of their own, and in the twelfth century that meant their own customary law, which might diverge from the old law as it existed in the countryside. Very early on the Flemish towns obtained from the ruler the right to modernize, change and 'improve' their customary law. For Bruges we know this through the testimony of a

---

existed in the time of Henry I, were in fact 'bad customs' and had to be abolished. See a typical statement in his charter for Barnstaple (Devon) where he says: 'Sciatis me concessisse burgensibus burgi Barnestapol omnes rectas consuetudines quas habuerunt in tempore regis H. avi mei, remotis omnibus pravis consuetudinibus post avum meum ibi elevatis', *Calendar of Patent Rolls of Edward IV, Edward V, Richard III, 1476-1485*, (London, 1901), p. 63 (confirmation by Edward IV of 8 February 1478).

[23] The canonists disagreed about the number of acts necessary for the establishment of a custom. Bernard of Parma and Innocent IV, following Johannes Bassianus, Azo and Accursius, deemed two acts for sufficient; this was accepted by Hostiensis also. Some authors went further and demanded ten, whereas others maintained that one was sufficient to bring to light the existence of a customary law (Johannes Andreae, Antonius de Butrio). See G. Le Bras *et al.*, *Age classique*, p. 543; the adage 'Quod semel placuit ceterum displicere nequit' may have played a role in this.

narrative source,[24] for other places through articles in borough charters.[25]

Here also we are confronted with problems. To begin with there is the fact that the towns asked the count to authorize them to improve their customs, i.e. to develop their urban law. This logically implies that without the consent of the prince the towns could not create their own law. Yet, this is belied by what we know of the creative activity of the cities in the earliest period of their emancipation. It is hardly credible that the gilds and towns shaped their institutions and rules in the eleventh and twelfth centuries only after obtaining the count's permission, even though often they afterwards obtained his confirmation. I am therefore inclined to accept, with Ebel,[26] that the town had the undisputed right to choose their own law (*willekeuren* = to will and to choose) and consequently to change the existing customs, initially at least. I believe, however, that in the course of the twelfth century the towns gained the impression that this freedom of initiative, was threatened by comital ambitions and have therefore obtained, in their borough charters, written confirmation both of their specific customs and their right to legislate – a right which they did not fail to use, as appears from the vast collections of urban statutes (*voorgeboden*) from the later middle ages.[27]

Another question concerns the exact significance of this 'improvement of the customary law'. It seems improbable that a gradual and unobtrusive adaptation, for example via case law, is meant here, but rather an open and express change in the law through legislation – or at least the abolition of *malae consuetudines*, of which there were many.[28] This entails that customary law does not stand here for law that originated exclusively in custom, but belongs rather to the sphere of traditional law, which grows organically and

---

[24] Galbert of Bruges, ed. H. Pirenne (Paris, 1891), c. 55, p. 87; the passage could be reminiscent of art. 7 of Gregory VII's famous *Dictatus papae*, ed. C. Mirbt, *Quellen zur Geschichte des Papsttums* (Tübingen, 1924), no. 278, p. 146.

[25] Arras, 1157-63, ed. Espinas, *Recueil*, no. 107, i, p. 272, art. 26; charter of Baldwin IX for Saint-Omer of 5 May 1199, ed. Prevenier, *De oorkonden der graven van Vlaanderen*, no. 104, p. 224: the aldermen were entitled 'iuri preterea suo quicquid voluerint, ad emendationem ville, superaddant, salvo iure meo et ville'.

[26] W. Ebel, *Die Willkür: Eine Studie zu den Denkformen des älteren deutschen Rechts* (Göttingen, 1953), pp. 46ff., against Planitz who believed that the privilege allowed the merchants to have a different law from the other citizens. Ebel quotes Lübeck 1163 and Bern 1191 as the oldest texts in Germany mentioning urban ordinances.

[27] Thus the charter of Aire of 1188 grants the citizens the *libertas* of conserving their ancient particular customs, ed. Espinas, *Recueil*, no. 20, i, p. 56.

[28] Abolition of *malae consuetudines* in Germany from the eleventh century onwards. Exceptionally there are traces already in the tenth, see the *mala consuetudo* in the charter of Conrad I for the bishop of Chur of 25 Sept. 912, ed. Th. Sickel, *Conradi I, Heinrici I et Ottonis I diplomata* (Hanover, 1879), no. 11, p. 2 (*MGH, Diplomata*, i); cf. H. Krause, 'Königtum und Rechtsordnung', pp. 91ff. Abolition of bad customs is known in France from the middle of the eleventh century, see F. Olivier-Martin, 'Le roi de France et les mauvaises coutumes au moyen âge', *Zeitschrift der Savigny Stiftung*, G.A., 58 (1938), pp. 108-137; the oldest text is from 1051, the next from 1105.

is not in conflict with it.²⁹ In this way internal contradiction is solved of the introduction of better 'customs' by way of legislation.

Flemish evolution reflected the European situation. Even if institutional development took place within narrow regional or local boundaries, it still mirrored great international mutations. This was especially the case in the twelfth century, which was most probably the most international and open of the whole medieval period. Flemish events of that century reflect the European transition from an older, more Germanic society to a modernized, more Roman-looking political organization. The decisive element was the position of the ruler.

According to the older view, authority was in the hands of several aristocratic potentates who rallied around the prince and whose activity – like that of the king himself – was dominated by ancient, sacred law. The king, as appears from his coronation oath, had the right and the duty to maintain the laws and nothing else: at most he could abolish bad laws or grant privileges.³⁰ He was the guarantor, not the creator of the law. According to the new concept, which made progress in church and state in the twelfth century, society knew only one central seat of power, to which all other bearers of authority were subject and from which they derived their power. This supreme ruler was, moreover, not himself under the law, as he was the *fons et origo* of all law and a sovereign lawgiver. Thus Philip of Alsace confirmed the law as it had been put in writing (*quoniam talis est lex eorum*),³¹ but he also issued new legal rules, which were openly introduced as such (*hec sunt precepta que statuit dominus comes*).³² He was not giving away his legislative power. Whereas William Clito had granted the citizens of Bruges the right to improve their customary law *potestative et licenter*, Philip of Alsace stipulated expressly in the last article of his great borough charter that urban changes in the existing law must be made in collaboration with the count.³³ The 'improvement' of the law of Bruges in 1127 was certainly meant to include the abolition of 'bad customs', even though this was, strictly speaking a princely prerogative (as appears in neighbouring countries), which William Clito had given away in his desire to win over Bruges during the struggle for the succession of Charles the Good.

---

²⁹ See below, 'Bookish Law and Customary Law', pp. 119-33.

³⁰ In the classic medieval coronation oath the king promised to protect the peace and the church, to maintain good laws and abolish bad ones, and to see to it that everyone's rights were guaranteed. See M. David, 'Le serment du sacre du IXe au XVe siècle', *Revue du moyen âge latin*, 6 (1950), and H.G. Richardson, 'The English Coronation Oath', *Transactions of the Royal Historical Society*, 4th series, 23 (1941), pp. 129-58.

³¹ Arras 1157-63, art. 1; cf. the charter for Ghent of Matilda of 1191, art. 5: 'Sunt autem hec eorum decreta'.

³² Ghent, shortly after 1178, Koch, *Vroegmiddelnederlands ambtelijk proza*, no. ii, pp. 16-20.

³³ 'Ad haec nec scabini nec burgenses aliquid addere, mutare vel corrigere poterunt nisi per consensum comitis vel illius quem loco suo ad justitiam tenendam instituerit.' *Corrigere* and (*com*)*mutare* is exactly what the citizens of Bruges were allowed to do in 1127, cf. n. 24.

Three forces assailed the omnipotence of customary law; the church through its doctrine and the Peace of God movement, the counts through the introduction of modern political principles, and the town through the construction of a more modern law and a privileged position. These forces put an end to the oldest phase of Flemish legal history, where custom reigned supreme. They, however, put an end to the role of custom, for the new norms concerned essentially what we would call public law, whereas private law remained for many centuries the almost exclusive domain of custom. An interesting early example of comital legislation on private law can be found in art. 3(4) of the *Precepta* of Count Philip of Alsace for Ghent (shortly after October 1178). Here we find that the surety of a condemned person, who does not pay the fine until he is condemned to do so, shall owe twice the double amount. The text then proceeds to stipulate: 'Similiter in aliis negotiis, quicumque fidejussor constitutus fuerit, et donec super [eum] placitetur satisfacere distulerit, puniatur in duplo', which meant an extension *per analogiam* to private law.[34] Nevertheless, a decisive experiment had been made, and the idea of a planned, directed development of the law had arisen at the side of customs with their conservatism and chance-induced variety.

---

[34] Ed. Koch, *Vroegmiddelnederlands ambtelijk proza*, no. ii, p. 18.

8

The Ghent Revolt of February 1128

The numerous revolts that shook Ghent between the twelfth and the sixteenth centuries are a spectacular element in the history of the Low Countries. Time and again the mighty industrial city took up arms and rebelled against the authority of the counts of Flanders. And every time the proud burgesses were beaten by the superior forces of their rulers, but not without putting up a long and stubborn fight. Ghent has been at loggerheads with the counts of the houses of Alsace, Dampierre, Burgundy and Habsburg, and not until the fall of the Calvinist Republic to Farnese's army, in 1584, was its old contrariness finally subdued. Some people will shake their heads over such misguided stubborness and hopeless resistance, while others may express their admiration for so much courage and love of freedom. It is legitimate to condemn Ghent's urban particularism and lack of pan-Netherlandish vision and statesmanship, but it is equally acceptable to stand in awe of this never-ending fight for democracy and autonomy. Whether one praises or condemns it, nobody escapes the fascination of this wayward and self-willed city.

The series of Ghent revolts was opened on 16 February 1128. The February Revolt of that year was directed against the castellan, Wenemar II, the local representative of the comital government. The burgesses accused him of treating them unjustly and vilely, by reimposing taxes which had just been abolished and which were associated by the townspeople with rural serfdom: a sensitive area for emancipated burghers. The revolt was violent and the castellan soon fled to his master, Count William Clito, for military assistance. Every reader of Galbert of Bruges' narrative of the murder of Count Charles the Good, on 2 March 1127, knows that the militia of Ghent, which that year took part in the struggle against the conspirators, was a solid and well-organized formation, equipped with modern and impressive arms. Count William and his knights went to Ghent, determined to beat the revolt, but he soon discovered that he had underestimated his opponents. A full-scale battle between the town militia and his band of knights was bound to lead to a bloodbath and possibly the destruction of one of his most important towns. Hence the confrontation was, for the time being, limited to a battle of words fought out in one of Ghent's large squares. Here, in the course of a mass meeting, the count had to listen, under the threatening glare of a restless crowd, to a lashing attack on his rule – just as Charles the Bold would be obliged, in 1467, to listen in the Friday Market to the list of injustices Ghent had suffered at his hands.

How had this rupture between count and town come about? William Clito was a young and inexperienced ruler. He had gained power in 1127 as successor of the childless Charles the Good and, although he belonged to the ruling house of Flanders through his grandmother Matilda (d. 1083), a daughter of Count Baldwin V (d. 1067), he was a foreigner who had mainly grown up in another world. He was the first count to find himself in this situation. From the ninth century until 1119 the counts of the first dynasty had followed each other in a direct line of succession, and even Charles the Good, a son of Adela (d. 1115), a daughter of the famous Count Robert the Frisian (d. 1093), had from childhood onwards lived in Flanders, after the murder of his father the Danish King Canute IV (d. 1086). In March 1127 William Clito had been imposed on his Flemish subjects, to the exclusion of the other pretenders, by the king of France, Louis VI, for reasons of international politics. Indeed, it might have been expected that Clito's hatred of his uncle, King Henry I of England, would lead Flanders into an anti-English and pro-French policy. William Clito was a Norman, the son of Duke Robert of Normandy, the nephew of King Henry I of England and grandson of William the Conqueror.

The Anglo-Norman Empire was his world and the focus of his greatest ambitions. It was a princely and feudal world, which had little understanding of the communal aspirations of the county of Flanders, where urban expansion was in full swing. Clito had no sympathy with ideas of urban liberty, let alone self-government. He had admittedly needed the Flemish towns in order to secure his debatable succession, but as soon as the latter seemed safe, he turned against urban aspirations.

There had already been a first revolt in Lille in August 1127, when the new count had disturbed the peace of the market by arresting a runaway serf of his; the swords of his knights had put it down. And one week before the troubles in Ghent, a revolt had taken place in Saint-Omer because Clito had tried to impose on the town a castellan who was a robber and an oppressor. The townspeople even accepted an anti-count, Arnold, a grandson of the forementioned Adela and a nephew of Charles the Good, but here again William's military preponderance had been too great and the town had submitted and paid a considerable fine.

In Ghent the situation was apparently different and military prowess useless. The count did not dare risk a frontal attack, which might lead to bitter street-fighting, and he also decided against a prolonged siege: after a violent exchange of words with the rebels he withdrew. Military preparedness was not the only trump in the hands of Ghent, which disposed of an excellent competitor to replace Count William. Flanders was inconceivable without a comital government. The county as a political unit had been created by an outstanding lineage of counts, who had originated as Frankish royal officials and turned an area which was economically, ethnically, ecclesiastically and linguistically diverse into a meaningful principality and a true fatherland. Whoever revolted against the count, the father of the land, had to produce an acceptable new father figure. This role Thierry of Alsace could easily assume, as he was a grandson of Robert the Frisian and, like his grandfather, not afraid of a bold stroke. He had already made clear his ambitions in March 1127 when he had written to express his claim to the county. He was a scion of the princely family of Alsace, in the German empire, because his mother, Gertrude, had married Duke Thierry II (d. 1115). His later career showed him to have the necessary qualities to be a good ruler; Ghent's candidate clearly was a pretender on a footing equal to William Clito.

The rebels disposed of yet another trump card: certain new and attractive ideas on public authority and the organization of the state that were circulating in their camp. The impact of ideas and slogans should not be underestimated, a fact of which cynical ministers of propaganda are better aware than some naive historians, who imagine they can write history as if the mental make up of the *dramatis personae* were irrelevant and people thoughtless automata in some process determined by iron laws. The remarkable and even revolutionary ideas which circulated among the disgruntled townsmen were expressed in a great speech pronounced in Ghent in the course of a mass meeting by one of the leaders of the revolt, Yvain of Aalst. It certainly belongs to the most important political speeches ever pronounced in the course of Flemish history, and deserves a special place beside the celebrated political and military addresses in Livy's Roman history. Its starting point was the conviction that political authority, in this case the monarchy, ought to rest on a legitimate base; which was none other than a pact, a contract between the ruler and his people. They owed the prince loyal service, but he was obliged to observe the law and to respect the rights of his subjects, who were free.

We are confronted here with the contractual relationship between equal partners, not with a vertical master-subject nexus. It meant that a ruler who did not fulfil his obligations, and who violated the rights of the people, had broken his contract and could be rejected by the people and replaced by a better prince.

All this was clearly enunciated, as a point of principle, by Yvain, who also explained what injustice the count and his castellan had committed against the citizens of Ghent. He concluded that Clito had forfeited his function. It is interesting to compare this reasoning with that of the famous 'Act of Abandonment' by which the northern Netherlands denounced their allegiance to Philip II in 1581.

The delicate question in all this was, of course, who could decide whether the government had indeed violated the fundamental rights of the population. It was obviously impossible to let all and sundry decide for themselves that the ruler had violated their particular rights and had therefore forfeited the throne. The Ghent speech of 1128 did not fail to address this aspect of the problem, and formulated the remarkable proposal that a great exceptional tribunal – a sort of constitutional court – should be convened at Ypres which, after objective and serious examination of the merits of the case, would pronounce judgment. The court at Ypres would consist of the existing *curia comitis*, the highest feudal court in the land, strengthened and completed by 'the wisest men from the clergy and the people'. If they gave judgment in favour of the count, he would keep his office, but if they decided that he had acted in bad faith, cunningly and as a perjurer, he would have to leave the county, which would be entrusted to a more law-abiding successor.

The effect of these surprisingly modern ideas can be imagined: they contained the principles of constitutionalism and the sovereignty of the people (even though these abstract terms themselves did not appear in the speech). William Clito rejected them angrily and, as a child of his time and his knightly environment, countered such ideas by a challenge to judicial combat: the sword against the word. This was rejected by the rebels, who insisted on a court hearing, and the meeting ended in a general uproar.

The Ypres tribunal never met: what had happened in Ghent was the beginning of civil war. Followers of William Clito and of Thierry of Alsace, the former recruited mainly from the feudal world, and the latter from the ranks of the burgesses, fought each other until William Clito died at the end of July 1128 from wounds incurred in a skirmish under the walls of Aalst, whereupon Thierry was generally acknowledged as the new count. Although he had entered Ghent on 11 March 1128, a band of followers of Clito continued to resist within the count's castle there and had even made a sortie on 2 May, causing fire and destruction in the town.

The intellectual background of Yvain's remarkable speech is still insufficiently known. It seems clear that the contractual theme stemmed from feudalism, which was based on a free covenant between lord and vassal. But other themes are also audible: the insistence on the role of *clerus et populus* and certain ideas on public office are most probably of Gregorian origin. We have more specifically the impression – although the question demands more profound research – that the ideas of Manegold of Lautenbach, who (by coincidence?) also came from Alsace (like Thierry), exerted a notable influence here. His *Liber ad Gebehardum* (1082-85) had become famous precisely because it contained the theory of popular sovereignty and gave the people the right of replacing an unjust ruler.

Yvain's speech admittedly left some points obscure, such as who would select the 'wisest man from the clergy and the people', but it contained interesting and positive ideas. However, ideas tend to remain a mere academic pastime unless they are propagated by certain powers and can serve certain interests. Which groups and interests were behind the Ghent revolt? It is not difficult to discover them.

The towns were displeased with Clito's rule, which had led to an English embargo and severely hit commerce and trade, particularly the cloth industry. But there was worse: Clito's regime was very feudal, betrayed incomprehension towards the movement for communal emancipation and sought to restore an agrarian and feudal world which the Flemish towns had just outgrown. In 1127 the new count had seduced the towns, *inter alia*, by the abolition of several tolls which had seriously hindered trade. When later on the knights, who had of old profited from these tolls, protested – the count had given away what was not his – Clito withdrew his concessions. His submission to his barons' demands made the latter so impudent that they began to treat the townspeople as if they were serfs on their manors. But if there was one critical point, it was that the burghers under no circumstances wanted to return under the *dominium* of the great landowners. The revolts in Saint-Omer and Ghent were panic reactions to this threat. The accession of the powerful house of Aalst to Thierry's camp also had other causes. Yvain of Aalst was a landowner who had great interests in the Ghent area, and the prosperity of the town concerned him directly. There was also the fact that he, just like Thierry of Alsace, came from the German empire, Aalst being situated in Imperial Flanders (and not in the larger, French part of the county known as Crown Flanders).

We owe it to Galbert of Bruges that we are so well informed of what was said and done in Ghent and Flanders in 1128. This comital official kept a diary during the whole drama, from the murder of Charles the Good to the triumph of Thierry of Alsace. The ideas expressed by Yvain interested Galbert so much that he had reported them in a lively and detailed way: reading him we have the impression of listening to the spokesman of the revolt himself.

In the short run the Ghent revolt was successful: Ghent's anti-count became victorious and the house of Alsace owed its short but brilliant Flemish career to the February Revolt. This does not mean that Thierry and his son Philip were 'democratic' rulers. On the contrary, whereas they allowed and esteemed the economic role of the towns, they did not yield them an inch in the political field. Hence their forceful rule led repeatedly to violent clashes with Ghent, and it is significant that Wenemar, with whom it had all started, was maintained by Thierry in his office of castellan of Ghent.

The first revolt of Ghent was the symptom of a fundamental problem: urban autonomy could not flourish in the feudal world. Powerful cities with democratic ideas were foreign bodies, at first in the feudal and knightly world and afterwards in the absolute monarchies. Such a foreign body leads, as we know from modern surgery, to a process of rejection. This explains the latent tension, which existed from the twelfth to the sixteenth century, between the difficult town of Ghent, which repeatedly cherished republican ideas, and the *Fürstenstaat* of the old feudal or the modern bureaucratic type. The starting shot for the long chain of Ghent 'troubles' which ended with the surrender of 1584, was given in 1128, a remarkable event which deserves to be commemorated.

9

The Pacification of Ghent

The revolt of the Low Countries – roughly present-day Belgium, Holland and Luxembourg – against King Philip II (d. 1598), who had inherited them (in 1555) together with Spain (in 1556) from his father, the Emperor Charles V (d. 1558), was a national reflex against foreign domination by a distant absentee ruler. The regime of the Spanish king caused resistance because he treated the Netherlands as a colonial province and not as an independent and important state of European significance. King Philip also disregarded established traditions and interests so flagrantly that his subjects gradually gained the impression that they lived in an occupied territory and under a dictatorial regime. When the king sent a general with full powers – at the head of a motley collection of mercenaries – to restore order, install a 'Council of Blood' which pronounced more than 12,000 condemnations (*c.* 2,000 of which led to executions), promulgate a new criminal code in the Spanish fashion and impose new taxes without the consent of the people or their representatives, a national resistance movement could be expected.

In personal terms also there was an incompatibility between the ruler and his subjects. Philip was a very Spanish monarch. The struggle for Catholic orthodoxy was at the forefront of his preoccupations, and he carried it on in a merciless manner which to the Low Countries was hardly imaginable: he came from a country which for centuries had fought a hard battle for Catholicism, first against Islam in the Reconquista and then against the heretics through the ruthless Inquisition. It is true that Philip tried to convince the Low Countries that orthodoxy was economically advantageous, but this message must have fallen on deaf ears. Indeed, when the citizens of Ghent heard the ruler explain in 1559 that 'the change of religion does not take place without the whole *res publica* being changed and that the poor, the have nots and vagabonds use that excuse in order to lay their hands on the goods of the rich', they must have wondered whether the Lutheran merchants in Antwerp did not respect property rights and whether Calvin was really aiming at a social and economic revolution (although, admittedly, the case of the Anabaptists of Münster seemed to support the king's contention). Many thought, on the contrary, that to defend Catholicism with bloody ordinances constituted the worst possible threat to the prosperity of the cosmopolitan Netherlands and their trade and industry.

The Pacification of Ghent was a crucial moment in the Revolt of the Netherlands against Spain. It was the last chance of establishing a united front and bridging the opposition between the Calvinist strongholds in Holland and Zealand and the rest of the Seventeen Provinces, in the hope that the Estates General, as the parliament of the whole of the Low Countries, would find a definitive solution for the political and religious problems.

The Revolt, revolutionary in its effect although conservative and even atavistic in its starting point, is a crucial event in Dutch national history. It belongs, however, equally to European and even world history, as it was the first of a series of great risings against modern absolutism, which shaped the constitutions of numerous important countries.

The modern European states were produced by the late medieval national monarchies, whose internal contradictions and tensions gave birth, in modern times, to several great national revolts or revolutions. Tension existed between the monarchic and the democratic elements. The medieval king was, on the one hand, an hereditary ruler by God's grace, supreme legislator and judge, as well as sovereign leader of the people who were entrusted to him. On the other hand, he understood that he was bound by the liberties and rights of his subjects (which he had sworn to uphold at his coronation); he had to respect their right of resistance and to rule with parliaments or estates, i.e. the people's representatives. In sixteenth-century Europe the authoritarian element was everywhere in the ascendant. Kings, supported by standing armies and a legalistic, bourgeois bureaucracy, freed themselves from old laws and traditions, and left the national assemblies – with their eternal complaints and demands – quietly at home. Against this absolutism, which installed itself in modern Europe, five famous revolts broke out successively, and each of them, however different their ideological inspiration, toppled an insupportable and oppressive regime.

The first in the series was the Revolt of the Netherlands. It was directed against the 'absolute' exercise of power by King Philip and spiritual uniformity imposed through torture and burning at the stake. It stood for a political regime of national inspiration, religious tolerance and a parliamentary constitution, in the form that was current at the time. The old estates were not really democratic, as the electorate and the elected representatives belonged to the better classes; they in fact maintained the rule of the notables, and the Revolt was no doubt caused to a large extent by the displeasure of the traditional elites. The old assemblies of estates were nevertheless the cradle of our parliamentary democracy. In the Northern Netherlands, which escaped reconquest by Alexander Farnese (d. 1592), the Italian general and statesman in Spanish service, the Revolt led to a radical solution: the abolition of the monarchy and the foundation of an independent and federal republic.

The second in the series was the English revolt against Stuart absolutism. Here again a national movement of resistance was directed against a conscious attempt – in the case of James I even defended with learned and theoretical arguments – to establish an absolute form of monarchy. Here also religious dissidents, who defended their rights against the established church, played an important role. The protracted conflict resulted in the Glorious Revolution of 1688 and the Bill of Rights of 1689: the unity of the kingdom and the monarchy were preserved, but the latter had to accept various far-reaching limitations and to recognize the supremacy of parliament; also, the Protestant denominations outside the Anglican church were tolerated, which meant the institution of ideological pluralism.

The third in the series is the American revolt, which led to the Declaration of Independence of 1776, exactly 200 years after the pacification of Ghent (the ensuing British-American conflict was, remarkably enough, finally put to rest by another 'Peace of Ghent', that of 1814). In the case of America we are dealing with a colonial population which refused any longer to be treated as such. It had had enough of being administered by governors of the distant British Crown, of living under laws voted by the Westminster parliament and, on top of it all, of being arbitrarily taxed by the impecunious mother country without being represented in its parliament. Therefore the thirteen American colonies founded an independent nation, with a federal organization, a congress and laws of its own, radical ideological pluralism and a democratic constitution, without hereditary monarchy or privileged classes.

The fourth in the row was the French Revolution of 1789. Nowhere had royal absolutism been such a brilliant success as in the land of the Sun King. Yet, here also the moment of revolt against arbitrary rule, religious monolithism and hereditary privilege arrived. Finally in the immense Russian lands, the February and October revolutions of 1917 put an end to the ancestral autocracy of the czars. A drastic modernization was embarked upon, inspired by one ideology and led by one party.

All five revolts were aimed against existing oppression, and all five were successful. They all fought a privileged state-supported church. There are, however, striking differences in their degree of success. The United Provinces, however republican, had preserved in the stadholders of the House of Orange a quasi-monarchy, which commanded strong feelings of personal loyalty. The English monarchy was preserved, but as a national symbol rather than a dominating political force. The American revolt abolished the monarchy and preferred an elected president with a limited term of office. The French Revolution was followed by various eliminations and restorations of the monarchy, which eventually resulted in a presidential republic. In the religious field the Dutch and the English revolutions led to toleration combined with an established church, American independence resulted in total ideological freedom without any official recognition of, or influence on, any denomination. The French Revolution resulted in regimes with very divergent attitudes towards the church. The Russian October Revolution went much further and was, like the dominant ideology of the Soviet state, anti-religious on principle.

The Pacification of Ghent was the last chance of success for the revolt of the whole of the Low Countries. Its aim was never achieved. An Erasmian, tolerant approach did not mean much to the radicals who – in the autumn of 1577 – had begun to establish a Protestant democratic dictatorship in Ghent, followed by drastic anti-Catholic measures in the first months of 1578 – all against the stipulations of the Pacification. In the agrarian south many nobles, who at first had formed the core of the anti-Philip front, were becoming more frightened of the 'democracies' of the large towns in Flanders and Brabant and the Calvinist 'rebels' in Holland than of the king of Spain, and they looked for a separate peace – if not with Philip, then with another acceptable Habsburg. In January 1579 the opposing Unions of Arras (southern, Catholic and ready for a rapprochement with Spain) and of Utrecht (northern, ideologically mixed and determined to continue the resistance) were founded. Under the Emperor Charles V the nobility had been royalist. In the first years of Philip II the tendency had changed, but now the fear of the turbulent spirits which the revolt had conjured up drove many back to the safety of the royal sceptre. The pan-Netherlandish outlook of William of Orange was not shared by those whose horizon was limited to their own region or town: is it not typical that the first demand of the Ghent Calvinist Republic, in October 1577, was the restoration of the old urban privileges, which had been lost at the time of the revolt against the Emperor Charles V?

The two states, into which his Seventeen Provinces were eventually divided, the Republic of the United Netherlands and the Spanish Netherlands, appear as each other's opposites. Nevertheless, each of them continued a late medieval tradition. In the North, that of urban autonomy, powerful bourgeois entrepreneurs and provincial or national assemblies of estates; in the South, that of monarchical rule and centralized administration – two tendencies which had already dramatically collided in fourteenth-century Flanders. The sixteenth-century separation was, moreover, no definitive and irrevocable development. On the contrary, modern Holland has, while preserving her traditions of political freedom and responsibility and ideological pluralism, returned to monarchy and a centralized and unitary constitution, whereas the South has added to its monarchy a parliamentary and constitutional dimension, combined with ideological freedom. In other words, in the nineteenth century the kingdom of the Netherlands recovered the monarchic, and the kingdom of Belgium the parliamentary element which they had abandoned in the sixteenth century. Consequently the two countries again combine today the two great traditions of their late medieval past and, since their respective constitutions of

1831 and 1848, show a striking similarity, in spite of their separate peregrinations in previous centuries.

I would like to conclude with a tentative question: is it possible to draw lessons from the events we commemorate? We are somewhat hesitant, because many people consider 'drawing lessons' an old-fashioned pastime, redolent of sermons and schoolmasters, whereas others find that the historian ought merely to describe and narrate, leaving the conclusions to his readers. Some historians have drawn only one conclusion from the study of the past and its recurrences: that humanity never learns from its mistakes. I wonder, however, what sense historical research – a mass industry producing tens of thousands of titles every year – can have if one is *a priori* convinced that it can be of no use to the reader. I believe therefore that it is legitimate to draw attention to a few aspects of the Revolt which might be a source of inspiration for our own time. There is, to begin with, the basic idea, that the state exists for the people and not the other way round. As was admirably and succinctly expressed in the famous Act of Abandonment of July 1581, in the northern provinces, where we read that 'the subjects were not created by God for the sake of the Prince and to submit to all his decrees . . . , but that on the contrary the Prince was created for the sake of the subjects, without whom he could be no Prince'. This is a just evaluation of human priorities, which to-day has lost none of its value.

The course of events in the sixteenth-century Low Countries also demonstrated how particularism can paralyze all efforts, even when considerable common interests are at stake. We shake our heads in condemnation of the blindness of our ancestors who could not overcome their provincial outlook in order to think in Netherlandish, 'Burgundian' terms. But what about the national reflexes in our own time, when thinking in European terms is called for – particularly in difficult moments. When friction with Philip started, the formation of the Seventeen Provinces was still very recent: Frisia, Groningen and Utrecht had been added to the Habsburg Netherlands in the 1520s and 1530s and Gelderland as recently as 1543. Were they really 'United Provinces' or might the description of 'collected provinces' be more suitable for the political 'multinational' assembled by the Burgundians? We are dealing with a very new and recent solidarity, when measured by the standard of the immemorial regional loyalties inspired by the mini-fatherlands that composed the Low Countries. There is possibly a lesson here for our time: we hope that our readers will not think it inappropriate if I conclude on this twentieth-century note.

10

Bookish Law and Customary Law: Roman Law in the Southern Netherlands in the Late Middle Ages

Around 1430 the reeve and the aldermen of the village of St. Peter near Ghent, the seigniory of the ancient St. Peter's abbey, faced a problem which they could not solve.[1] Before this important court of law, itself the court of appeal to a number of courts in other seigniories of the abbey, appeared as plaintiff Rogier De Draeyer, a monk of the abbey, accompanied by a judicial patron (*dyngheleke vooght*), a counsellor (the barrister Jan De Backer) and a pleader (*taalman*); Rogier carried a power of attorney from the abbey to represent it in the lawsuit. As the abbey's pittancer[2] he was responsible for the distribution of food, and was thus engaged in the administration and control of certain sources of income, among which was a cherry orchard, a plot of land belonging to the office of the pittancer which we will meet later on. As a cleric acting before a secular court, he had to be represented by a lay patron, the *dyngheleke vooght* of our case. He demanded to receive 'purgation' of a plot of land, called the cherry orchard, situated near the abbey and belonging to his office, 'according to the custom of the aforesaid seigniory', i.e. the customary law of the seigneurial court of the aldermen of the village of St. Peter.

The purgation (*purge, sueverynghe*) is a procedure by which an owner or purchaser obtains a judicial confirmation that the property is undeniably his and free of all real charges. When after a prescribed number of proclama-

---

[1] The text of their judgment, dated 4 October 1431, from which we obtained our information, can be found in D. Berten, *Coutumes de la seigneurie de Saint-Pierre-lez-Gand* (Brussels, 1905), no. x, pp. 80-89. The edition is not always correct, as appears from the original, conserved in the State Archives in Ghent, 'Fonds St. Pieters', 1st series, no. 1655. A document concerning the jurisdiction of the aldermen of Ghent, which previously was joined to the sealed judgment of St. Peter's, is apparently lost. Berten prints it (p. 86, n. 1) and until a few years ago it was still in its place, but when I tried to see it at the beginning of 1966, it could not be found. There is a not very accurate summary of the judgment in A. Van Lokeren, *Chartes de Saint-Pierre*, no. 1655, 11 (Ghent, 1871), p. 192.

[2] Ibid., no. 1685, ii, p. 212, document of 12 August 1437. Accounts of R. De Draeyer are conserved for the period 1430-32 in the series 'Rekeningen van de Pitanciers', Ghent, State Archives, Fonds St. Pieters, 1st series, nos. 1688-1690.

tions nobody comes forward to make a claim, the property is declared 'purged' by the court. This procedure is very clearly described in the custom of Veurne of 1615 (lxii, 1), one of the most complete and careful of all Flemish customs, under the title 'Van Purgen ende Suyveringhe van Wetten'.³

To find out where the cherry orchard was situated we can consult old maps of the village, which give us a clear picture of the situation. The abbey church of St. Peter was to the west of the steep bank of the River Scheldt and quite close to it. To the north was the parish church of Our Lady. The land of the pittancer was situated along the river, to the east of the church of Our Lady, and is clearly marked on the map.⁴ In the area one finds an orchard, but not specifically a cherry orchard. On another map we find a cherry orchard, but too far from the Scheldt and the lands of the pittancer to be identified as the cherry orchard of our lawsuit.⁵

The pittancer's request was granted and, after the usual public announcement in church on Sunday, he again appeared before the court and repeated his claim to the free and full ownership of the cherry orchard, except for a right of way for two named plots of land. At that moment one Jacob Tornoey appeared, accompanied by counsel, *taalman* and guarantors, and claimed a right of way for another built-on plot of land, situated next to the cherry orchard of St. Peter's abbey and called the parsonage of St. Nicasius. This passage ran towards the Scheldt, right across the pittancer's cherry orchard. Jacob Tornoey had founded a service in honour of St. Nicasius in a chapel of the Lady church and had endowed his foundation, *inter alia*, with a house whose revenue was destined for the priest. Tornoey's demand of the recognition of 'eenen wech ende borreganc' was therefore a claim to a servitude of right of way, ensuring access to the water of the Scheldt for one plot of land through another.⁶

We are here dealing with very old types of servitude; in Roman law also rights of way and servitudes of water were the oldest among the *servitutes*

---

³ L. Gilliodts-Van Severen, *Coutumes de la ville et châtellenie de Furnes*, ii, (Brussels, 1896), p. 262. See for French customary law the references under the entry *purge des droits réels* in the index of Olivier Martin, *Histoire de la coutume de la prévôté et vicomté de Paris*, 2 vols. (Paris, 1922-30). There is an interesting case of opposition against such a procedure, because of rents, in a judgment of the Parlement of Paris of 23 December 1484 (Paris, AN, xia 119, fo. 157v-159) in an appeal from the aldermen of Lille and from the Council of Flanders.

⁴ Ghent, State Archives, 'Fonds Kaarten', no. 263. The 'pittancy', a square plot of land between the church of Our Lady and the Scheldt, is clearly marked on Map IV of a plan of Ghent from 1534; *La ville de Gand en l'an 1534*, facs. by A. Heins, text by V. Van Der Haeghen (Brussels, 1896). The following maps in the aforementioned 'Fonds Kaarten' were also consulted: nos. 206, 253, 259, 265, 293, 972 and 1035, all from the sixteenth to the eighteenth century.

⁵ Map no. 205.

⁶ E. Verwijs and J. Verdam, *Middelnederlandsch woordenboek*, i, (The Hague, 1885) under *borneganc* and *bornewech*; K. Stallaert, *Glossarium van verouderde rechtstermen*, i (Leyden, 1890; Handzame, 1978) under *bornewech*.

praediorum rusticorum. J. Tornoey based his claim on peaceful possession during 'ten years and ten days, twenty years and twenty days, thirty years and thirty days', in other words on the acquisitive prescription of thirty years, a *praescriptio longissimi temporis*. He added that there was no need for him to show a title of possession for this very long term, and in this he was right: indeed, according to Roman law, the source of the *praescriptio longissimi temporis*, no *justus titulus* was required.[7] He expressly admitted the abbey's ownership (*ervachtichede*) of the orchard, but he demanded that the priest's house should retain its aforesaid right of way. The monk-pittancer did not deny the thirty-year possession of his adversary, but argued that it could not be alleged against the abbey. Indeed, so he said, against churches only a prescription of a hundred, or at least forty years, could be invoked.

He also was right: the Emperor Anastasius, in the late fifth century, had raised the *praescriptio longissimi temporis* against churches to forty years, and this had been incorporated in Justinian's *Corpus*. The pittancer therefore knew very well what he did when he said that, if the rule on which he based himself was put in doubt (not the facts but the law was in dispute), he would request an enquiry by experts, which would show that the rule he referred to was indeed the law. As the text puts it, he 'appealed to clerics and masters of written law that that was written law'.

This put the aldermen in a quandary, as they were suddenly confronted with Roman law rules on prescription, terms and titles and their application. They were expected to see the light, but it was an unreasonable expectation, not so much because the case was complicated but because they knew no Roman law, and had never dealt with a similar problem before. For judges who were wont to decide according to custom and precedent the situation was hopeless. They postponed their judgment, then again, then a third time, because, as the text explains: 'such allegations of written laws had never before been made before them, and the aldermen of St. Peter knew of no customary law on the case, and consequently they were ignorant (*niet vroet*)'. So they decided to ask the aldermen of Ghent for advice, who decided that the pittancer should be allowed to prove his claim by the testimony of learned jurists. This was done, and five experts were heard, Master Jan van Culsbrouc, Master Lieven van den Huffele, Master Gillis van Lennoet, Master Joris Nevelync and Master Zeger Wuerem. Their pronouncement was as decisive as it was correct. They found that in written law possession of at least forty years was required against churches. This was decisive: judgment was given in favour of the pittancer and enacted and sealed on 4 October 1431.

The terminology of the judgment is interesting, as Roman law terms are very inconspicuous. This is particularly striking as in a case on property and real rights, such as servitudes, one would expect Roman law terminology, as

---

[7] Cf. Ph. Godding, 'Courtes et longues prescriptions aux XIIe et XIIIe siècles, principalement en Brabant', *Hommage au Prof. P. Bonenfant* (Brussels, 1965), pp. 151-67.

the aldermen of St. Peter in no way constituted a minor, obscure or remote village court. For the contrast between property and servitude only terms from customary law were used: *ervachtigheid* against *recht, wech* or *recht van wege*, not 'property' against 'servitude' – the latter word turns up later, when the report of the learned jurists is mentioned. On the other hand, De Draeyer (or his counsel) appears to have known the learned terminology, as appears from terms such as *posses, termine, titel van posses, paysivel posses, sonder titel vercrighen* and *prescriptie van tide*; on the part of a cleric alleging canon law this is not surprising.

The message of the text is interesting and surprising. Here we find, well into the fifteenth century, the important law court of the village of St. Peter being confused by the allegation of an elementary rule of Roman and canon law: 'the aldermen do not understand; they do not know that rule; it is not customary' and they have never before been confronted with it. After several postponements they were obliged to consult the urban aldermen of Ghent, but even they gave no final judgment but advised that learned 'masters' should be consulted. So it was as late as the fifteenth century, and so it had been for ages. Countless generations of aldermen or vassals had judged according to the traditional, native customary law. If they were startled by some appeal to the *leges* – either the 'clerical laws'[8] or the laws of the Romans – they found that they were 'ignorant'; they had to declare themselves incompetent.

Many a reader of this fifteenth-century text will be reminded of another lawsuit, which had taken place six centuries before in the Loire area, which is known to us through a detailed narrative in the *Miracula Sancti Benedicti*. There also the judges, who were wont to decide according to Frankish customary law, were at a loss when they were asked in a suit between churches to judge according to Roman law: 'cum litem in eo placito finire nequirent, eo quod Salicae legis iudices ecclesiasticas res sub Romana constitutas lege discernere perfecte non possent'. In that ninth-century case also the suit was passed on to others, in the hope of finding people who knew Roman law.[9] However much customary law had developed in the meantime, and in spite of the progress in the study of Roman law, the situation in the ordinary courts had changed remarkably little: the aldermen gave judgment according to custom and precedent. A sudden quotation of

---

[8] The term occurs in the affixed document mentioned in Berten, *Coutumes de la seigneurie de Saint-Pierre-lez-Gand*, p. 86, n. 1.

[9] Suit for a number of *mancipia* living in Gâtinais, between the abbeys of Fleury (Saint-Benoît-sur-Loire) and Saint-Denis, from 818-40, in Adrevald's *Miracula Sancti Benedicti*, c. 25 (ed. O. Holder-Egger, *MGH, SS*, xv, 1 (1887), p. 490). The case had first appeared before local judges under the chairmanship of two *missi dominici*, Jonas, bishop of Orleans, and Donatus, count of Melun. Because of the indecision of the judges, the *missi* ordained that the case be transferred to Orleans, in the hope of finding there *iudices* who knew Roman law. See the commentary in F.L. Ganshof, *Een kijk op de verhoudingen tussen normatieve beschikkingen en levend recht in het Karolingische rijk* (Brussels, 1965), p. 7.

Roman law, the invocation of a ghost from another world, caused consternation and confusion.

The Southern Netherlands in the 'Second Middle Ages' (the period from the twelfth to the fifteenth century) had made enormous progress in comparison with the 'Dark Ages'.[10] Monarchic rule and urban expansion were the twofold foundations of a typical and remarkable civilization. The law had followed social progress, being adapted to new requirements. This new law, however, was based on ancient custom and was itself customary; it had grown organically and gradually, with solid roots in regional and local circumstances, needs and languages. The learned 'law of the clerics' was happily left to the small and peculiar world of professors and bishops' officials. To the general public, for whom courts of aldermen and vassals were the bearers of the living law, the *exceptio Divi Hadriani* and the *exceptio senatus consulti Vellejani* were irrelevant concepts from an unreal world. For the mass of the people, customary law simply was the law which regulated the life of every day.

It may be useful to pay some attention here to the concept of customary law. The position is in fact not so simple as it seems at first sight. 'Customary law is a legal custom which has become binding through uninterrupted peaceful application over a long period of time, and as such is opposed to law based on legislation or a judicial pronouncement' – this description might serve as an acceptable, even obvious definition. It may satisfy lawyers, but it is insufficient for historians who want to go more deeply into the matter. I believe that it would be historically more correct to define as customary law what the people themselves at any given time felt and considered as such, even if it had in reality been introduced through the legislative process (as privileges from the ruler or as urban statutes). The medieval definitions of customary law are not very useful, since they are copied from Roman or canonical sources, which are themselves based on classical authors such as Cicero. It is an elementary rule of historical criticism that we should not be misled by such borrowings. What people felt in their bones was customary law; it had grown organically, in a piecemeal fashion, constantly building on older native materials and the solid foundations of society itself.

There are clear examples of legal rules whose legislative origin we, modern historians, can precisely demonstrate, but which contemporary society considered as customary law. In 1953 J. Gilissen pointed this out in an article on 'Law and Custom'. In this he referred to an example from the town of Ypres, which clearly showed how a rule of legislative origin was

---

[10] Historians realize more and more that the middle ages until and after the twelfth century constitute two distinct historical periods, which it is impossible to consider as forming one single epoch. No proper names for these two ages have yet been coined, so we use provisionally the neutral appellations of 'first' and 'second middle ages'. Cf. the expressions *premier* and *second âge féodal* used by Marc Bloch.

considered as a norm of the urban customs. Indeed, a town ordinance (*schepenvoorbod*) of 9 September 1293 ordained that henceforth bastards would be included in the peace concluded between two families after a feud. This rule was literally repeated in the Custom of Ypres of 1535, but as a customary norm (*by der costume*).[11]

An analysis of various legal texts from the time of the Flemish Count Philip of Alsace shows that rules which were represented as the record of the existing custom of a given borough were in fact newly introduced law. In 1157-63 the city of Arras received a borough charter from the count, whose title said: 'talis est lex et consuetudo quam cives Attrebatenses tenent'. While this suggests a record of various points of law from the old customs of the city, a scrutiny of the articles indicates the exact opposite. Indeed, we are here confronted with a new and, for the first time, progressive law that constituted a real break with numerous ancient and primitive rules and concepts.[12] This is not so amazing if one abandons the all too common idea that all customs were very old and customary law immobile: whereas custom could remain immobile for a long time, it was also flexible and could be quickly adapted. Thus Galbert of Bruges tells us that the new count of Flanders in 1127 expressly granted the burgesses of Bruges the right freely to improve and adapt their customary law: 'ut potestative et licenter consuetudinarias leges suas de die in diem corrigerent et in melius commutarent secundum qualitatem temporis et loci.'[13]

It even happened that certain rules of Roman law origin came to be considered or represented as customary, if they were sufficiently integrated in the practice of a certain court or area, or if people wanted them to be applied. I refer, for example, to the interesting lawsuit between the collegiate church of St. Piat at Seclin on the one hand and Jacques d'Olhain, lord of Estaimbourg, and Jean Boucault, his bailiff at Gondecourt, on the other, which led to a judgment in appeal by the parlement of Paris on 14 August 1469. Jacques d'Olhain and his bailiff, the defendants, alleged the prescription of forty years against St. Piat, but without referring to Roman law

---

[11] J. Gilissen, 'Loi et coutume', *Tijdschrift voor rechtsgeschiedenis*, 21 (1953), p. 275.

[12] Ed. of the borough charter of Arras of 1157-63 in G. Espinas, *Recueil de documents relatifs à l'histoire du droit municipal, Artois*, no. 107 (Paris, 1934), pp. 268-72. The problem of Flemish twelfth-century legislation deserves a thorough study; a start was made in a series of seminars in Ghent from 1964 onwards.

[13] Galbert of Bruges, *De multro . . . Karoli comitis Flandriarum*, ed. H. Pirenne (Paris, 1891), c. 55, p. 87. Cf. the peace charter of Saint-Amand of 1164, granted by Count Philip of Alsace at the request of Abbot Hugh, which stipulates that the abbot of Saint-Amand is empowered to make changes, additions or eliminations in the *pax* whenever it is useful: 'Verum huic paci quicquid ad meliorationem visum fuerit proficere licebit abbati adicere detrahere et mutare', art. 19, ed. H. Platelle, *La justice seigneuriale de l'abbaye de Saint-Amand* (Paris and Louvain, 1965), p. 433. Similarly Count Baldwin IX on 5 May 1199 granted the aldermen of Saint-Omer the freedom of improving their law; 'iuri preterea suo quicquid voluerint ad emendationem ville superaddant, salvo iure meo et ville', W. Prevenier, *De oorkonden der graven van Vlaanderen* (1191-aanvang 1206), ii (Brussels, 1964), no. 104, p. 224.

(never an intelligent move, at least openly, when pleading before the parlement of Paris), or to canon law (which they could easily have done). They based themselves on the said prescription of a rule of the custom of the Salle de Lille, the comital feudal court of the castellany of Lille: strange customs of Lille, taken from Anastasius and Justinian.[14] Again, the technical problem of the origin of the rule – whether legislation, case law or jurisprudence – was less important than the incorporation of the rules into the structure of the living, organic custom: anything rather than an alien and undigestible mass of bookish law.

Another striking opposition existed between customary and written law. The distinction was made consciously in the medieval texts, which used the expressions *jus scriptum* and *ghescrevene rechten*. In the Southern Netherlands customary law remained indeed to a very large extent unwritten, right up to the end of the middle ages, in spite of various expositions and commentaries: homologation (i.e. the official recording and promulgation of the old customs by the government) did not come about until the sixteenth century.[15] How did this situation arise? The question deserves to be asked, since the disadvantages of unwritten law, such as the ignorance of the law and the consequent uncertainty, which is the opposite of the rule of law are obvious.[16] If one asked a historian how to explain this early medieval situation, he would probably refer to the low cultural level which left less room for writing than in developed societies. He might also point out that the extraordinary diversity of the customs made it an almost hopeless task to put them all in writing: it took a legal genius to discern the essential principles in that enormous diversity, or a monster of patience to record them in all their details.

Medieval authors sometimes posed the question themselves. One of the most interesting answers is given in the treatise known as *Glanvill*, after Ranulf de Glanvill, a royal justice in the time of King Henry II of England. Writing in 1187-89, the author wonders why English law, although a legal system on a par with others (even though it was unwritten), was not described in books as was that of Rome. His answer is interesting and does not differ much from the explanation we just suggested. He begins with blaming the *ignorancia scribentium*. This is an ambiguous explanation, which probably does not mean that those who could write were ignorant, but rather that the general state of ignorance was such that very few people could write (in Latin) – or could the author possibly have referred to the ignorance of Roman law? The author then explains that the *multitudo*

---

[14] Judgment of the Parlement of Paris of 14 August 1469 (Paris, AN, xia, 101, fo. 153-55 v). Gondecourt and Seclin are in the arrondissement of Lille, département du Nord; Estaimbourg is in the arrondissement of Tournai, in the Belgian province of Hainaut.

[15] Cf. J. Gilissen, 'La rédaction des coutumes en Belgique aux XVIe et XVIIe siècles', *La rédaction des coutumes dans le passé et dans le présent* (Brussels, 1962), pp. 87-111.

[16] Idem, 'La preuve de la coutume dans l'ancien droit belge', *Hommage au Prof. P. Bonenfant* (Brussels, 1965), pp. 563-94.

confusa of English legal rules makes it impossible to put them all in writing.[17] When working on this passage of his prologue, the author clearly had before him, or in his memory, the *prooemium* of Justinian's Institutes, for the beginning of his *prologus* literally repeats that of the *prooemium*. This must have sharpened the contrast between the 'ignorance' of his time and the situation at Constantinople in the time of Justinian, for in the *prooemium* Justinian mentions the *sacratissimae constitutiones antea confusae*, the confused mass of imperial constitutions which he has harmonized, and he also talks of the *immensa prudentiae veteris volumina*, which he has put in order (in the Digest) and collected and reshaped into a new, ordered whole, 'a hopeless undertaking, as he puts it, like crossing an ocean of troubles, but now happily carried out with God's help'.

Twelfth-century Europe was not yet capable of an undertaking on that scale. It took ages before in a number of countries, codifications of customary law emerged. When this customary law was homologated, it had gone through an organic development of many centuries and was miles away from the primitive Germanic tribal *leges* of the Frankish period. The comparative lawyer realizes, of course, that the predominance of custom is a frequent phenomenon, following, in the words of the late Professor Romein, the 'common human pattern'.

While in the Southern Netherlands, as in so many other countries, customary law was developing organically, another body of legal rules, a totally different system, was being elaborated, based on books from Antiquity and on bookish commentaries by scholars and clerks. This was a divergence from common human experience, as, seen in the perspective of universal history, this is not the normal pattern of legal development. Medieval Roman law was *stricto sensu* bookish law, for its essential component was the collection of books in which the Emperor Justinian had brought together the whole law of Rome. It was also bookish in a broader sense, as it was developed and elaborated in the medieval lecture rooms by means of learned commentaries on learned books. Ultimately this strange evolution was a consequence of the very nature of medieval culture, as the daughter of Antiquity and a derivative civilization. It was the heir of Antiquity and always conscious of it. Hence the predominance of various classical texts, considered to contain the ultimate truth and upon which great constructions were built by the glossators and commentators from the twelfth century onwards, in the theological and philosophical as well as in the legal field. What could be further away from the evolution of living customs than the activities of these limited circles of clerks, who on the dead texts of a bygone world built a legal system that originally did not even pretend to be in any way relevant to their own society? Their law was also bookish in the

---

[17] G.D.G. Hall, *The Treatise on the Laws and Customs of the Realm of England Commonly called Glanvill* (London, 1965), p. 3.

sense that the commentaries were not orientated towards practical problems, but towards the exegesis of texts, using the well-known techniques of scholasticism. Nor ought we to forget that for the man in the street the clerical milieu, where Roman law flourished, was a world apart, which fell outside the jurisdiction of the ordinary courts and the grasp of the ordinary collector of taxes.

It is remarkable that two such different systems, customary and Roman law, developed at the same time and side by side, in one and the same culture yet were nevertheless so distant from each other that they might have belonged to two different worlds. It was not until the fourteenth-century commentators that civilians began to be interested in the practical problems of their own time. For the people of the Southern Netherlands at large Roman law remained a closed book well into the fifteenth century. What then was the law for the vast majority? It consisted of rules followed time and again in various circumstances and usually without thinking about them; which could be confirmed by judgments of aldermen of feudal courts. The results of their application were found in innumerable acts and court registers, large and small. They were the norms known to and sometimes described by practitioners who avidly collected formularies and precedents. To medieval people this living custom was binding and flexible, fixed and yet evolving, omnipresent but hardly subjected to reasoned and systematic analysis. As a social phenomenon this law was comparable to the vernacular that people spoke and the traditional remedies they used. Nobody would have considered reforming the living language, which could quickly evolve, on the authority of some system conceived by a caucus of scholars.

What was going to happen when these two legal worlds collided? One can imagine the confusion and astonishment of practitioners when the law, which had been for centuries the cement which held society together, was put in jeopardy because it disagreed with the heavy and esoteric folio volumes of Justinian and Azo. The message 'Chi non ha Azzo, non va al Palazzo' must have sounded very ominous. Was it possible to change the law that regulated society – or the language that people spoke – simply on the strength of some Latin quotations, or to elude, corrupt and enervate it by using erudite subtleties – the famous reproach 'Juristen, böse Christen'?

How great the disarray in traditional circles was and how sharply they realized the true nature of this learned law of the books appears from the words of Maarten van den Bundere, a practitioner from Ghent (1451 to after 2 Jan 1533), who spoke for a whole school of customary lawyers. Van den Bundere criticized the learned law and its main followers, the judges in the Council of Flanders. The latter were inimical to custom, which, so he maintained, 'they want to divert from its ancient nature and foundation'. Little good would come, so he continued, from all these innovations, and he concluded that the gentlemen of the Council planned to change the custom of Ghent 'after the teaching of their books'. Hence his striking reproach: book-learning was being used to subvert ancient rules rooted in society. The author expected nothing positive from such attacks on traditional institutions, launched by intellectuals. Writing in 1510 he voiced a typical conservative idea, maintaining that 'it is wiser to let countries and towns enjoy their rights, privileges, customs and usages . . . rather than to cause the people to murmur against the rulers because of novelties, as murmuring leads to discord and suffering for the peaceful, whereas little advantage is gained by such novelties'.[18]

The collision of these two systems in the Southern Netherlands took place in the fifteenth century. It was at that time that learned jurists appeared in not inconsiderable numbers among the judges (as opposed to the clerks and pensionaries). In the Council of Flanders university-trained lawyers were not yet in the majority in the first half of the fifteenth century. Generally speaking, at that time the nobility and the practitioners without degrees were still the predominant element in the higher provincial courts of justice. But things changed. The example was set by the parlement of Mechelen (Malines), the highest court of law in the Burgundian Netherlands (1473-77), where the predominance of the jurists was striking. Besides the duke, his chancellor, his *chef de conseil* and two presidents, the court contained the following members: four knights, who were no jurists, six *maîtres des requêtes*, of whom three were jurists, eight spiritual councillors, all graduates, and twelve *conseillers-loiz*, all masters. There were moreover a first advocate-fiscal, who was a graduate, and another who was not, a procurator-general and a substitute, both graduates, three clerks of the court, all graduates, and four secretaries, also all graduates. Even among the seventeen ushers there were two masters.[19]

For the courts of aldermen the following figures and dates may be quoted. On the bench of Ukkel we find, in a first phase (1197-1431), not a single learned jurist. From 1431, the date of a reform of this important court, until the end of the sixteenth century there were sixteen out of a total of eighty-two.[20] In the town of Kortrijk the first graduate alderman appears in 1436, followed by others in 1457 and 1471. In the latter year, and for the first time, two learned aldermen sat on the bench, out of a total of nine.[21] Among the 143 known medieval aldermen of Huy only one had been at university.[22]

---

[18] E.I. Strubbe, 'Het "Motyf nopende der costumen ende husagen van den sterfhuuse van Ghend" door M. van den Bundere', *Handelingen van de koninklijke commissie voor de uitgave der oude wetten en verordeningen van België*, xvii, 1 (1950), pp. 24-5.

[19] P. Wielant, *Antiquités de Flandre*, ed. J.J. De Smet, Corpus chronicorum Flandriae, iv, (Brussels, 1865), pp. 136-37.

[20] J. Gilissen, 'Le droit coutumier d'Uccle', S. Bartier-Drapier, S. Gilissen-Valschaerts and S. Petit, *Une commune de l'agglomération bruxelloise* (Brussels, 1958), p. 239.

[21] Figures from an unpublished thesis by J. Bauwens, 'Bijdrage tot de geschiedenis der stadsinstellingen van Kortrijk tot 1494' (University of Ghent, 1962).

[22] M. Yans, *Les échevins de Huy* (Liège, 1952), p. 179.

For Ghent during the years 1384-1468 we can give the following figures: in most years none of the twenty-six aldermen was a learned jurist; in eighteen years there was one; in nine years there were two; and in two years three jurists.[23] Among the aldermen of the sovereign court of Liège we find for the whole of the middle ages only one learned jurist, and he was a member of the short-lived court founded by Charles the Bold.[24]

The extent of the changes that came about in the fifteenth century can be gauged from the increasing prestige of academic studies in law. Although for a long time jurists had been working in the entourage of rulers and in the service of cities, the vast majority of the personnel of the courts – judges as well as bailiffs – in the fifteenth century still consisted of men who had been trained in practice, who had learned their trade through trial and error, and who therefore were dominated by the spirit of the native customs. The most intelligent among them were certainly aware of the learned jurists and found it normal to consult these specialists of the *leges*, but that was as far as it went. When, for example, Jan van den Berghe discusses a difficult aspect of dower, he writes: 'If I had to give judgment on this, I would postpone the case and in the meantime talk to legists, for I believe that the *leges* speak of it, and whenever custom is not opposed to the written laws, one ought to give judgment according to the latter.'[25]

Consequently these people thought it superfluous to prepare their sons for a public career otherwise than by giving them a practical training, teaching them the official French language – important in the Burgundian Netherlands – and the polite manners to which the milieu of top officials were accustomed. E.I. Strubbe pointed this out when studying the aforementioned Jan van den Berghe (d. 1439), author of the *Juridictien van Vlaenderen* and a man with practical experience. Van den Berghe was convinced that knowledge of customary law could not be acquired by studying in books, only through practice and the advice of experienced people. 'The more one has seen, the better an expert one is' was his motto, by which he meant that one became a lawyer as one became a master in any other trade, by learning from an older member of the craft; 'old people', he said, 'are obliged by law to teach the young'. Hence it never crossed Jan van den Berghe's mind to send his son Joos to a university. Instead he sent him to a noble lady, Johanna of Harcourt (who usually lived in Béthune), in order to learn French and aristocratic manners.[26] The education of Phi-

---

[23] Figures from the unpublished thesis by F. Buvens, 'Het gerechtelijk leven der stad Gent, weerspiegeld in de stadsrekeningen (1384-1467)' (University of Ghent, 1963).

[24] C. De Borman, *Echevins de la souveraine justice de Liège*, 2 vols. (Liège, 1892-99).

[25] *Juridictien van Vlaenderen* [from 1431-39], p. 192, ed. E.I. Strubbe; 'Jean van den Berghe, écrivain et juriste flamand', *Bulletin de la commission royale des anciennes lois et ordonnances de Belgique*, xii, 3, 1926.

[26] E. I. Strubbe, 'De briefwisseling tussen Jan van den Berghe en Johanna van Harcourt', *Handelingen van de Koninklijke Commissie voor Geschiedenis*, cxxv (1960), pp. 523, 524.

lippe de Commynes, who reached a high position thanks to his intelligence and experience, was similar: he did not go to university and spoke with a mixture of admiration and envy of learned men who 'à tous propos ont une loi au bec, ou une histoire'.[27]

Towards the end of the fifteenth century parents began to have other ideas. Fathers carefully looked around for the best careers for their sons and the way to obtain them – to what extent the sons shared the fathers judgment is another matter. Thus Willem van der Tanerijen (d. 1499), again someone who had received a practical training and reached a high position on the bench (just as Jan van den Berghe, but in the duchy of Brabant and not the county of Flanders), considered the study of Roman and canon law as the best preparation for his son Andries. Indeed, the author of the *Boec van der loopender practijken der raidtcameren van Brabant* concludes his prologue with a general appeal to parents to send their children to a university.[28]

This change of heart is striking, for not only was another way of learning the law advocated – university versus practice – but also the study of another legal system: written and learned law instead of the traditional products of the practice of the courts; bookish law instead of customary law. From then onwards the jurists occupied an increasing number of seats on the local and provincial benches.[29] Hence the negative reactions from the customary lawyers: what did those heads crammed with book-learning know of the real law of their fellow citizens, when they returned from the university to take their seats among the judges and officers of the courts?[30] How did they cope with the intricacies of customs, which were poorly described or not at all, and without appropriate commentaries? Were they not bound to try and impose the superior *jus commune*? This collision between customary and learned law indeed materialized.

In the second half of the fourteenth century the courts of aldermen started in difficult cases to consult learned jurists. In 1369 the aldermen of the town of Ypres, who found no solution in the local custom, decided to consult 'masters of laws'; after which they gave judgment 'according to what the *leges* and the written laws indicate and hold'. A similar case again presented itself in Ypres in 1381. In both instances the aldermen themselves took the initiative in the consultation. In a comparable case in Antwerp at the beginning of the fifteenth century, one of the parties alleged the

---

[27] G. Charlier, *Commynes* (Brussels, 1945), p. 9.
[28] Ed. E.I. Strubbe, i, (Brussels, 1952), p. 3.
[29] Idem, 'De verordening van 1483 voor den Raad van Vlaanderen', *Annales de la Société d'Émulation de Bruges*, lxxiv (1931), pp. 162-4 describes the composition of the Council of Flanders in 1483.
[30] See the ironic complaints, in a later period, by G. De Ghewiet, 'Méthode pour étudier la Profession d'Avocat, art. 2', *Institutions du droit belgique*, ii (Brussels, 1758), pp. 403-4.

learned law and produced written advice.[31] For major courts, which were not subjected to a superior 'head' and therefore could not ask for a pre-judgment when they were 'not wise', this was the only way out of their problems.

In the course of the fifteenth century more and more local aldermen were graduates, while in the second half the jurists became numerous in the provincial and central courts. The foundation of the university of Leuven caused more young people to study law, who then occupied judicial seats, particularly in the courts of appeal. There was therefore a real chance that around 1500 the learned law might be introduced, 'received', *in toto*, beginning with the higher courts and consequently elsewhere in the land, where aldermen and judges would not want to see their judgments reversed in appeal. The German example shows how real this possibility was. It should moreover not be forgotten that medieval Roman law itself had developed from a superior but irrelevant system, studied for its own sake (in a sort of *art pour l'art* attitude) into one that took account of the shape and needs of modern European society and was applicable in the life of every day.

It was around this time that a book was completed which should be seen in that light, the aforementioned *Loopende practijke* by van der Tanerijen. This work, completed in Dutch in 1496, is a remarkable exposé of the doctrines of written law. To what extent it reflects the practice of the Council of Brabant (as the title suggests) is hard to establish, as the archives have been insufficiently studied. In any case the book is a good exposé of learned written law, particularly civil law and civil procedure. In spite of the real possibility of a 'Reception', the confrontation of the two systems in the Southern Netherlands took a different course. Instead of a wholesale adoption of the learned law, the country decided upon the homologation of its customary law: following the French example, customary laws were put in writing at the ruler's command, and those texts, amounting in some cases to real codifications, were then promulgated as law by the government. Was this a victory for customary law? This was undoubtedly the case, but only to a certain extent. The number of customs was reduced by rationalization and unification; they were revised by academic jurists, most customs containing a stipulation that the learned laws were to be applied wherever the custom was silent. Roman law was thus the *ultima ratio*: it played the same role vis-à-vis customary law it had played for centuries vis-à-vis canon law. This had already been ordained by Philip the Good when the customs of Burgundy were confirmed. A decisive step was taken in the sixteenth century and the Southern Netherlands remained what they were, a land of custom and legal

---

[31] E.I. Strubbe, 'De receptie in de Vlaamse rechtbanken van midden veertiende tot einde vijftiende eeuw', *Tijdschrift voor rechtsgeschiedenis*, xxix (1961), pp. 447ff.

parochialism, where strong learned influences were exerted by judges and authors with university degrees. Old Belgian law was essentially customary and remained so, in spite of substantial impact of learned law, particularly in the field of obligations and in legal writing (as appears from a comparison of modern works with the sometimes stilted language of the medieval law books). On the other hand this influence may have hindered the autonomous development of Dutch as a legal language.[32]

Having seen what happened, we may ask the reason: no historical analysis is complete without a quest for the causes. It is clear that the decisive step was the homologation of the local and regional customs, as this gave them binding force in the courts. The principal advantage was that it put an end to existing uncertainty, which had been caused, on the one hand, by ignorance as to what exactly the custom contained and, on the other hand, by the uncertainty to what extent the learned law could be applied and what was to be done when the customs provided no (clear) solution. One of two steps had to be taken: either the adoption of the *Corpus juris* as a common law for the Burgundian and Habsburg Netherlands; or the homologation of the customs. Both trends were in line with the general demand for a *Verwissenschaftlichung*, supported notably by the progress of the printed book.

That the decision was made in favour of homologation can, I believe, be explained by two circumstances: the high qualitative level of customary law in the region; and certain innate reflexes of the historic Netherlands against every manifestation of a unifying and centralizing policy. By 1500 native law had already gone through a considerable evolution. From the twelfth century, we can follow an uninterrupted process of modernization and adaptation through which customary law lost many of its primitive traits, so that by about 1500 it belonged to the more sophisticated of Europe. One important factor was the openness of society which thanks to the large towns was in constant contact with new trends coming in from all quarters (even of Roman law origin). Thanks to the formal adaptation and substantial enrichment provided by homologation, the law could be considered adequate for the time. It also responded to the fundamental particularism (or parochialism) of the country. A local custom was the palladium of local autonomy. The aldermen of the big towns and the country courts played a role which was elsewhere in the hands of the central authorities of the state. Roman law, sovereign councils of the monarch, centralization and unification were

---

[32] See for example, c. 85 and c. 110 of the ordinance on the Council of Flanders of 1483, ed. E.I. Strubbe, *De verordening*, pp. 177, 180.

so many aspects of one and the same princely greed for power. Charles the Bold, the conqueror of Liège, abolished the ancient custom of that unfortunate city and replaced it by Roman law – a short-lived but significant measure.³³

---

³³ Art. 4 of the condemnation of 28 November 1467 of the vanquished city of Liège by Charles the Bold, ed. S. Bormans, *Recueil des ordonnances de la principauté de Liège*, 1st series (Brussels, 1878), p. 618. On the return to customary law upon the abolition of the Parlement of Mechelen in 1477, P. Fredericq, *Essai sur le rôle politique et social des ducs de Bourgogne* (Ghent, 1875), p. 186. It is at present impossible to go beyond these reflections because of the lack of detailed studies. Amongst older works the following remain important: W. Modderman, *De receptie van het Romeinsche regt* (Groningen, 1874) and P. Van Heijnsbergen, 'De receptie van het Romeinsche recht in de Nederlanden', *Verspreide opstellen* (Amsterdam, 1929), pp. 293-322. That I have managed to go this far is to a large extent because of the important research carried out by Feenstra, in Leiden, Gilissen, in Brussels and Strubbe, in Ghent. I would also like to mention the contribution of the Belgian-Dutch study group for the history of Roman law, which was founded by Professor Feenstra. A Belgian-Dutch study group for the institutions and the law of the Old Netherlands does not yet exist, but the aforementioned group has already produced significant results.

11

Witchcraft in the Low Countries

It is not superfluous to remind the reader that witchcraft – and also the witch-craze – were religious phenomena. For the people in the past, who were familiar with the invisible world, this was self-evident, but for modern man, whose feeling for the numinous element is much weaker or even altogether absent, things are different. Many people nowadays find it difficult to imagine religious thought and action, and are inclined to look for material motives for the religious behaviour of the past. They would, for example, tend to explain the action of the iconoclasts as a social and economic event, a reaction of the poor to the high price of grain. The belief in witches, the paroxysm of fear and prosecution of witches, which we call the witch-craze, were steeped in religion and should be understood in the light of the feeling for the supernatural that then prevailed. Belief in witchcraft was inseparable from religious life, and even though some aspects of the behaviour of witches may well be related to what we now call paranormal or psychic cases, it would be inconceivable to declare the whole phenomenon as the sixteenth- and seventeenth-century form of extra-sensory perception or psychokinetics. On the contrary, we are in the presence of an aspect of Christianity as it was then perceived.

Magic – notably the black magic which was the target of the witch-hunt – is a universal phenomenon which can be found both in the great civilizations, such as Greek and Roman Antiquity, and in obscure primitive tribes. It is based on the belief in forces or beings which fall outside our ordinary sensory perception but influence events in our world, at the request, or even at the command, of people who are particularly gifted or initiated. As far as western civilization is concerned, witches are mentioned in the Old Testament as well as in the Roman world – notably in Justinian's *Corpus Juris* (c. 9.18.7). Witchcraft was known to the Germanic peoples (see the Salic Law), and medieval and post-medieval Christianity was familiar with it; in Frankish times prohibitions were published against taking part in the flight of the witches (to their sabbath). In that Christian world black magic was naturally coloured by Christian belief in the devil as the personal and eternal antagonist of God and enemy of mankind. It is therefore understandable that a certain assimilation was made between witches and heretics, as both were marginal persons, moving outside the normal perception of the faithful. Nevertheless, heresy and witchcraft were essentially different. The former was a deviation within Christianity, but based on faith and veneration for Christ; the latter worshipped the devil, the arch-enemy who, as the New Testament witnesses, had not hesitated to tempt Jesus himself to try and seduce him into apostasy.

It is because witchcraft belonged so clearly to the religious sphere that the church authorities and in particular the ecclesiastical courts were so active in the prosecution of witchcraft or what looked like it. And because this outspoken diabolical and anti-Christian behaviour undermined the religious foundation of society it was natural that the lay rulers and courts joined in the prosecution of witchcraft. Religion was the ideological cornerstone of the 'magic', thaumaturgic monarchy by God's grace, and no anti-religion or anti-magic could leave the monarchy indifferent. It is no different in our own time and age: a socialist state will not tolerate anti-socialist behaviour or propaganda while a witch-hunt against communists is not unknown even in countries devoted to freedom and a free economy.

Like every other aspect of religious life witchcraft was part and parcel of the medieval and Old European world in which it manifested itself. It was, in other words, coloured by the judicial machinery, the organization of church and state, the ideological currents and the social and economic circumstances in which the devil-worshippers lived and were prosecuted. No religion is practised in a void, and all its manifestations are rooted in the everyday reality of working and thinking people. It is therefore appropriate to examine how social data have influenced and shaped the witchcraft of the Old European epoch.

The attitude of the judicial authorities played an important role in the ups and downs of the witch-craze. We repeatedly find that directives issued by the highest, central authorities encouraged the lower courts to be more vigilant and goaded them into active prosecution. Quite often the slowness and traditionalism of the courts, which did not discern the real threat of witchcraft, had to be overcome. The continuous harping on the danger of witches, the frequent admonitions to the officials of the persecution not to leave any suspect women in peace, certainly inflamed a psychosis which was bound to lead to the discovery of suspects and a consequent increase in the number of cases. The fact is so clearly established that some scholars have described the witch-hunt as, to some extent, a product of judicial zeal – or rather 'excess of zeal'. It has thus been pointed out that Roman law and Roman legists played an important role in this context. It was not in vain that the *Corpus Juris* took the prosecution of witches seriously, nor was it unimportant that the learned inquisitorial procedure of Roman inspiration knew torture as a mode of proof in criminal matters. Innumerable witches confessed under torture and – possibly as a consequence of hallucinations produced by torture and the hellish atmosphere of the torture chamber – admitted the mad crimes mentioned in the judges' textbooks.

The reader should, however, beware of blaming the learned law and its followers too rashly: in the common law countries outside the realm of Roman law and with the jury as mode of evidence the witch-craze was as bad as elsewhere. It would be wrong to simplify the situation to the extent of picturing the witch-hunt as the product of the inquisitorial procedure and blaming the whole craze on a few judges who, holding the 'little red book' in their hands – the *Malleus maleficarum* or Delrio – , created and maintained the ghastly business. It is moreover a fact that in many cases the fatal machinery was set in motion by popular initiatives and denunciations and that in some cases the mad crowd took the law into its own hands and killed witches without any form of process – a fate that also befell heretics.

The idea of a link between *lèse majesté divine* and *lèse-majesté humaine* comes readily to mind. The contempt for divine majesty shown by the devil-worshippers implied contempt for the religious foundation of the monarchy and was therefore a form of lese-majesty aimed at the rulers crowned by God as much as God himself. The power of the ruler was based on the Christian dogma and the uniform orthodoxy; absolute royal power was based on absolute religious uniformity. Hence the apparatus of the state went into action parallel with that of the church against whoever committed the *crimen majestatis*. The state acted against heresy – in Spain this was pursued so vehemently that it possibly explains why the witch-hunt was less intensive there. The state also acted against witchcraft: the former crime rejected God's true church, the latter God himself.

The absolute monarchy disposed of powerful weapons in its struggle against witchcraft: a centrally directed judicial apparatus and judicial torture, the latter being no doubt responsible for numerous confessions and lurid details on the unmentionable goings-on at the witches' sabbath. It was no mere coincidence that amongst the most outspoken absolutists one finds also the most pronounced witch-hunters, such as Philip II and James I. This link between Christian absolutism and witch-hunting is, at first sight, supported by chronology. The worst excesses of the witch-craze do not belong to the middle ages, but to modern times, the classic period of the absolute monarchs. Another indication of the causal nexus between absolutism and witch-craze can be found in the fact that republics and large free towns reacted to witchcraft with greater tolerance. Even the evident anti-feminist streak in the witch-craze fits well into the general picture of a militarist, intolerant and imperialist society based on the personality cult.

The reader should, nevertheless, beware of rash conclusions and exaggerated generalization. There are, indeed, a few facts that should incite us to prudence. The chronology, when scrutinized more closely, does not work out. The witch-craze was over by about 1650 when society returned to the old situation, in which from time to time a case turned up of casting of spells or freeing people from them, of soothsaying and various other forms of superstition and swindle, which the authorities usually punished with leniency. This was quite unlike the panic of the real witch-craze which had cost thousands of lives. Absolutism, however, was far from finished by 1650: Louis XIV's heyday was still in the future. Henry VIII's absolutism on the other hand, one of the most tyrannical examples of the species, afflicted England before the great witch-craze and was even free of witch-hunting, except that the accusation and execution for witchcraft was occasionally used to eliminate politically obstreperous figures. Even worse for the equation between witch-craze and absolutism is the fact that savage prosecution of the devil's servants occurred also in countries and periods that were free of absolutism. We refer to the American colonies (the witches of Salem), inhabited by Puritans who had fled modern English absolutism, and we recall that among the enemies of the witches one finds people like Sir Matthew Hale (d. 1676), a famous common lawyer and Puritan, who in 1651 became a member of Cromwell's commission for legal reform and was appointed around 1654 as justice of the common pleas (he is known, *inter alia*, for the condemnation and execution of two witches at Bury St. Edmunds in 1661). Also, the republic of Geneva, free from royal absolutism, if not from religious fanaticism, zealously took part in the extermination of witches. Numerous others were executed in common law lands, where the jury was used as mode of evidence instead of confession under torture. Scholars who view the witch-hunt as a form of terrorization in the service of absolutism need also to explain why this terror was not aimed at or limited to political opponents rather than peculiar women who travelled by night on their broom-sticks. The impression one gains is that whereas some aspects of royal absolutism favoured the witch-craze, it was not necessarily a by-product of absolute forms of government and also occurred outside the latter's domain. We search elsewhere for a deeper cause.

It is natural to look for a relation between the triumphalism of the Counter-Reformation and the witch-craze: the ultimate destruction of the followers of 'the enemy in hell' went hand in hand with the exalted triumph of Christ's only true church, so exuberantly and luxuriously expressed in architecture and painting. Whereas the victorious Counter-Reformation manifested itself in the visual arts, the impact of the popular missions made itself felt ever more deeply and led to a less exalted but steadier form of triumph of the true faith in the hearts of the people – a battle which was waged by the catechism-carrying Jesuits. Here again the chronology is right and for some areas, such as the Spanish Netherlands, strikingly so: the last years of Albert (d. 1621) and Isabella (d. 1633) witnessed counter-reformatory exuberance, unbridled Jesuit activity and a delirious witch-hunt. But here again not everything turns out quite right. Whereas the Jesuit order has indeed produced some of the most notorious learned witch-hunters, it can also be proud of some famous critics of the craze. Above all there is the fact that the hunt was no less virulent in Protestant lands, so that the simple equation witch-hunt = Counter-Reformation does not stand up to scrutiny.

It was rather than the ideological struggle exacerbated the religious feelings and interests, in both the protestant and the Catholic camps, raising disputes to a pitch of fanaticism. Latent religious sentiment was whipped up by an endless stream of controversy and sermons poured over the people's heads. As against this interpretation, however, it should be recalled that at the height of the Protestant controversy, when Henry VIII broke with Rome, and Lutheranism and Calvinism broke up the unity of the Roman church, witchcraft preoccupied people's minds much less than in the seventeenth century. Nor should we forget that the first wave had been unleashed as early as the late fifteenth century by the famous bull of Pope Innocent VIII and Sprenger and Institoris's 'Witches' Hammer', long before there was any mention of Luther and Calvin. This means that the witch-craze cannot be simply explained as a spin-off of Reformation and Counter-Reformation.

There have been attempts to explain the witch-craze in social and economic terms, but the results have been questionable. The reductionists clearly face a difficult task here. The witch-craze should allegedly have been a consequence of the conversion in depth to true Christianity of the villagers, who previously had lived by all sorts of superstition but underwent a second and more profound process of conversion around the time of the witch-hunt. The persecution of witches is also supposed to have been caused by the impoverishment of the population, the rise of a class of rich peasants and the consequent chasm between them and the dispossessed victims of this early capitalism: rejected beggar-women are said to have cursed the heartless rich and thus become suspect of witchcraft whenever something went wrong in wealthy families. These hypothetical explanations raise more problems than they solve. Why was a more profound and comprehensive conversion bound to lead to a mad prosecution of devil worshippers rather than, say, adulterers, usurers or hoarders? Also, as every medievalist knows, the middle ages had witnessed, at the time of the foundation of an extensive network of parishes, a second wave of Christian conversion, after the 'official conversion' of the kings and the elders in previous centuries. This phenomenon, so carefully studied by J.F. Lemarignier, did not lead to any witch-craze, nor did it put an end to peasant superstition and gullibility. The campaign against blind faith in werewolves, elves and the evil eye was a struggle for centuries. Besides, the middle ages knew periods of great shortage and poverty (the fourteenth century, for example) without a witch-craze, and the opposition between poor and rich in the villages is much older than modern times – with or without merciless rich peasants being cursed by poor old women. One might wonder, moreover, whether the more profound conversion and intensive preaching of the sixteenth and seventeenth centuries ought not to have led to greater charity rather than harshness towards marginal wretches. The cursing of the heartless rich by the disappointed poor is a phenomenon of all times; it is unclear why it should have been specifically linked to witchcraft and witch-hunting. Nor are other periods than those of the witch-craze lacking in which sickness, epidemics, mortality, starvation and destructive wars have raged without resulting in any obsessional witch-hunt. What could have been worse than the sea of misery that engulfed the fourteenth century? And yet, precisely then popular magic was hardly taken seriously and the 'silly women' who practised it often got away with a small fine and a contemptuous note in the bailiffs' accounts.

The big question remains as to why the western world – Protestant and Catholic – entered at a given moment into a new phase in the history of witchcraft. The pact with the devil was a very old theme and Thomas Aquinas, supported by the Old Testament, had maintained that witchcraft was real; yet bewitching, lifting spells, superstitious behaviour, quack medicine and the whole gamut of extra-ecclesiastical appeals to the supernatural – a mixture of folklore, relics of the *vecchia religione*, superstition and massive gullibility – had seldom been really taken seriously. It was only when royalty was threatened or when witchcraft in some other way acquired a political significance (Templars, Joan of Arc) that the authorities acted mercilessly. For the silly behaviour of the ignorant plebs a fine or, at most, a few lashes followed by banishment were deemed a sufficient punishment and warning. Carrying amulets with incantations was superstitious, and invoking spirits with strange, mysterious names did not suit Christian people who could always turn to God and his saints. However, if no further harm was done and no scandal caused, and the simplicity of the culprits was manifest, there was no cause for alarm and heavy penalties. It is obvious that at that time nobody saw witchcraft as a threat to society or an attack on its Christian foundations; it was not all that frequent or dramatic when compared with the whole gamut of criminal behaviour (even though the excesses of a Gilles de Rais deeply upset public opinion).

The witch-craze of the sixteenth and seventeenth centuries, however, particularly the years *c.* 1590 – *c.* 1650, was an entirely different business. Here we are witnessing collective and orchestrated madness. A madness which claimed thousands of victims, lasted for about three generations and ended quite suddenly, when the manipulation of public opinion and the judicial organs was stopped and the conductors had signalled that enough was enough. It is indeed striking how quickly, after the middle of the seventeenth century, society returned to the normal situation: again witchcraft became the domain of the ordinary superstitious folk, who love being cheated by anyone who promises good health and announces, with a serious face, that against payment of the modest sum of 30 écus to a named devil, a treasure of one thousand florins will turn up. This sort of stupid behaviour led, except in some backward areas, only to light punishments (possibly the pillory), for swindling rather than insulting God's majesty. Delrio and Jean Bodin were put back in the bookcases (which they should never have left) and were only fit to be covered with ridicule and disbelief by the rising Enlightenment.

It seems clear to me that a long-term but unimportant substratum of social life was fanned into an uncontrollable psychosis by an orchestration from the top, the whipping up of popular fear and of authoritarian impulses in the judicial machinery. After a few generations and countless deaths at the stake, this psychosis suddenly subsided into the insignificant phenomenon it had been before and should normally have remained: henceforth the leading circles talked of the 'prétendu crime de sorcellerie' and, at least in the Southern Netherlands, from around 1645 called a halt to the persecution. Hence it is understandable that the witch-craze was at its worst where the rulers were personally most involved: James I, the Archdukes Albert and Isabella, Gustavus Adolphus, Charles IX and several prince-bishops. This orchestration from the top provides the key for a just understanding of the witch-craze. Of course, this psychosis of the leading circles would have met with no response but for the Christian background: the belief in the reality of the devil and his omnipresent threat and keenness to devour human souls was the necessary but not sufficient condition for this sort of outburst, and this also applies to the presence of a strongly organized judicature. In order to fathom correctly the reason for this orchestration, which manifested itself in bulls, ordinances, royal treatises, instructions to the lower courts and demonological reference works by top lawyers and theologians, one should remember that it was common to the whole of western Christendom. The great manipulators are therefore not only to be found among the Catholic *maîtres à penser* of the absolute monarchs, but in all the leading Christian circles of the time. In the late sixteenth and the first half of the seventeenth century the responsible leader and the notables, in other words the establishment, convinced themselves that there existed an extremely dangerous threat to Christendom, engineered by a diabolical conspiracy. They believed that they were confronted with a universal antichurch, a devil's church, which attempted in the darkness of night to topple Christianity itself and replace religion by devil-worship. This amounted to a regular attack on Christian civilization as it was then known and without which no culture was conceivable. It meant perversion, chaos and the triumph of evil incarnate; it also meant the end of morality and the family. On this point the Puritans and many crowned heads agreed with each other: they all cared about the strict morals of the population. Success of the devil's church, to which the witches belonged, would lead to the universal triumph of immorality. Philip II's ordinance said so in so many words, where it talked of 'la ruyne et confusion du monde' and the activities of 'certains vrays instrumens du diable'. How serious the threat was and how powerful the devil, was demonstrated by the resistance offered to torture by numerous suspects: the fact that they did not confess in spite of terrible suffering (which sometimes resulted in death) could only be explained by the extraordinary power at the disposal of the devil's armies. Light would eventually conquer, but the children of Light were expected to show great vigilance and unceasing devotion.

Witchcraft was much worse than heresy. Protestantism was another form of religion, another ecclesiastical organization, but it was Christian, it adored one God, venerated Christ and believed in his message. The cult of the devil was a totally different, much more pernicious apostasy.

The conspiracy theory is a well-known technique of historical explanation. It is based on the belief or the sentiment that behind the events on the surface some world-wide occult conspiracy is busy causing the perdition of mankind. In our century Jews, freemasons, capitalist war-mongers and the communists of the world revolution come easily to mind. In the days of the witch-craze it was the worshippers of the devil.

But why this obsessive panic in the day of Delrio, Bodin and James I? Far be it from us to propose one single causal explanation for such a complex phenomenon. All we intend to do by way of hypothesis is to suggest that it was one of the consequences of the unimaginable shock that our ancestors experienced in the sixteenth century. It was a time when institutions and convictions, which had seemed solid and even eternal, collapsed, and the familiar world of many generations disappeared, as did the traditional cosmology. It was an epoch that witnessed the falling apart of the one Latin church, for a thousand years the moral and ideological foundation of public life and private morality. So many values were questioned or even ridiculed, so much that was unthinkable had taken place, that everything, even the worst: the triumph of satanism, seemed possible. Against this ghastly prospect only the most merciless measures and never-abating vigilance could bring salvation, and they had to be directed against Satan's adorers and their nightly meetings. The middle ages had also known grave crises. Great institutions had been torn apart, when two or even three popes fought each other. There had been doctrinal rifts concerning the true meaning of Holy Writ. The result had been a struggle against schismatics and heretics, not against witches. The battle against the devil's church had to be a crusade against its servants, male and female. It is understandable therefore that the struggle against the pact with the devil and his adoration was much more important at that stage than the old concern over popular magic: damage to man, milk and cattle, or the silliness of women who thought that a black mass would bring clients to their brothels.

The end of the great witch-craze came, around the middle of the seventeenth century, because Europe had found a new balance and a new hope. It appeared to be possible to maintain a Christian society in spite of the 'scandalous' division of the faithful. Catholic and Protestant states could manage to live in peaceful coexistence, leaving everyone to practise his own religion in his own country. The treaties of Westphalia had proved it. Europe was no more the Europe of the middle ages, but it still was a Christian Europe, and far from being a victim of Satan and floundering in an abyss of sin, it generally enjoyed a life of strict Christian morality. The diabolical church had not triumphed – there possibly had never been a real chance that it might. The bad dream was over and the witch-hunt had become senseless. Witchcraft and magic could again occupy their true place, that of superstitious goings-on endemic amongst the illiterate. The *Malleus maleficarum* henceforth was the concern of the historian, not the magistrate or the politician.

12

Chivalrous Ideals and Religious Feeling

To take the years 'from the twelfth to the fifteenth century' as one historical period possibly deserves a word of explanation. The twelfth century is taken as the starting-point not only because of the – still hesitant – appearance of the vernacular languages,[1] and the fifteenth not only because of the 'waning of the middle ages': there were other and more fundamental changes (the emergence of the vernacular being only a symptom) to justify the chosen chronological limits. The problems of historical periodization – and the solutions proposed – depend largely on the point of view one occupies and the historical vision one has shaped or accepted, which necessarily means that subjective considerations are bound to be important.[2] Nevertheless the historian is capable of producing arguments and facts to support his conclusions in a solid and objective way. It thus seems to us that most medievalists at present agree that medieval society experienced a profound change around A.D. 1100, which ended the more archaic, primitive 'First Middle Ages' and led Europe into a new era – the 'Second Middle Ages' – with a very different face and habit of mind. There is no consensus on the appropriate name of the 'developed' (if this is an acceptable description) middle ages, and the descriptions as 'First or Second Middle Ages' are so neutral that they can be no more than provisional. Nevertheless there is a real measure of consensus on the reality of the different configurations of these two sub-periods of the middle ages.[3]

The Second Middle Ages started with the violent attack on the old post-Carolingian order, known as the Gregorian Reform, and the consequent Investiture Struggle. They also witnessed a striking economic, political and

---

[1] At least on the Continent. See on this point, and the Old English 'deviation': R.C. Van Caenegem (with the collaboration of F.L. Ganshof), *Guide to the Sources of Medieval History* (Amsterdam and Oxford, 1978), pp. 120-26 (Europe in the Middle Ages: Selected Studies, 2).

[2] See, besides the classic analysis by H.J. Van der Pot, *De periodisering der geschiedenis: een overzicht der theorieën* (The Hague, 1951), C. Van de Kieft, *La périodisation de l'histoire du moyen âge*, C. Perelman (ed.), *Les catégories en histoire* (Brussels, 1969), pp. 41-56.

[3] See the discussion in R.C. Van Caenegem, *De instellingen van de middeleeuwen* (Ghent, 1978), i, pp. 12-4.

intellectual breakthrough which put an end – according to the criteria of that time – to Europe's status as an underdeveloped area and allowed her to emulate her great neighbouring civilizations, the Byzantine Empire and the world of Islam. It was the time of the rise of the national monarchy and its junior brother, the territorial principality, but also of the rise of the towns, motors of a new economy, and of a new social order and intellectual climate. The universities were born and the study of Greek and Greco-Arabic speculative and scientific thought caused considerable enthusiasm. Besides this rather elitist preoccupation was a massive reduction of illiteracy and of various irrational techniques, which had previously been important in the life of the law courts.[4] This new society, characterized by international trade and industry, urbanization, growing freedom and literacy, flourishing universities and a semi-bureaucratic state, differed profoundly from the old world of knightly landowners, closed manors and subjected peasants, when literate people were as rare as atomic scientists today and lived their secluded lives in a few and scattered abbeys. The proper face of the Second Middle Ages is easily recognizable and was obviously a Netherlandish as well as a European phenomenon. It could hardly have been otherwise, when one considers that the Low Countries were unusually open to all currents that traversed Europe, often colliding there. Thus the Gregorian and the anti-Gregorian waves, arriving from France and Germany respectively, met in this area, the territories to the west of the Scheldt precociously welcoming the papal reform and the others remaining strikingly loyal to the emperors.[5]

If the four centuries after A.D. 1100 have a profile of their own, is it possible to go a step further and discover for each of those centuries a distinctive face? There is no doubt that certain centuries evoke in later generations a striking and distinct image – the textbooks contain any number of 'centuries of misfortunes' and 'golden ages', and even if one is

---

[4] See, *inter alia*, the papers devoted to the law of evidence in the middle ages and modern times in *La preuve*, ii, *Moyen âge et temps modernes* (Brussels, 1965) (Recueils de la Societé Jean Bodin).

[5] Whereas the Gregorian Reform met with early success in Flanders, to the west of the Scheldt, Sigebert of Gembloux, in the neighbouring duchy of Brabant, situated on the eastern, German side of the Scheldt, remained loyal to the emperor. Cf. J. Beumann, *Sigebert von Gembloux und der Traktat de investitura episcoporum* (Sigmaringen, 1976); in 1977 Beumann also published a new edition of the treatise in *Deutsches Archiv*, 33, pp. 76ff. It is well known that the activities of the 'heretic' Tanchelm, who met with great success during his *Wanderpredigten* in Zealand and Flanders, and the opposition of the chapter of the cathedral of Utrecht, can also be seen in the light of the imperial loyalty of that city, at a time when the Flemish diocese of Thérouanne was reformist. See J.M. De Smet, 'De monnik Tanchelm en de Utrechtse bisschopszetel in 1112-1114', *Scrinium Lovaniense: Historische opstellen E. van Cauwenbergh* (Leuven, 1961), pp. 207-34; J. Lampo, 'De Antwerpse ketters: Een bijdrage tot de studie van de middeleeuwse ketterijen in de Nederlanden', *Handelingen van de Koninklijke Zuidnederlandse maatschappij voor taal- en letterkunde en geschiedenis*, 34 (1980), pp. 189-201.

allergic to this sort of whimsical and subjective approach, one can hardly deny, for example, that 'the nineteenth century' (which ended in 1914) constituted a clearly-marked phase in the development of modern Europe. I find it therefore legitimate to examine which fundamental characteristics can be attributed to each of the centuries between about 1100 and about 1500 and to discover in each a sort of basic colouring. In doing this I am obviously leaving the safe path of historical certainty, in the sense of the individual, well-established fact, with its concomitant footnote referring to narrative and non-narrative texts: anyone who demands this sort of certainty as a *conditio sine qua non* for serious historiography, might as well part company here. It should, however, be understood that demanding that sort of certainty implies automatically the reduction of one's area of interest to less complex and less comprehensive fields and problems, and the elimination of speculation and interpretation.[6]

When considering the events of the twelfth century, I am struck by the resolution with which our ancestors turned their backs on the archaic middle ages and by the new unbridled optimism that pervaded innumerable fields of human endeavour. There was more than optimism, there was self-confidence: people were building a new society, and they knew and wanted it. I cite, for example, the twofold emancipation – external and internal – which then took place. The external movement consisted in vanquishing the pressure and threats which had weighed heavily on the West for a long time: Norsemen, Magyars, Arabs, Slavs. The roles were reversed and the West went onto the offensive, extending its sphere of influence to the south, east and north.[7] Internal emancipation was caused by the decline of serfdom. This was, in an agrarian society, a most important development, comparable to the struggle against big landowners in present-day Latin America. The emancipation of the west-European serfs in the twelfth and following centuries was a human and social gain of great significance.[8] It was made possible, *inter alia*, by a twofold political development, the rise of the centralized monarchy (*Fürstenstaat*) and of the towns. The latter is mentioned in every textbook and it is not necessary to go into it here – even

---

[6] See above, pp. 27-35.

[7] For a survey of this secular movement and its medieval origin, see G.V. Scammell, *The World Encompassed: The First European Maritime Empires, c. 800-1650* (London, 1981).

[8] M. Bloch, *La société féodale*, i, *La formation des liens de dépendance* (Paris, 1949), pp. 367-428; F. Lütge, *Geschichte der deutschen Agrarverfassung vom frühen Mittelalter bis zum 19. Jahrhundert* (Stuttgart, 1963); B.H. Slicher van Bath, *The Agrarian History of Western Europe, A.D. 500-1850* (London, 1963); idem, 'Vrijheid en lijfeigenschap in Agrarisch Europe (16e-18e eeuw)', *A.A.G. Bijdragen*, 15 (1970), pp. 75-104; R. Boutruche, *Seigneurie et féodalité*, ii, *L'apogée (XIe-XIIIe siècles)* (Paris, 1970), pp 11-150 (Coll. Histoire, dir. by P. Lemerle).

though the situation was not as simple as the oft quoted phrase 'Stadtluft macht frei' might lead one to believe.[9] The role of the *Fürstenstaat* is less well known and not so often referred to in the textbooks, but it was nevertheless a powerful lever of social emancipation. In various countries – quite clearly in England, France and Flanders, for example – the rulers employed, for the organization of their central administration, the most competent and devoted officials they could find. They did not hesitate to employ unfree people and to promote them to high office. That this could lead to conflict with the nobility, who felt slighted, was a natural symptom of social irritation. I will not go into this here, and merely refer to the tragic story of the Erembalds under Count Charles the Good.[10] The twelfth century was a time of new initiatives and somewhat uncoordinated experiment; anything seemed possible. Where, for example, was urban autonomy going to lead to? It is at this time that the foundation stone was laid both for the independent city-states and at the same time for the modern bureaucratic *Fürstenstaat*.[11] In intellectual endeavour also everything seemed suddenly possible. The *Corpus Juris Civilis* was discovered – in more than one sense of the word – and the possibility loomed large that Europe might exchange its feudal customs for the learned law of the university of Bologna.[12] Suddenly the Arab world stopped inspiring fear and abhorrence – the twelfth century overcame several obsessive anxieties – so that it became acceptable to translate the Koran into Latin and to study it as an object of rational discussion.[13] The century, in short, appears as a period in which plans were made and foundations laid, in an enthusiastic and somewhat uncontrolled way, as often happens at the start of new historical eras.

The thirteenth century offers the very different picture of a more mature, controlled and balanced society. The options taken in the twelfth century were worked out in the thirteenth, and imposing structures were built on the foundations of the previous century. Classic constructions were

---

[9] H. Mitteis, 'Über den Rechtsgrund des Satzes "Stadtluft macht frei"', *Festschrift E.E. Stengel*, (n.p., 1952), pp. 342-58. This famous adage, which is not medieval but formulated by modern historians, was not applied so universally as one might be inclined to believe.

[10] E. Warlop, *De Vlaamse Adel voor 1300*, i, *Historiche studie* (Handame, 1968), pp. 215-46; R.C. Van Caenegem, 'De ondergang van een ambitieus geslacht', *Galbert van Brugge, grafelijk secretaris. De moord op Karel de Goede. Dagboek van de gebeurtenissen in de jaren 1127-1128* (Antwerp, 1978), pp. 13-27. Similar events involving royal top officials of lower social origins took place around the same time in France (the Garlande clan) and England. See E. Bournazel, *Le gouvernment capétien au XIIe siècle* (Paris, 1975), pp. 35-39.

[11] See an attempt to describe the main outline of this development in R.C. Van Caenegem, *De instellingen van de middeleeuwen*, ii (Ghent, 1978), pp. 170-218.

[12] See the fundamental and encyclopedic work directed by H. Coing, *Handbuch der Quellen und Literatur der neueren europäischen Privatrechtsgeschichte*, i, *Mittelalter (1100-1500): Die gelehrten Rechte und die Gesetzgebung* (Munich, 1973).

[13] R.W. Southern, *Western Views of Islam in the Middle Ages* (Cambridge, MA, 1962).

erected, made to last for hundreds of years. This is true not only of the obvious example of the Gothic cathedrals, but also of intellectual life, in, for example, scholastic philosophy, and in institutional realizations, such as the semi-bureaucratic nation states, the oligarchic autonomous towns and the early synthesis of Roman and customary law. Thirteenth-century France is the textbook illustration. Organization, harmonization and the synthesis of hardly compatible elements took place frequently. Under Louis IX the monarchy reached a culminating point as the social key-stone rooted in consensus, and a balance was established between the elements of the realm: the towns in particular were constructively integrated in the monarchy. It is understandable therefore that L. Genicot, in his well-known sequence of *aube*, *midi* and *vesprée*, calls thirteenth-century France the most successful moment, the zenith of the European middle ages.[14]

This resting point was, however, only provisional, as became clear at the beginning of the fourteenth century, the great age of crisis in the millennium which people were just then beginning to call the time of *tenebrae*, the 'Dark Ages'.[15] The crisis was caused by broken equilibrium, within the existing structures as well as between them. In the French monarchy, that most successful product of the preceding centuries, things went seriously wrong and a period of internal dissension and conflict began: the country which Pierre Dubois had proclaimed as the natural leader of Europe, became a toy of French factions and of the English enemy – a tragedy not overcome until the fifteenth century.[16] The religious crisis was no less acute. The great curial church, erected by popes and canonists as the most imposing supranational organization since the Fall of Rome, ended in the subjection of the exile of Avignon and – worse still – in the schism and conciliarism, which attempted to place the Roman *curia* under the tutelage of the fathers of the oecumenical council.[17] Even within the prosperous and self-governing towns things went wrong: the established oligarchy was challenged, the *popolo minuto* grabbed power and created severe tension, aggravated by economic problems. The epoch of the 'captains' who oper-

---

[14] The appellations of this series appeared in the first editions of Genicot's *Lignes de faîte du moyen âge* (in the 7th edition, Tournai, 1975, they are called *transition, accomplissement* and *crise*). See, specifically for the thirteenth century, his *Le XIIIe siècle européen* (Paris, 1968).

[15] The appellation *tenebrae* was already used by Petrarch, see T.E. Mommsen, *Medieval and Renaissance Studies* (Ithaca, NY, 1959) (ed. E.F. Rice), 7: 'Petrarch's conception of the "dark age"', pp. 106-29; L. Varga, *Das Schlagwort vom 'finsteren Mittelalter'* (Vienna and Leipzig, 1932).

[16] See the remarkable and profound analysis in J. Favier, *La guerre de cent ans* (Paris, 1980).

[17] See, besides older and well-known works of K.A. Fink, B. Tierney and E.F. Jacob, the excellent survey in W. Ullmann, *A Short History of the Papacy in the Middle Ages* (London, 1972), pp. 279-305. For the medieval relation between the papacy and the ecumenical council seen in general, J. Leclerc, *Le pape ou le concile: une interrogation de l'église médiévale* (n.p., 1973) (series Unité Chrétienne).

ated outside the constituted framework had arrived.[18] The nominalist crisis, which eroded the scholastic system with its razor-sharp criticism, was equally profound, and necessitated a new order.[19]

Among the nation states troubles also occurred. In the days of Louis IX, France and England had fixed their mutual spheres of influence by arbitration (as, for example, the frontiers of the English possessions in France), but in the following century they involved themselves in an endless war in order to impose an uncompromising solution. It was all or nothing, for either the English crown would become victorious and England and France would be united under the English sceptre, or the French monarchy would win and the English would be chased completely from the soil of France.[20] The Anglo-Scottish relationship developed on similar lines. There had for a long time been a danger zone here the English crown claimed supreme authority over Scotland, which the Scots rejected. During the thirteenth century neither party pushed the other to extremes: the king of Scots attained the highest dignity by becoming an anointed ruler, while the English crown was content with verbal claims on principle. All this changed towards the end of the century. The king of England was content with nothing less than a complete and explicit subjugation of the Scottish kingdom, which however refused to give up its national identity. Here again it was a policy of all or nothing. If the English succeeded, Scotland would be absorbed (as happened to Wales) or reduced to the status of a vassal kingdom; if they failed, Scotland would not only become an independent

---

[18] N. Kamp, *Konsuln und Podestà, ballivus communis und Volkskapitäns in Viterbo im 12. und 13. Jahrhundert* (Viterbo, 1960) (Ital. transl. with add., 1963); G. Brucker, *Florentine Politics and Society, 1343-1378* (Princeton, 1962); P.J. Jones, 'Communes and Despots: The City State in Late-Medieval Italy', *Transactions of the Royal Historical Society*, 5th series, 15 (1965), pp. 71-96; G. Fasoli, 'Gouvernants et gouvernés dans les communes italiennes du XIe au XIIIe siècle', *Gouvernés et gouvernants*, iv, *Bas moyen âge et temps modernes*, ii (Brussels, 1965), pp. 47-86 (Recueils de la Société Jean Bodin). *Florentine Studies: Politics and Society in Renaissance Florence* (London, 1969); M. Mollat and Ph. Wolff, *Ongles bleus, Jacques et Ciompi* (Paris, 1970); G. Volpe, *Studi sulle istituzioni comunali a Pisa: città e contado, consoli e podestà, secoli XII-XIII* (Florence, 1970); L. Martines (ed.), *Violence and Civil Disorder in Italian Cities, 1200-1500* (Berkeley, CA, 1972); J.K. Hyde, *Society and Politics in Medieval Italy: The Evolution of the Civil Life, 1000-1350* (New York, 1973); R. Celli, *Studi sui sistemi normativi delle democrazie comunali: secoli XII-XV*, i, *Pisa, Siena, Firenze* (1976); G. Brucker, *The Civil World of Early Renaissance Florence* (Princeton, 1977); R.C. Trexler, *Public Life in Renaissane Florence* (New York, 1980); G. Guidi, *Il governo della città repubblica di Firenze del primo quattrocento*, 3 vols. (Florence, 1981). It is well known that the Netherlands, and in particular Flanders, have produced comparable popular movements and leaders in the fourteenth century.

[19] See for the impact of fourteenth-century philosophy – in particular that of William Ockham – on political organization: A.S. McGrade, *The Political Thought of William of Ockham: Personal and Institutional Principles* (Cambridge, 1974).

[20] J.R. Strayer, *The Reign of Philip the Fair* (Princeton, 1980), pp. 317ff, examines the reason for the sudden rupture of the Anglo-French status quo and the outbreak of war in 1294.

but even an inimical neighbour (which is, of course, what happened after Bannockburn).[21]

Something comparable took place between the leading monarchy of the time – the French – and the leading spiritual power, the papacy. Here also the thirteenth century had not pushed the latent conflict of interests to extremes and had established a *modus vivendi*, which satisfied both the monarchy and the curia. But under Philip IV and Boniface VIII the existing equilibrium was broken, the former trying to dominate the national church to such an extent (in such matters as taxation and the appointment of bishops) that the latter was led to extreme counter-measures and pronouncements, which are among the most eloquent programmatic expositions of medieval papal theocracy. As is well known, the rupture between the two superpowers was brutal and the papacy experienced a political *capitis diminutio* which turned out to be irreversible, even though the victory won by the French monarchy also proved to be short-lived, as this most powerful country on the European scene soon became the subject of foreign ambitions.[22] That the European economy also experienced a rupture of the existing equilibrium is well known; this was particularly the case in that between agrarian productivity and demographic development and resulted in a chain of catastrophes from *c.* 1300 onwards.[23]

The question as to the cause of these crises has not yet been answered, *inter alia*, because of the extreme specialization of historical research. As a partial contribution to the debate I would like to offer the following considerations. I have the impression that many of these fourteenth-century conflicts were caused by a syndrome which could be described as 'logical extremism'. By this we mean that in various fields the mechanisms that were initiated around A.D. 1100 were pushed to their extreme consequences, neglecting real parameters and the limits of human tolerance.[24]

In France the dynamic of the monarchy, effectively ruling over the whole national territory and all subjects (Kienast's *Intensivierung des Staatsbetriebs*),

---

[21] See, besides the classic monograph of E.M. Barron, *The Scottish War of Independence* (1934) and the additions and corrections in G.W.S. Barrow, *Feudal Britain: The Completion of the Medieval Kingdoms, 1066-1314* (London, 1956), pp. 386-410, E.L.G. Stones and G.G. Simpson, *Edward I and the Throne of Scotland*, 2 vols. (London, 1978), and additional material in E.G.L. Stones, 'English Chroniclers and the Affairs of Scotland, 1286-1296', *Essays Presented to R.W. Southern* (Oxford, 1981), pp. 323-48.

[22] See the two studies of the conflict between Boniface VIII and Philip the Fair in J. Favier, *Philippe le Bel* (Paris, 1978), pp. 343-93 and J.R. Strayer, *The Reign of Philip the Fair* (Princeton, 1980), pp. 237-313.

[23] See the surveys in the *Cambridge Economic History of Europe*, 3 vols. (Cambridge, 1965-1966) and in H. Kellenbenz (ed.), *Handbuch der Europäischen Wirtschafts- und Sozialgeschichte*, ii, *Europäische Wirtschafts- und Sozialgeschichte im Mittelalter* (Stuttgart, 1980).

[24] Huizinga pointed out, albeit in another context, that 'ideas that once had been meaningful could go mad and develop into grotesque obsessions', see W.E. Krul, p. 105 in A.H. Huussen Jr., E.H. Kossmann and H. Renner (eds.), *Historici van de twintigste eeuw* (Utrecht, Antwerp and Amsterdam, 1981).

clearly arise under Louis VI, in the first half of the twelfth century, but the realization of all its logical consequences did not take place until the time of Philip IV. Philip even attempted to place the clergy under the national government and, *inter alia*, to subject the county of Flanders to royal officialdom. This was no doubt a logical step, considering the fact that 'Flanders under the crown' (i.e. the part of the county situated to the west of the Scheldt) was French territory, but one that Philip's predecessors had always shirked.[25]

The ambitions of papal curialism, the claim of the Roman curia to exercise central control over the whole Latin West and to offer moral and political leadership to all Europe, was equally obvious. The starting point of this movement was provided by the Gregorian Reform, while subsequent centuries witnessed the practical elaboration of its principles, of theocracy and centralization. The pontificate of Boniface VIII, the pope of the Jubilee of 1300 and of the bull *Ausculta fili*, can be seen as the extreme logical consequence of the Gregorian principles. However, both the monarchic and the theocratic conclusions, which flowed from their respective premises, were so extreme that there was no room for manoeuvre left between them. The 'peaceful co-existence' of previous times could not be maintained.[26]

Economic historians do not have to look far to discover comparable developments. In material civilization also certain mechanisms were pushed to extremes, to the neglect of economic viability. We remind the reader of the vast process of land reclamation by drainage and deforestation and generally obtaining new land for agriculture, which had been going on for a considerable time and which, around A.D. 1300, reached a temporary climax. Extensive areas of poor and unprofitable land had been brought under cultivation, and subsequently were abandoned again because of their low productivity: here again a secular trend had been pushed to an untenable paroxysm. We have the impression that urbanization underwent a similar development. It had started in the late eleventh century and, in the early fourteenth the demographic concentration in the industrial towns reached a temporary – and untenable – maximum: urban-based industrialization had exhausted its dynamism and had even overshot its target, which

---

[25] See W. Kienast, *Untertaneneid und Treuvorbehalt in Frankreich und Deutschland* (Weimar, 1952) and *Deutschland und Frankreich in der Kaiserzeit, 900-1270*, 3 vols., (Stuttgart, 1974-75). See also C. Petit-Dutaillis, *La monarchie féodale en France et en Angleterre* (Paris, 1971) and the recent survey by B. Guenée, *L'occident aux XIVe et XVe siècles: les états* (Paris, 1971). On the Franco-Flemish conflict under Philip IV the reader may consult the relevant chapters in Favier, *Philippe le Bel*, pp. 223-49 and Strayer, *The Reign of Philip the Fair*, pp. 324-46 (both authors unfortunately took insufficient account of studies in the Dutch language).

[26] See the excellent analysis of the bull *Ausculta fili* and its impact in Favier, *Philippe le Bel*, pp. 344-49, 353-56. For a general survey of the relations between the papacy and the monarchies the reader may consult J.B. Tierney, *The Crisis of Church and State, 1050-1300* (Englewood Cliffs, NJ, 1964). On the rise of curialism and its legal arguments, see the classic volume by G. Le Bras, Ch. Lefebvre and J. Rambaud, *L'âge classique, 1140-1378: sources et théorie du droit* (Paris, 1965).

resulted in social and economic crises in the towns and the rise of competing industries in the countryside.[27]

If it is (relatively) easy to form a *Gesamtbild* of the fourteenth century, I find it difficult to interpret the fifteenth and to draw its 'face'. The danger of anachronism is particularly acute here, because – according to the traditional periodization – we all know that this was the last century of the middle ages and are therefore inclined to view it as the decline, if not the collapse of a civilization: the 'waning' of a great period. We should, however, not forget that the break between middle ages and modern times is to a large extent arbitrary and was in no way absolute: it is quite reasonable to view the 'Old-European phase' as one historical period, stretching from the twelfth century to the epoch of the Industrial and the French Revolutions.[28] We readily admit that various fifteenth-century phenomena can be interpreted as the last manifestations of a typical medieval way of life; the question is whether they are fundamental or even important aspects. This certainly does not apply to the Renaissance, which in that century was triumphant in southern Europe and looked like the beginning of a new world. Also the commercial expansion (Antwerp and southern Germany) and the explorations of Henry the Navigator were the harbingers of a new era, whereas the shaping of the Seventeen Provinces was similarly a constructive and forward-looking development.[29] In short, I am rather inclined to view the fifteenth century as an era of renewal, which had turned its back on the crises of the fourteenth. In this respect the following aspects come to mind.

Firstly, renaissance and humanism not only led to new forms of art but

---

[27] See D. Nicholas, *Town and Countryside: Social, Economic and Political Tensions in Fourteenth-Century Flanders* (Bruges, 1971). For the demographic element: N.G.J. Pounds, 'Overpopulation in France and the Low Countries in the Later Middle Ages', *Journal of Social History*, 3 (1970), pp. 225-47. It is well known that monetary history is one of the most striking indicators of the contrast between the stable thirteenth and the turbulent fourteenth century. On the stability of the Flemish penny which lasted for more than a hundred years see C. Wyffels, 'Contribution à l'histoire monétaire de Flandre au XIIIe siècle', *Revue belge de philologie et d'histoire*, 45 (1967), pp. 1113-41.

[28] A new periodical has been launched specifically devoted to the study of the later middle ages and modern times viewed as one historical period, from *c.* 1100 to the middle of the eighteenth century: *Zeitschrift für historische Forschung: Halbjahrschrift zur Erforschung des Spätmittelalters und der Frühen Neuzeit.* It is based on the following periodization: 1) *Archaisches Zeitalter* (until *c.* 1100), 2) *Alteuropäisches Zeitalter* (twelfth-eighteenth centuries), 3) *Das industrielle Zeitalter.* See also the arguments in R.C. Van Caenegem, *Geschiedkundige inleiding tot het privaatrecht* (Ghent, 1981), pp. 28-30. I am not alone in seeing the 'Old European period' as one continuous phase of legal history, as appears from a recent pronouncement by a leading specialist: 'Beaucoup d'observations peuvent nous mener à la conclusion qu'en réalité la pensée juridique forme une même idée de l'époque des Glossateurs . . . aux juristes de l'*usus modernus pandectarum* du 18e siècle', H. Coing, 'L'application des "Libri Feudorum"', *Diritto comune e diritti locali nella storia dell' Europa* (Milan, 1980), p. 23.

[29] See, besides the bibliography in n. 23 H. Van Der Wee, *Conjunctuur en economische groei in de Zuidelijke Nederlanden tijdens de 14e, 15e en 16e eeuw* (Brussels, 1965).

also to a new way of life, created by people who did not hesitate to break with existing concepts and traditions.[30]

Secondly, the conciliar movement was a daring ecclesiastical experiment in democracy, as it was a conscious attempt to conquer the papal crisis caused by the Schism, and put the government of the church in the hands of the faithful, or at least of their spokesmen. The great councils of the first half of the fifteenth century, with hundreds of participants – clergy and laymen from all countries – were not only a remarkable anti-curial experiment in government by consent, they were also the earliest – and for many centuries the only – international assemblies of representatives from all parts of the western world, real prefigurations of the European parliament of our own time. The conciliar phase was admittedly no permanent success, but this does not detract from the importance of this daring innovation.[31]

Thirdly, when we turn our attention to political life, we are again struck by the progress of government by consent. English parliamentarianism reached a provisional summit in the fifteenth century, while in Spain and the Low Countries representative assemblies achieved an unparalleled importance. The French monarchy recovered from the disasters of the Hundred Years War, which had almost been fatal, while towards the end of the century Germany, full of optimism and ardour, made all sorts of plans to establish a forceful modern nation state.

Fourthly, the economy had resolutely turned the depressing page of the preceding century and experienced a remarkable advance, if not necessarily in the old centres. Southern Germany profited more from the new international trade than the old Rhineland, and Brabant and Antwerp more than Flanders and Bruges, but generally speaking the crisis was overcome and the expansion started which would receive an unimaginable impulse from the great voyages of discovery. It is no exaggeration to conclude that towards the end of the fifteenth century the rejuvenated nations of Europe were ready for the conquest of the world and for an unheard of industrial and commercial expansion.[32]

The foregoing considerations concerned the general physiognomy of Europe; let us see now whether they are applicable to the old Netherlands.

---

[30] See, for example, the outspoken criticism by the Humanist school of Roman law of its immediate predecessors, the Commentators, H. Coing, *Handbuch*, ii, 1, (1977), pp. 615ff,; R.C. Van Caenegem, *Geschiedkundige inleiding*, pp. 48-51.
[31] See, *inter alia*, B. Tierney, *The Foundations of the Conciliar Theory* (Cambridge, 1955) and R. Bäumer (ed.), *Die Entwicklung des Konziliarismus: Werden und Nachwirkung der konziliaren Idee* (Darmstadt, 1976). It is well known that the conciliar phase came to an end under Pope Pius II (1458-64), who had previously been a moderate conciliarist himself.
[32] For the importance of the role of Antwerp, see H. Van Der Wee, *The Growth of the Antwerp Market and the European Economy*, 3 vols. (The Hague, 1963).

For the twelfth century the answer is certainly positive. Various foundations were then laid and certain outlines became visible which were decisive and remained typical for centuries. The events in Flanders in 1127 and 1128 showed that the big towns were a political, and not only an economic power, of the first order. The comital government had seriously to take this into account. The rulers from the House of Alsace, who then came to power – in particular Philip of Alsace (1157-1191) – made it clear on the other hand that they were determined to turn comital authority in Flanders into an efficient and modern institution: they thus laid the basis for the long-term power-sharing of towns and counts.[33] The seed of French-Flemish tension also was sown at this time. The failed intervention of Louis VI in Flanders and particularly the death of his candidate for the succession, William Clito (d. 1128), prevented the annexation of the county by the French monarchy, so that in the late fourteenth century it could form the basis for the independent Netherlandish state of the Burgundians and the Habsburgs.[34] The fundamental economic pattern – with its urban industry and trade connected to France, England and the Rhineland – was already clearly recognizable.

The thirteenth century witnessed the institutionalization of princely as well as urban power; thus the centrally supervised bureaucracy had its roots in the twelfth, but received its clear organizational pattern and standardized nomenclature in the thirteenth century. Demographic expansion continued and reached a temporary peak; the emancipation of the countryside, encouraged by the rise of urban liberty, made striking progress and was officially recognized and confirmed. Franco-Flemish relations went through an undramatic phase of latent tension: the county underwent strong French influences, but even after Bouvines its existence was not threatened and the French monarchy – until Philip IV the Fair – was not tempted to the extreme step of outright annexation. The expansion of the main towns was led by an oligarchy of entrepreneurs and *viri hereditarii*, who occupied a

---

[33] See R.C. Van Caenegem (ed.), *Galbert van Brugge*, chapter 6: 'De bakens zijn gezet', pp. 68-71. For the interpretation of the Great Borough Charter of Philip of Alsace as an expression of the power-relations between count and town, see R.C. Van Caenegem and L. Milis, 'Kritische uitgave van de 'Grote Keure' van Filips van de Elzas, Graaf van Vlaanderen, voor Gent en Brugge (1165-1177)', *Bulletin de la Commission Royale d'Histoire*, 143 (1977), pp. 213-19, and R.C. Van Caenegem and L. Milis, 'Kritische uitgave van de "Precepta" van Graaf Filips van de Elzas voor de stad Gent (1178)', *Handelingen van de maatschappij voor geschiedenis en oudheidkunde te Gent*, new series 33 (1979), pp. 99-116.

[34] F.L. Ganshof, 'Le roi de France en Flandre en 1127 et 1128' *Revue historique de droit français et étranger*, 27 (1949), pp. 204-28; idem, 'Les origines du concept de souveraineté nationale en Flandre', *Revue d'histoire du droit*, 18 (1950), pp. 135-58; idem, 'Trois mandements perdus du roi de France Louis VI intéressant la Flandre', *Handelingen van het genootschap voor geschiedenis gesticht onder de benaming 'société d'émulation' te Brugge*, 77 (1950), pp. 117-33; R.C. Van Caenegem, *Galbert van Brugge en het recht* (Brussels, 1978), pp. 18-26.

stable position of power and were confronted by confrontation only towards the end of the century.[35]

This thirteenth-century image of balance and expansion was sorely battered in the following hundred years. The agrarian optimum was left behind and urban industry went through a profound crisis from which – in Flanders at any rate – it never really recovered. Violent conflicts broke out between the old urban oligarchs and the mass of the people, led by new men. Franco-Flemish relations turned sour and the sharp conflict reached a dramatic and decisive climax in 1302: the greater part of Flanders escaped French rule and became, as we have seen, the corner stone of an anti-French Burgundian state. In the meantime tension between the count and the main towns also reached breaking point and it looked for a while as if the county of Flanders would, after the Italian model, reject its monarchical constitution and turn into a group of three urban republics, led by captains (*hoofdmannen*). Even in the relations between the Netherlandish principalities harmony was lost, as is shown by the alliance of Hainaut and Holland against Flanders and the war of Duke John III of Brabant against the grand coalition of his neighbouring enemies.[36]

The contrast with the fifteenth century, where harmony and construction dominated instead of tension and destruction, is very striking. Political patience allowed the erection of the state of the Seventeen Provinces, provided with common central institutions as well as a common ruler. This Burgundian state was not merely a continuation or resumption of older traditions. It was, on the contrary, strikingly original, as will be seen from the following analysis.

Firstly, the constitution was monarchic, yet the Burgundian and Habsburg state of the Netherlands was federal and not unitary. The principalities retained their own identity and institutions but were held together by their common ruler and the organizations that grew up around him.[37] Nor was the monarchy absolute; it strongly resembled the modern parliamentary model. Few political decisions were taken without consulting the assemblies of estates.[38]

Secondly, the role of the nobility also deserves attention, for, although

---

[35] See the innovative publications by R. Van Uytven, 'Plutokratie in de "oude demokratieën der Nederlanden"', *Handelingen van de koninklijke zuidnederlandse maatschappij voor taal- en letterkunde en geschiedenis*, 16 (1962), pp. 373-409; 'Sociaal-economische evoluties in de Nederlanden voor de Revoluties (14e-16e eeuw)', *Bijdragen en mededelingen van de geschiedenis der Nederlanden*, 87 (1972), pp. 60-93, and 'Politiek en economie: de crisis der late XVe eeuw in de Nederlanden', *Belgisch tijdschrift voor filologie en geschiedenis*, 53 (1975), pp. 1097-1149.

[36] See chapter II: 'De koalitie tegen Brabant (1332-1334): een keerpunt', P. Avonds, *Ideologie en politiek: Brabant tijdens de regering van Hertog Jan III, 1312-1356*, i (Ghent, 1981), pp. 361-492.

[37] See J. Van Rompaey's chapter, 'Instellingen en recht, 1384-1482', *Algemene geschiedenis der Nederlanden*, iv (Haarlem, 1980), pp. 135-81.

[38] See the fundamental study of W.P. Blockmans, *De volksvertegenwoordiging in Vlaanderen in de overgang van middeleeuwen naar nieuwe tijden (1384-1506)* (Brussels, 1978).

knightly romances were popular and their romanticism was consciously stimulated by the dukes, the state of the Netherlands was anything but an aristocratic republic. Philip the Good was, of course, prepared in a bout of chivalrous feelings, in the midst of a glorious banquet, to promise a crusade against the Turks, but there the matter rested. The Burgundian state was run in a very pragmatic way and its aristocracy was mainly a nobility of service, created by the prince; it was given various administrative tasks and was seen as a symbol of the union of the Low Countries (this was particularly the role of the Order of the Golden Fleece).[39] Those noble families whose lands and offices were distributed over several provinces undeniably played a centripetal role. The Burgundian dukes understood this and were content to let them play an important social role in their provinces and domains. The nobles, however, came to realize the importance of their contribution to the cohesion of the Low Countries: in the sixteenth century they considered themselves as the natural spokesmen of the country and defenders of its interests. I have often wondered why the towns, which had previously been the traditional leaders of popular action, were so clearly outstripped by the nobility in the resistance against Philip II. I believe the explanation lies in the fact that the Burgundians themselves had given the nobility a real, though limited, role as leaders and representatives of the people of the Low Countries. When Philip attempted to degrade them and turn them into mere subjects, placed under the authority of a few bureaucratic confidants of his choice, he provoked resistance which eventually turned into a revolt. The Burgundian state had tamed the towns, with the exception of the stubborn and unmanageable Ghent. This is not to say that the towns ceased to carry political weight, but such influence as they wielded made itself felt in the representative institutions of the state, the organs of deliberation assembled by the ruler.[40]

So far I have dealt with political and social and economic developments. It is time to extend the survey to cultural life and, more particularly, to pose the question of the nexus or interrelation between the political and social and economic strands on the one hand and the cultural developments on the other. I risk producing platitudes by pointing out that the rise of a literate class of burgesses and knights necessarily led to the breakthrough of the vernacular in writing, or that the enhanced role of the cities naturally resulted in a strongly urban culture (chambers of rhetoric, an ironic attitude towards the nobility, criticism of the clergy, success of didactic literature). I would equally force already open doors by pointing out that a flourishing culture is most likely in a prosperous society or that political democracy was bound to have a positive effect on the position of the vernacular. It is not my

---

[39] Cf. R. Van Uytven, 'Vorst adel en steden: een driehoeksverhouding in Brabant van de twaalfde tot de zestiende eeuw', *Bijdragen tot de geschiedenis*, 59 (1976), pp. 93-122.

[40] On various occasions the normal process of consultation failed, and pent up tensions led to open revolt, cf. Blockmans, *De volksvertegenwoordiging in Vlaanderen*, pp. 342-76.

intention to minimize these causal relations, let alone to deny them, but I feel justified in warning against exaggerating the closeness of these ties. It struck me, when studying the main lines of cultural development, that they are no mere reproductions or reflections of the political or economic events and that cultural evolution even possesses a marked autonomy and follows a dynamic and a logical pattern of its own. Nor is it my intention here to go deeply into this most tantalizing problem, for it appears in many fields (in the history of science, for example) and has wide ramifications.[41] I will limit ourselves to a few preliminary remarks and concentrate my attention on the Low Countries of the late middle ages. We are faced with two theses, two historical visions, which can be described as follows.

One interpretation, which can – for lack of better terms – be described as 'reductionist', 'holistic' or 'synchronic', believes that all manifestations of social life – particularly cultural and economic – form one vast current; they are interrelated and connected, follow parallel lines of development and influence and explain each other. They could, in that sense, be called synchronized.

The other view, which can be described – again for lack of a better word – as 'autonomist' or 'dyschronic', believes in the internal dynamic of each of those lines of development, whose ups and downs are self-determined and may easily move in opposite directions: they are, in other words unsynchronized.[42] (The reader will realize that I am not thinking here of the old and well established distinction between the synchronic and the diachronic approach.)

The autonomist interpretation can, for example, easily accept that some great scientific breakthroughs went against the general trend of society, whereas the reductionists cannot conceive of scientific progress in a society that does not – for political or economic reasons – need or demand it.[43]

[41] The historians of science speak of a debate between 'autonomists' (discoveries follow their own independent course) and 'derivationists' (discoveries automatically produced by new social circumstances and needs). Among the latter one finds, for example, the famous historian of Chinese science, Joseph Needham, cf. particularly his *The Grand Titration* (Toronto, 1970); in the former school we find, for example, R.K. Merton, *Sociology of Science: Theoretical and Empirical Investigations* (Chicago, 1974). See also P. Mathias (ed.), *Science and Society, 1600-1900* (Cambridge, 1972).

[42] As far as I know the terms dyschronic or dyschronism are neologisms. I nevertheless use them tentatively in analogy with 'synchronic', because they so clearly express the idea of various lines of development which, although coeval, have essentially nothing in common with each other or are even conflicting and, in that sense, unsynchronized, i.e. not attuned to each other. I thank my Ghent colleague, Prof. G. Sanders, for a fruitful discussion on the linguistic aspects of this terminology.

[43] Many historians are, often unconsciously, convinced of the connection between the various threads of history, which is conceived as proceeding in one comprehensive movement. Hence, for example, Toynbee's amazement when he found that in the nineteenth century there existed a 'perverse parochialism' (he refers to nationalism), which fought against and was in contradiction with the process of modernization, industrialization and democratization of the time. See on this P.B.M. Blaas in Huusse, Kossmann, Renner (eds.) *Historici van de twintigste eeuw*, p. 124,

When I reflect on the Netherlandish cultural development in this light, some very provisional impressions arise. Thus I am struck by its great autonomy or, in other words, by the dyschronism between the permanent character of cultural life and the violent political and social upheavals. It is noteworthy, for example, that many of the main artistic manifestations of the later middle ages had only tenuous ties with the state of society at any given time and had a timeless character, above the contingencies of the moment. This is particularly true of Gothic architecture and of Dutch literature, especially in the latter's great lyrical and mystical works. I readily admit that there is here wide scope for discussion.

who rightly points out that Toynbee "was at a loss when faced with an historical development in which phenomena coincided chronologically which ought 'logically . . . not to have done that, something which is nowadays sometimes described as the contemporaneity of what is not contemporaneous'". There are, of course, other examples of dyschronic evolutions in the nineteenth century, not least in England itself, where the social and economic and also the technological developments were extremely modern, but the legal system, the common law, very old-fashioned and to a large extent even medieval.

13

Henri Pirenne: Medievalist and Historian of Belgium

Opinion on Pirenne is nowadays divided.[1] In 1984, a few weeks apart, I happened to hear two diametrically opposite judgments about him. In a casual conversation the well-known American medievalist T.N. Bisson told me that he was a warm admirer of Pirenne and reread his *Histoire économique et sociale du moyen âge* (rev. ed. by H. Van Werveke, Paris, 1963) every year. Soon afterwards, A. Derville, professor of medieval history in the university of Lille, sent me an off-print of his *Les échevins de Douai, 1228-1257*[2] (Mémoires de la Soc. pour l'Agriculture, les Sciences et les Arts de Douai, 8, 1980-82, pp. 39-48), where I read the following about Pirenne (p. 39): 'De cet historien prestigieux, plus sans doute par la puissance de son imagination et de sa rhétorique que par la solidité de son érudition, que reste-t-il cent ans plus tard? Très peu de choses'. These two pronouncements are typical of the division in the scholarly camp. It is statistically impossible

---

[1] The fiftieth anniversary of Pirenne's death, on 24 October 1935, and the hundredth anniversary of his appointment in the university of Ghent, where he taught from 1886 till 1930, led several scholars to reflect on that famous historian's role and significance. As a pupil of one of Pirenne's most famous alumni, Professor F.L. Ganshof, I also found it a suitable moment to put in writing some ideas on Pirenne's work with which I had, of course, been acquainted for many years. I welcome the opportunity to present them to your attention in this essay. All I have to offer are some reflections on his career and importance. I shall produce no new facts from archive material and I have based my ideas merely on Pirenne's own writings and the well-known publications devoted to his life and significance. C. Verlinden, 'Henri Pirenne', *Architects and Craftsmen in History: Festschrift für A.P. Usher* (Tübingen, 1956), pp. 85-100; F.L. Ganshof, 'Pirenne (Henri)', *Biographie nationale*, 30 (1959), col. 671-723; B. Lyon, *Henri Pirenne: A Biographical and Intellectual Study* (Ghent, 1974); J. Dhondt, 'Henri Pirenne: historien des institutions urbaines', *Annali della fondazione italiana per la storia amministrativa*, 3 (1966), pp. 81-129; H. Sproemberg, *Mittelalter und demokratische Geschichtsschreibung: Ausgewählte Abhandlungen* (Berlin, 1971), pp. 375-446: 'Pirenne und die deutsche Geschichtswissenschaft'; B. Lyon, 'A Reply to Jan Dhondt's Critique of Henri Pirenne', *Handelingen der maatschappij voor geschiedenis en oudheidkunde to Gent* n.s., 29 (1975), pp. 3-25; B. Ebels-Hoving, 'Henri Pirenne (1862-1935)', A.M. Huussen Jr., E.H. Kossmann and H. Renner (eds.), *Historici van de twintigste eeuw* (Antwerp and Amsterdam, 1981), pp. 26-40; 'La fortune historiographique des thèses d'Henri Pirenne', *Archives et bibliothèques de Belgique*, special no. 28 (Brussels, 1986).

[2] *Mémoires de la société pour l'agriculture, les sciences et les arts de Douai*, 8 (1980-82), pp. 39-48.

without an organized poll to be sure which opinion is predominant. My hunch, however, is that the detractors may be gaining the upper hand, because one so often comes across the phrase, in books and articles: 'in contrast to what Pirenne maintains, we find that . . .'

It is, however, necessary to make an important distinction. It is the most natural thing in the world that in the course of time a scholar is overtaken by new research: if this were not the case, science would be stifled by sclerosis. It is normal that a learned opus which is several decades old is corrected and revised by recent research. Scholars would be judged against their own epoch and for what they have realized with the means at their disposal: one does not judge the mid nineteenth-century discoveries of F.A. Kekulé about the structure of benzene with the yardstick of present-day chemistry.[3] It is obvious that pioneers can err or neglect certain phenomena more easily than following generations: Pirenne was – certainly in his own country – a pioneer of social and economic history. I shall take care not to follow the example of Richardson and Sayles, who had an easy task in demolishing the image of William Stubbs, the pioneer of modern scholarship in medieval studies in Victorian England.[4] Yet, I readily admit that the adulation of Stubbs could easily seduce some modern and critical scholars to an iconoclastic exercise, just as in Belgium the songs of praise for Pirenne led the late Prof. Jan Dhondt to his famous 'demythologizing' article of 1966. I believe that it is senseless to keep myths alive, since they hinder the search for truth, but a systematic and merciless denigration of the achievement of our predecessors is equally wrong-headed: my aim in this essay is to present a sober and unprejudiced evaluation, not demolition for demolition's sake.

The Personality of Pirenne

All witnesses agree that Pirenne had an enthusiastic disposition and that he wished to introduce, with great dynamism and conviction, the message of modern medieval research to his country. His enthusiasm affected not only colleagues and students with whom he was in personal contact, but also readers who lived thousands of miles away and had never seen or heard him personally. His biographer, Professor Bryce Lyon, told me that reading

---

[3] Kekulé (1829-96) taught chemistry in Ghent from 1858 to 1867 and became famous through the discovery of the formula of benzene, cf. J. Gillis in *Nationaal biografisch woordenboek*, 1 (1964), col. 645-48.

[4] H.G. Richardson and G.O. Sayles, *The Governance of Mediaeval England from the Conquest to Magna Carta* (Edinburgh, 1963), chapter I: 'William Stubbs, the Man and the Historian', pp. 1-21. The authors blame Stubbs mainly for his 'gross anachronisms', through which he 'projected into the past the image of the constitutional monarchy which he saw working under his own eyes and to which he attributed the greatness of his country' (p. 6, a quotation from C. Petit-Dutaillis). The authors conclude their chapter with the contention that Stubbs's oeuvre is 'a mountain of chaff'.

Pirenne while he was a student in the American Midwest fired his imagination so strongly that he decided to become a medievalist.

Where could one find critical medievalists, except for the Bollandists, in Belgium in the 1880s? Nowhere. The historians were romantic *littérateurs*, who normally taught literature as well as history. The impact of Pirenne, who had seen the new light in France and Germany, was understandably strong and explains to a large extent his meteoric career. Who, for example, has ever heard of his immediate predecessor in Ghent, P.J. Wouters (1830-86)? This honest plodder became, after spending some time as a teacher, extraordinary professor in 1871 and ordinary professor in 1875. He succeeded Serrure in the chair of political history of the middle ages and also taught the political history of Belgium from 1874 onwards. Wouters' main interest was literature and he wrote poems, some of which were published (for example, a collection called *Dromen*, in the *Nederduitsch letterkundig Jaarboek* of 1849). His scholarly production was strikingly inconspicuous and consisted of abstracts of courses in Belgium and Antiquity, as well as an essay on the previous greatness of Belgium in navigation, trade and industry, published in 1869 in the year-book of a local cultural organization, the Willemsfonds, of which he was a member. This meagre harvest is excused in the *Liber Memorialis* of the university of Ghent with the following words: 'Consacrant tout son temps à son enseignement Wouters ne publia pas de recherches scientifiques: on lui doit toutefois quelques livres d'enseignement'. The notice ends as follows: 'Wouters était un savant modeste' – to which one is inclined to add that he had every reason to be.[5] This is the 'scholar' whom Pirenne succeeded in Ghent. Nor was his case unique: in the then learned world, around the time of Pirenne's appointment, Belgium was a provincial no man's land between France and Germany. Pirenne alone worked on the best European level. It is not surprising that this prophet of the new science made an enormous impression, quickly receiving various national prizes and already in 1891, not yet fully twenty-nine years old, becoming a member of the Royal Commission for History and in 1907 its secretary and the main inspiration of its activities. The Ghent medievalist believed strongly in science in general and in history in particular, and was also full of hope. This explains, partly at least, how the optimistic and confident Pirenne, courageous – or bold – enough to assume many heavy and varied tasks, became a tragic figure.

The tragedy of his life was firstly of a personal nature. Henri Pirenne, who was happily married, had four sons: three, of whom one fell at the IJzer in 1914, died before their father. It is hard to imagine what it means to a father to have to mourn three of his four children. In the funeral oration for his pupil Guillaume Des Marez, who had died on 2 November 1931, Pirenne said that it was monstrous for a father to survive his sons and for a master his

---

[5] *Université de Gand: Liber Memorialis. Notices biographiques*, i, *Faculté de Philosophie et Lettres. Faculté de Droit* (Ghent, 1913), pp. 173-75.

pupil.⁶ When, in 1935, he lost a third son, Henri Edouard, the scholar's vitality and possibly the will to live were lost in spite of his iron constitution, and he died a few months later, on 24 October 1935, almost seventy-three years old. Secondly, there was the ideological tragedy in Pirenne's life. The foundations of his conviction, everything in which he had believed before 1914, became uncertain: several pillars of his *Weltanschauung* have collapsed in that and the following years. Pirenne was very much a child of the nineteenth century, which disappeared with the First World War. We have his following convictions in mind.

A belief in progress, the role of the social sciences, the rule of law and European civilization. Pirenne shared with many Europeans the idea that the incessant progress of humanity – which meant essentially European humanity – had eliminated barbarian methods of settling international conflicts, such as warfare, and had relegated them to museums and books on military history: modern Europe had recourse to the Peace Palace in The Hague and not to the battlefield. Western civilization had reached such heights that the rule of law was safe. To Maurice Prou, who had been pessimistic about the international situation in 1905, Pirenne wrote, 'Croyez-vous vraiment à la possibilité d'une guerre? Il m'est impossible pour ma part d'avoir la moindre crainte à cet égard'.⁷ The German invasion of Belgium in 1914, in spite of the overvalued 'bit of paper' of the guarantees of the treaties, and the unleashing of modern barbarism consequent to the First World War, were shocking events, which Pirenne could not cope with and which left only rancour against the Germans – including his fellow historians – as a bitter aftertaste.

Pirenne also believed in liberalism, and especially in free enterprise and parliamentary democracy. Here also the post-war years led to bitter disappointment. Far from conquering the world, liberalism was rejected or even eliminated by the masses. Pirenne witnessed the victory of proletarian dictatorship in Russia as well as the early successes of the Nazi party in Germany. In his own country the liberal party, which once upon a time had ruled Belgium, was reduced to a small faction, operating in the shadow of socialists and Christian democrats.

Pirenne admired imperial Germany and Germany's culture and scientific prestige throughout Europe. After the French-speaking world, in which he was born and educated, Germany had become Pirenne's second cultural fatherland. During his studies there (1884-85) he met so much friendliness and acquired so many new ideas (particularly in the field of social and economic history) that German science became his polar star. He was born in Verviers, close to the German border, in an area that did much business with Germany and he mastered the language sufficiently to give talks in German during his stay there at medieval seminars. When his son, who

⁶ B. Lyon, *Henri Pirenne*, p. 361.
⁷ Ibid., p. 142.

studied in Germany just before the war, told him about the militarism that was rampant among the students, Pirenne could not believe his ears. The true nature of German militarism and imperialism was revealed to him in a shocking way in 1914 and so another of his illusions was lost. Where was the time when he described the 'national culture' of Belgium as 'le riche et harmonieux assemblage des meilleurs éléments de la civilisation franco-allemande'?[8]

Above all Pirenne believed in the excellence of French civilization. The nineteenth century witnessed the apogee of French cultural influence in the world, but the enormous role of the Anglo-Saxon powers in the victory of 1918 and in the Paris peace conference of 1919 was a clear indication that the twentieth century would see the rise of the English-speaking world and the English language as the main global means of communication. The signs of this change could not have escaped Pirenne's notice as he travelled in the United States in the years after the war.

In this same connection Pirenne believed in the necessity of Belgian unity, cemented by the French language. He had faith in and was proud of the unitary Belgian state dominated by the French-speaking bourgeoisie. He could muster little sympathy for the demands of the Flemings that their language – Dutch – should be placed on an equal basis with French. He had opposed the poisoned gift of the von Bissing University in Ghent, which had led to his exile in Germany, but even after the war, when the legitimate gift of a Dutch-language university in Ghent was being debated by parliament in Brussels, he was opposed to it and became the honorary president of the *Ligue Nationale pour la Liberté des Langues*, an organization that fought for maintaining a French university in Ghent.[9] Nevertheless, he lived to see linguistic laws guaranteeing to a large extent the use of Dutch in Flanders and Dutch becoming the language of teaching in his own, previously French, university of Ghent.

So much that was dear to Pirenne was lost or endangered and it all happened in his last twenty-one years. After childhood and studies, his life consisted, from his appointment in Ghent onwards, of twenty-eight years of uninterrupted happy progress, until 1914, and from then on twenty-one years of mourning and misfortune. Seldom were prosperity and adversity in one human life so sharply separated. The prosperous years witnessed excessive prosperity and Pirenne had the temerity, in 1912, when he was honoured in Brussels, to tempt fate as it were by publicly calling attention to his extraordinary luck. He put it in this way:

---

[8] Ibid., p. 143, quoting from the preface of vol I of the *Histoire de Belgique*.
[9] J. Dhondt, *Henri Pirenne*, p. 106. On Pirenne's attitude towards the Flemish movement one can consult the nuanced article 'Pirenne' In *Encyclopedie van de Vlaamse beweging* (Amsterdam, 1975), ii, pp. 1252-53, by Professor A. Verhulst.

'Il y a, n'est-ce pas, en ce monde, deux sortes de destinées: celles qui, contrariées par le sort, se déroulent dans une lutte constante contre la mauvaise fortune, dans un effort perpétuel de la volonté tendue vers l'idéal à atteindre, et celles qui, aidées par les circonstances, n'ont qu'à s'abandonner au bon vent qui les favorise et accomplissent sans encombre la traversée de la vie. La mienne, je dois bien le confesser jusqu'aujourd'hui du moins, a été de ces dernières. Elle n'a point connu les tempêtes qui mettent à l'épreuve le courage et l'énergie et permettent seules d'apprécier la valeur d'un homme'.

Five years later, imprisoned in Germany, he remembered his words of 1912 and wrote (to J. Cuvelier): 'Je me félicitais d'avoir été constamment heureux jusqu'alors, et c'était vrai. La destinée s'est vengée. Et j'aurais bien dû me rappeler le vers de Sophocle dans Oedipe "Ne proclamons heureux nul homme avant sa mort".'[10]

The Work

After the personality it is Pirenne's oeuvre which now deserves our attention. It contains several main elements. Pirenne was first and foremost a highly trained and erudite professional who knew the latest heuristic techniques and the rules concerning the criticism and edition of medieval source material. Here he proved himself to be an excellent pupil of his French and German masters, whose influence he first underwent indirectly in G. Kurth's seminars in Liège and afterwards directly during his studies in France and Germany. Pirenne always remained an erudite savant: even after launching himself into very broad themes and interpretations, he never stopped publishing detailed critical studies of various texts.

Pirenne was also the founder in Belgium of social and economic history. It is hard for us to imagine, after the enormous expansion of this discipline, how new it was a hundred years ago, when history was still a form of *bellettrie* of the romantic sort, devoted to the heroic deeds of political and military leaders. It is quite plausible that Pirenne's birth in the textile town of Verviers as the son of an industrialist gave him a natural interest in economic history, particularly that of the medieval textile industry. Nevertheless, it was mainly the influence of Gustav Schmoller and Karl Lamprecht which aroused Pirenne's enthusiasm for economic history. One of his earliest plans was to write a history of the Flemish textile industry; that history he never wrote, but he did publish, between 1906 and 1924, in collaboration with Georges Espinas, four volumes of the *Recueil de documents relatifs à l'histoire drapière de Flandre* (which was continued by Professor H. Van Werveke and Dr. C. Wyffels). Pirenne's work on the great economic and social developments and structural changes led not only Belgian but also French historiography into new fields. It is known that Pirenne, for

---

[10] B. Lyon, *Henri Pirenne*, p. 195.

whom Marc Bloch had the greatest veneration, was a father figure of the founders of the *Annales* (and what later became the *Annales* School) and that numerous ideas of Karl Lamprecht reached France via Pirenne.[11]

Finally it was Pirenne who secured an important place in international scholarship for Belgian medieval studies and, in particular for the school of Ghent. He opened the gates of the temple of internationally recognized scholarship for innumerable Belgian medievalists. He did so by studying three great themes and launching new visions which have made a worldwide impression and which, even if they have not met with general acceptance, have certainly led to universal discussion. These themes are, of course: the origin of medieval towns; the history of Belgium; and 'Mohammed and Charlemagne'. Without these wide themes Pirenne would have been a positivist scholar like so many others and would have published interchangeable technical studies of limited appeal, which might just as well have been written by his colleagues. Studies on great problems and a personal vision of whole sketches of world history are not interchangeable, but marked by the strong personality of their authors.

The Origin of Medieval Towns

Everyone knows that the agrarian society of the early middle ages was followed by a phase of urbanization, which was particularly important in Northern Italy and the Low Countries and the adjacent Northern-French and Rhineland areas. Nineteenth-century scholarship was full of theories which were supposed to explain 'the origin' of 'the medieval town'. To us this is somewhat surprising because we do not share their obsession with the origins of all sorts of phenomena, are less inclined to believe in a single origin and are not enthusiastic about building theories (a habit taken over from the natural sciences). The nineteenth century was different and numerous scholars forcefully produced various theories on the origin of towns, epic literature, parliament and so on: historiography was to a large extent a battle of theories. It is in this context that Pirenne developed his own theory on the origin of towns, following the example of German books which he had reviewed and had thus introduced to the French-speaking world. Several of these theories he rejected – those of W. Arnold, K.W. Nitzsch, G. von Below, R. Sohm and F. Keutgen – but with one, that of S. Rietschel, he largely agreed. Towns were very important to Pirenne because they certainly played a dominating role in social and economic develop-

---

[11] idem., 'Henri Pirenne and the Origins of Annales History', *Annals of Scholarship: Metastudies of the Humanities and Social Sciences*, 1 (1980), pp. 69-84; L. Schorn-Schütte, *Karl Lamprecht: Kulturgeschichtsschreibung zwischen Wissenschaft und Politik* (Göttingen, 1984), pp. 309-16 and 320-28. The author announces the publication of new items from the Pirenne-Lamprecht correspondence (p. 320, n. 146).

ment, as centres of production and distribution and cradles of a new type of men: even if one is less interested in towns as juridical corporations, one cannot fail to grasp their role in the economy. Medieval towns were also, according to many scholars, important because they created modern liberties and democracy, as well as modern capitalism.

Pirenne defended the thesis that there was no continuity between the Carolingian and the late medieval town (for him the Carolingian period was the absolute economic nadir, particularly for urban and commercial life) and that west European towns had in the course of the eleventh century risen from nothing. This had been caused by the revival of international trade and the foundation, by international traders gathered from various corners, of agglomerations on sites which were geographically favourable (and not, for example, next to abbeys and castles and existing merely to provide monks and knights with commodities). This idea of towns as creations *ex nihilo* by rootless merchants has today been abandoned. Historians do not believe any more that all towns originated along one definite scheme: various circumstances caused urbanization, which cannot be classed in any one category. Some towns grew out of the manorial world, others originated as fortified boroughs, yet others as suppliers of large abbeys. Nor is it correct that eleventh-century towns had no roots in the past. More and more appear to have Carolingian or even classical antecedents, as was recently shown by Professor Verhulst for Ghent and Antwerp.[12] It is also clear that for his theory on the origin of towns Pirenne was too exclusively preoccupied with the north west of the Continent. He seems hardly to have heard of the English boroughs and of their well-documented history. The same applies to the towns of northern Spain, whereas his first contacts with Italian towns took place shortly before the First World War. This means that he generalized on too narrow a basis. If little is left of his theory, Pirenne's lasting merit was that he pioneered urban history in his country, broke out of the old purely juridical or institutional framework and, last but not least, secured for medieval Flemish towns a place of honour on the map of world history. He was, of course, not the first to comprehend their importance (the famous historian of Antiquity Barthold Georg Niebuhr drew Leopold August Warnkoenig's attention to the importance of Flemish urban history in 1823),[13] but I believe that no one else has described the role of those cities as strikingly as Pirenne or excited the imagination of the whole historical world as he did.

---

[12] A. Verhulst, 'Neue Ansichten über die Entstehung der flämischen Städte am Beispiel von Gent und Antwerpen', *Niederlande und Nordwestdeutschland: Studien zur Regional- und Stadtgeschichte F. Petri zum 80. Geburtstag*, ed. by W. Ehbrecht and H. Schilling, (Cologne and Vienna, 1983), pp. 1-17. See also A. Verhulst, 'An Aspect of Continuity between Antiquity and Middle Ages: The Origin of Flemish Cities', *Journal of Medieval History*, 3 (1977), pp. 175-206.

[13] G. Wild, *Leopold August Warnkönig, 1794-1866: Ein Rechtslehrer zwischen Naturrecht und Historischer Schule und ein Vertreter deutschen Geistes in Westeuropa* (Karlsruhe, 1961), p. 28.

The History of Belgium

The success of the *Histoire de Belgique*, loudly praised by scholars and those in authority, was, of course, to a large extent caused by its intrinsic quality. It was the work of a very gifted historian who had, by pointing out some major lines of development, given meaning to the chaotic history of the old principalities in question – the main line being their social and economic evolution. Here also Pirenne was the pioneer of serious historiography. One has only to compare his oeuvre with that of his predecessors, J.J. De Smet, Baron de Reiffenberg, H.G.P. Moke, J.B. David, Th. Juste, A.J. Namèche and Baron Kervyn de Lettenhove, who after Pirenne were quickly forgotten. Nevertheless, Pirenne's success, particularly with Belgian readers and the Belgian establishment, should also be viewed in connection with the political climate of the time, when the *âme belge* was receiving a good deal of attention. Pirenne did not use the expression himself, although he talked of a *civilisation belge*; it was Edmond Picard who had baptized the 'Belgian soul' in an article called 'L'âme belge' in the Paris *Revue encyclopédique* of 24 July 1897. Pirenne was a product and an exponent of the Belgian state of 1830, which can be described as liberal (provided with the most liberal constitution of the time), unitary (the constitution knew neither Flemings nor Walloons) and Walloon-dominated (because heavy industry was in Wallonia and French was the language of the state in the whole country). In that kingdom Pirenne felt at home. Thus he found it normal that Walloon scholars taught in French in Flanders, the Dutch-speaking part of Belgium. When in the university of Ghent this anomaly came to an end in 1930, it appeared that, having lived there for forty-four years, he knew insufficient Dutch to teach in that language; so he left his adoptive Alma Mater. Witnesses of his last seminar heard him say, about his leaving: 'C'est la loi, donc je m'y conforme.' They had no doubt that Pirenne meant that since he was incapable of teaching in Dutch, the introduction of that language put an end to his teaching in the university of Ghent.

Pirenne had no sympathy for Flemish demands. I have already mentioned that he was honorary president of the *Ligue nationale pour la liberté des langues*, an organization for the defence of French in Flanders; his son Jacques was known as a leader of demonstrations in favour of *Gand français* and the orchestrator, together with Viscount Terlinden, of the *Ligue nationale pour l'unité belge*, whose aim it was to protect the French-speakers in Flanders.[14] It would, however, be wrong to conclude from all this that Pirenne had no Flemish sympathies. On the contrary, his love of Flanders and Flemish cities is well known (and earned him Walloon criticism), but this

---

[14] H. Hasquin, *Historiographie et politique: essai sur l'histoire de Belgique et la Wallonie* (Charleroi, 1982), p. 68.

feeling did not go as far as sympathizing with the aims of the Flemish movement and its demand of the official use of Dutch in Flanders. If I recall these facts it is not to give good or bad marks to Pirenne's political attitude (he acted according to his own insight and was no doubt sincerely concerned with the national interest as he saw it), but to draw attention to a strange contradiction between one of his best-known historical pronouncements and his attitude as a citizen. He pointed out in a glowing passage that Belgium had always been a meeting-place of Germanic and Romanic culture and he clearly found it a positive point that in Belgian history neither of these cultures or cultural groups had attempted to dominate or oppress the other.[15] This was a correct appraisal as far as the old principalities are concerned. Although the central government often strengthened French influence, no attempts are known by the French-speaking population of the county of Flanders, the duchy of Brabant or the prince-bishopric of Liège to put their Dutch-speaking fellow-citizens under cultural pressure; nor did the Walloon provinces of the Austrian Netherlands try to force their language upon the Flemings. This is, however, exactly what happened for the first time (if one leaves the years of French invasion and annexation out of consideration) in the nineteenth-century kingdom of Belgium, which practically from the start imposed French as the only language of the state even on the Dutch-speaking areas, in spite of all the best historical traditions. It is remarkable that Pirenne did not understand this and that he deplored the linguistic laws which were intended to restore that equilibrium and the juridical equality of Romanic and Germanic culture and the balanced interplay which he had admired so much in earlier times. What could one expect from the much vaunted Romanic-Germanic encounter and mutual fertilization when one culture dominated the other and at most tolerated it in the role of Cinderella?

Pirenne, who had Hegelian sympathies,[16] thought that Belgium was the outcome of a secular and logical development, which had left nothing to chance. The idea that nineteenth-century Belgium was the excellent fruit of the march of the centuries was a miniature version of the widely-held belief that western civilization was itself the result and crowning achievement of world history: a teleological interpretation out of favour today. Pirenne's Belgium was, however, threatened by external dangers.

Most Belgians before the First World War were afraid of French annexation plans (which had been real enough in the days of Napoleon III and were implicit in various French pronouncements about Belgium as a temporary set up, doomed to return sooner or later to French rule, *inter alia*,

---

[15] H. Pirenne, *La formation de la nation belge: extraits et notice par Albert Counson* (Paris and Brussels, 1912), p. 19. Counson came from the same area as Pirenne and was his colleague in Ghent. He was a doctor of Romanic philology and started teaching Romanic literature there in 1907.

[16] See Ganshof's statement in *Biographie nationale*, 30 (1959), col. 720.

because of the 'natural frontiers' policy). Others in the late nineteenth century were more foresighted or better informed and feared Prussian militarism more.

There were internal dangers also, particularly the Flemish-Walloon divide and the strong regional feelings in these two parts of the country ('Il n'y a pas de Belges', as Jules Destrée put it in 1912). It is understandable that people who were worried about Belgian unity and considered the existing unitary system as indispensable for the continuation of the state hailed the publication of the *Histoire de Belgique*, because here a scholar of great authority revealed that the Belgian kingdom of 1830 was in reality an old nation and from the middle ages onwards Flemings and Walloons had worked together to produce a Belgian civilization.[17] For this thesis Pirenne needed a common characteristic that went deeper than the recent political unity. He was not the first to look for it. Some of his predecessors had found it in the Germanic character of the Belgian population and had claimed that the Walloons, in spite of their language, were of Germanic descent. This should not unduly surprise us, as the ethnic factor played a great role in nineteenth-century historical writing. The same attitude had already been adopted in the eighteenth century by Montesquieu, who claimed descent from free Germanic warriors for the French nobility, the common people descending from the subjected Gallo-Roman peasantry. In Belgium in the nineteenth century Kervyn de Lettenhove, author of a multi-volume *Histoire de Flandre* (1847-50), was one exponent of this form of ethnic interpretation. Count de Liedekerke went so far as to write, in 1867: 'Si les Wallons et les Flamands diffèrent par la langue, ils sont frères par le sang, car les uns comme les autres sont issus de la même race germanique'.[18] Others, such as Mgr. Namèche, considered the Catholic faith as the eternal cornerstone of Belgium's national existence. Pirenne rejected both the ethnic and the religious national principle and found the unifying element, as one might expect, in a social and economic factor: the importance of the towns. No one will deny the latter's role in Belgian history, but one ought not to forget that medieval urbanization was a phenomenon that transcended the Belgian frontiers and stretched over a great zone between Rhine and Seine.[19] Nor can anyone deny that the Low Countries also contained agrarian zones, where towns were not essential: Hainault had really only one town of importance, Valenciennes, and the principalities of Namur and Luxembourg had none.

How is the *Histoire de Belgique* viewed today? Criticism of what has been called Pirenne's belgicism started early. It came, as is well known, from

---

[17] B. Lyon, *Henri Pirenne*, p. 194.

[18] 'La nationalité belge', *Revue générale*, 15 (1867), p. 382, quoted by H. Hasquin, *Historiographie et politique*, p. 30.

[19] Professor Ganshof extended this zone to the Loire. See his classic *Étude sur le développement des villes entre Loire et Rhin au moyen âge* (Brussels, 1943).

Flemish quarters, but in Wallonia also Pirenne was very early on attacked on two counts. He was criticised because he identified Belgian history too much with the history of the medieval county of Flanders (Belgium a microcosm of Europe, Flanders a microcosm of Belgium) and underestimated the role of the Romanic and French-orientated part of the population. He was also reproached for anachronism, since he already discerned in medieval times an embryonic Belgium that was not there at all. The most authoritative voice in this camp was the famous Liège professor Maurice Wilmotte, who wrote in 1903: 'En mettant tout en oeuvre pour nous montrer dans l'histoire de ces siècles lointains les progrès successifs d'une nationalité en marche, l'auteur a été opportuniste avec bonheur: il a trop vu, à mon sens, la Belgique de demain, ou d'après demain, dans les Pays-Bas de la veille et surtout dans les Etats sans attaches fermes, sans cohésion durable de l'avant-veille.'[20] A recent author speaks of Pirenne's teleology and repeats the accusation of anachronism. Indeed the Brussels historian Hasquin wrote in 1982: 'Projeter dans le passé l'image d'une situation qui n'existait que depuis 1830 et, comme corollaire, prêter aux Belges d'autrefois les sentiments des Belges d'aujourd'hui c'était tomber dans un anachronisme incontestable.'[21]

The reproach is indeed justified that Pirenne saw a Belgian society already growing up in the middle ages, whereas in fact there was a vast zone in the north of the kingdom of France and the north west of the kingdom of Germany that escaped from the rule of these two monarchies and was divided into a number of autonomous principalities, dominated by feudal dynasties and their power games. The territories or at least their towns were, of course, sometimes driven towards each other, often by common economic interests, such as the safety of the great trade route from Bruges to Cologne, which was equally important for Flanders, Brabant and Liège. This did not prevent their going to war with each other and did not stop soldiers from Brabant, for example, taking part in the Battle of the Golden Spurs, not on the Flemish but on the French side. Anything was possible with this shapeless magma and it takes a Hegelian belief that what is had to be, to maintain that the Burgundian Netherlands were the normal or logical outcome of the feudal era. A permanent annexation of the Flemish fief by the French crown in 1300 – after several others – would have been a more logical result of history, and the resurrection of Flanders as an autonomous state in 1302 went against the normal pattern. Nor was it written in the stars that the duchy of Brabant would completely disappear from the German political firmament: Duke John III, for example, had a policy that was strongly involved with the Empire.

---

[20] *La Flandre libérale* (5 June 1903), quoted by H. Hasquin, *Historiographie et politique*, pp. 90-91.
[21] Ibid., p. 12.

The truth is that the Burgundian Netherlands have emerged, between France and Germany, as the fruit of a dynastic policy and not of the spontaneous desire for unification of the people of the Low Countries. This prefiguration, not of Belgium but of the Benelux countries, was torn apart in the sixteenth century. One could imagine that then at least a territory was constituted in which present-day Belgium can be recognized (particularly in the Austrian Netherlands after the amputations under Louis XIV). It is a fact that the inhabitants of the Austrian Netherlands called themselves Belgians and even founded the ephemeral 'Etats Belgiques unis'. Even then it is somewhat early to see present-day Belgium, as the prince-bishopric of Liège (about the size of one third of present-day Belgium), was an autonomous state that had nothing to do with the 'Belgian States'. Liège was foreign territory and until the mid nineteenth century Histories of Belgium were written leaving it out. It is typical that both the Austrian Netherlands and Liège knew a revolution in 1789, but their characters were entirely different, one being a conservative revolt against a progressive ruler, the other a progressive revolt against a conservative one. The only similarity is that both were suppressed, the one by Austrian and the other by Prussian troops. 'Belgians' and Liégeois were brought together for the first time when they were all annexed by the French republic and empire and they remained together under King William I (united with the Northern Netherlands), so that it was only in 1830 that they formed their own common state. The role of chance in all this has been very considerable: the link with Spain, for example, which became fatal for the unity of the Seventeen Provinces under Philip II, was the consequence of an unimaginable number of deaths which placed Philip the Fair, against all probability, on the Spanish throne.

There was nothing providential about the Seventeen Provinces, which a British historian called a few years ago 'this hotchpot of duchies, counties and lordships' with 'nothing natural or inevitable about them' and which 'owned their existence entirely to the energies of their rulers'.[22] Around the same time a Dutch historian explained, from a similar vantage point, how different it could all have been and concluded: 'A residue of teleology in us still possibly resists this sentiment, but with the disappearance of a historiography inspired by patriotism it will become ever clearer that the three little Benelux states in the northwestern corner of Europe in fact were unexpected and even unwanted children.'[23]

It is not because the kingdom of Belgium was only established in the nineteenth century that it is impermissible to write the history of the area and its inhabitants: Ganshof even published a little book called *La Belgique*

---

[22] A. Duke, 'From King and Country to King or Country? Loyalty and Treason in the Revolt of the Netherlands', *Transactions of the Royal Historical Society*, 5th series, 32 (1982), p. 113.

[23] P.N.M. Boy reviewing the new *Algemene geschiedenis der Nederlanden, Kleio*, 23 (1982), p. 33.

carolingienne (Brussels, 1958), which enquires what the situation in those areas was at the time of Charlemagne (when Pirenne himself would hardly have discerned Belgium).[24] The important thing is not to project this young Belgium back into periods when it did not exist and nobody had the foggiest idea that it would ever be created, which was the meaning of Leopold I's pronouncement in a letter to Jules van Praet in 1859: 'La Belgique n'a pas de nationalité et vu le caractère de ses habitants ne pourra jamais en avoir.'[25]

In recent times Belgian historiography has moved away from the Belgian framework, in Flanders as well as in Wallonia, with this difference, however, that the *Histoire de Wallonie* triumphs in Wallonia whereas in Flanders, besides the history of Flanders, it is the history of the whole of the Low Countries that is seen as the most 'intelligible field of study'.

Mohammed and Charlemagne

Until the drama of the Great War, the historian Henri Pirenne was the prisoner of his *Sitz im Leben*: north-west Europe, especially Belgium, and the two great neighbouring countries where he had studied and made friends. Although he travelled to Italy shortly before 1914, it was only during the World War that his vision was widened and he began really to think in European terms. His contacts with fellow-prisoners from the world of Greek-Russian culture focused his attention on the great historical significance of Byzantium, whereas before the war he used to say 'Byzance c'est la prolongation de l'Antiquité, il ne faut pas s'en occuper.'[26] At the same time as Byzantium the Arab world began to receive his attention, as it was the third 'daughter civilization' of Antiquity, together with Greek and Latin Christendom. That Antiquity was the civilization of the Mediterranean. Thus Pirenne became ever more interested in the question of how the classical Mediterranean world had become divided and had handed its

---

[24] The author warns against any anachronism that could be associated with the title of his book and writes in the introduction: 'Il est assez paradoxal de consacrer un volume à "La Belgique carolingienne", alors que ni la Belgique, ni aucune préfiguration de celle-ci n'ont existé au VIIIe et au IXe siècle. Nous croyons même que parmi les événements qui se sont produits à l'époque carolingienne, on n'en peut discerner aucun qui ait préparé, fût-ce de loin, la naissance des anciens Pays-Bas ou de la Belgique.'

[25] Quoted in H. Hasquin (ed.), *Histoire et historiens depuis 1830 en Belgique* (Brussels, 1981), p. 9. King Albert sent Pirenne a letter of thanks on the publication of vol. III of the *Histoire de Belgique*, calling the work 'cette éloquente affirmation de notre nationalité', B. Lyon, *Henri Pirenne*, p. 144.

[26] This is a quotation from a course on medieval history given in 1913-14, which the late Professor Ganshof used in a discussion in the Class of Letters of the Belgian Academy of Sciences on 9 Nov. 1974.

hegemony over to the Atlantic world.²⁷ More precisely he began to wonder what the role of the early middle ages had been in all this. Had Antiquity perished in the West at the time of the Germanic invasions or later? As is well known, Pirenne developed the thesis, publicly expounded for the first time shortly after the war in a conference at Lille in December 1922,²⁸ that after the Germanic invasions, during the Merovingian period, classical life continued in Gaul and relations with the East over the Mediterranean were carried on. It was the great Arab expansion of the seventh century which cut the east-west contact in that area and so caused the end of Antiquity and the real beginning of the middle ages. The Carolingian empire, cut off economically from its classical sources, became a land power with a closed manorial economy and feudal structure: without Mohammed there would have been no Charlemagne. This opinion went against the *communis opinio*. Whether one believed that the world of Antiquity perished by its internal weakness (whether through the fault of Christianity, as Gibbon thought, or because of a social and economic crisis, as Rostovtzeff believed), or was killed by a Germanic 'stab in the back', no one had thought of blaming the Arabs for the rise of a truly medieval society in Carolingian Europe. The 'Pirenne thesis' caused a sensation, but at present it is safe to state that this long drawn-out polemic has subsided and that the Pirenne thesis has failed to find general acceptance. This is not the occasion to discuss the innumerable points in Pirenne's position that were denied or refuted. A few examples will suffice. Far from being an economic nadir the Carolingian period saw an important revival, *inter alia*, of international trade, mainly around the North Sea and via Scandinavia with the East, nor did the Arab expansion put an end to trade in the Mediterranean. Pirenne also attached too much weight to the superficial appearances of classical culture in the Merovingian world: it was not because the illiterate Clovis wore imperial purple and received the (minor) title of *consul* from the emperor in Constantinople that he became a classical ruler and his government the continuation of the Roman empire. Rather than quoting all the aspects of this controversy, which raged for decades,²⁹ I will simply refer to the pronouncement of Pirenne's biographer and admirer, Professor Bryce Lyon, who recently wrote: 'It is enough to

---

²⁷ Dhondt's 1966 attempt to trace the origin of the theme of *Mahomet et Charlemagne* to the years before the First World War was unsuccessful. See B. Lyon, 'Reply to Jan Dhondt's Critique', p. 9; on this point Lyon was followed by W. Blockmans, *Hommes et pouvoirs: les principales études de Jan Dhondt sur l'histoire du 19e et du 20e siècle* (Ghent, 1976), p. 57. In an article entitled 'Mandarijnenhulde en wetenschapsgeschiedenis' published in the *Handelingen der maatschappij voor geschiedenis en oudheidkunde te Gent*, n.s. 29 (1975), pp. 27-38, Blockmans had in general followed Dhondt rather than Lyon.

²⁸ J. Dhondt, *Henri Pirenne*, p. 107. The first publication was an article in the *Revue belge de philologie et d'histoire* of the same year.

²⁹ As general surveys and presentations of the problem the following two books will be found most useful: A.F. Havighurst, *The Pirenne Thesis: Analysis, Criticism and Revision* (Lexington, MA, 1969) and B. Lyon, *The Origins of the Middle Ages: Pirenne's Challenge to Gibbon* (New York, 1972). The older discussion in C. Verlinden, *Henri Pirenne*, pp. 95-100 remains very valuable.

note that Pirenne had fewer defenders than opponents and that most medievalists would agree that there is no longer any profit in the continuation of the debate. Pirenne's book has had its day.' Lyon goes on to say that Roman continuity had not lasted until the advent of the Arabs: 'The decisive change came in the sixth century. Charlemagne's reign coincided with a renewal of long-distance trade in Carolingian lands and Scandinavia, a conclusion quite contrary to Pirenne's view.'[30]

The intriguing question remains how a learned medievalist like Pirenne could go so wrong. One forms the impression that he suddenly conceived a new vision on a very complex and wide-ranging historical process and that he stuck to that intuition, even when the facts contradicted him. Why attribute this important role to Islam? Was it in order to reduce the role of the Germanic invaders? Did Pirenne react against certain German historians who praised the contribution of the young Germanic nations in the decadent world of late Antiquity? One can only guess, as clear evidence is, as far as I know, not available on this point. Nevertheless, I believe that there is one clear indication in that sense, in the speech which Pirenne gave as rector of the university at the solemn inauguration of the academic year 1921-22 in Ghent. The text deserves closer examination, since I am not aware that anyone has drawn attention to it in the context that occupies us here. The title of Pirenne's address was *Ce que nous devons désapprendre de l'Allemagne*. Two elements in it are relevant to our present problem. To begin with (and I believe this to be very striking), Pirenne sketches a contrast between the Germans who invaded the Roman empire in the west and the Arabs in the east. The latter are credited with an enthusiasm and a religious fervour which allowed them to cause a 'radical transformation' in the conquered areas. In sharp contrast the Germans are depicted as devoid of all culture and living in pure 'barbarism': from their *âme enfantine* no cultural contribution could be expected. Medieval civilization therefore consisted exclusively of elements from the Romanic world, which was the continuation of (Latin) Antiquity, and from Christianity. Pirenne attacked the German medievalists (Waitz being expressly named) who had thought differently and had attributed to the Germanic invaders an original contribution in the field of institutions and the economy. Of this there was, according to Pirenne, no question when it was all too obvious that those Germans were mere barbarians, or to put it in his own words: 'Ce qui les caractérise essentiellement c'est qu'ils sont des barbares, des barbares analogues à ceux que l'on observe à toutes les époques et sous les climats les plus divers, et que leurs institutions tant vantées ne sont simplement que ce que l'on a si bien appelé les institutions internationales de la barbarie.' Those barbarians, he goes on, had the physical strength to topple the Roman state, but 'ils n'avaient ni

---

[30] Reviewing R. Hodges and D. Whitehouse, *Mohammed, Charlemagne and the Origins of Europe* (Ithaca, NY, 1983), *Speculum*, 60 (1985), p. 682. See in the same sense F.L. Ganshof in *Biographie Nationale*, 30 (1959), col. 710.

assez de vigueur morale, ni assez de vigueur intellectuelle pour élever sur ses ruines une civilisation nouvelle'. And Pirenne concludes the passage with the words: 'Mais ce qui reste vrai, c'est que l'époque des invasions n'a point germanisé l'Europe occidentale: elle l'a seulement barbarisée – et ce n'est pas la même chose. Dès que l'on écarte les broussailles de cette barbarie on retrouve, supportant toute la civilisation médiévale, les substructions romaines et chrétiennes.'[31]

No Germanic culture, no Germanic cultural contribution, only barbarism. What had happened to the time, just before the World War, when Pirenne described Belgium's originality as the meeting of Romanic and Germanic culture? Germanic culture was unmasked: it was barbarism. What did the listeners on that 18 October 1921 make of it? Was Belgium the meeting place of Romanic culture and Germanic un-culture, Germanic barbarism? One can understand the feelings of Pirenne, who shortly before had been a prisoner in Germany and burnt the German gods he had adored before 1914, but the change is so striking that it casts doubts on the scientific grounds for Pirenne's thesis. The only possibility I see to save something of the 'Pirenne thesis' is, I believe, the following. It is only through the rise of Islam as a great Mediterranean power that the division of the inheritance of Antiquity had been concluded. It is from then onwards that the classical world belonged definitely to the past and was taken over by her three 'daughter civilizations' – Byzantium, the West and Islam – and a new power equilibrium was created which dominated the world until the fall of Constantinople.

We have seen that none of Pirenne's three great themes is accepted by present-day medievalists. Nevertheless, his research has been of lasting value. Much in his work on urban history, where he was a great forerunner, remains valuable. The *Histoire de Belgique* repays attentive reading and is a monument of the historiography of the time. The 'Pirenne thesis' on Mohammed and Charlemagne, the most daring of the three constructions, is the one that in the judgment of learned opinion has suffered most damage. The urban theory fitted in with the period: the air was full of theses on the origin of medieval towns and, as a child of his time, Pirenne added one of his own, which followed from his interpretation of history, which was social and economic rather than legal and institutional. His theory doubtlessly enriched historical studies. In writing the history of Belgium Pirenne was also very much a child of his time (national history was very popular and the young kingdom of Belgium seemed to deserve a scholarly history of its own, written by an author of European stature), but what was wrong with that? Can an historian be expected to write history from a space satellite in

---

[31] *Université de Gand: ouverture solennelle des cours et remise du rectorat 18 octobre 1921. Discours de M. le Recteur H. Pirenne*: 'Ce que nous devons désapprendre de l'Allemagne', (Ghent, 1922), pp. 12-14.

order to distance himself sufficiently from his subject? This is still a pipe dream. On 'Mohammed and Charlemagne' the influence of the *Zeitgeist* is less obvious. Although several authors were at the time engaged on themes of decline in general and the decline of Antiquity in particular, the great role attributed to the Arabs is an oddity and hard to explain. The fact remains that *Mahomet et Charlemagne* has been the starting point of one of the longest and most captivating debates in modern historiography, so that here also Pirenne's *felix culpa* has contributed to medieval research, just as three centuries ago the exaggerated criticism of the Bollandist Daniel van Papenbroeck led to the celebrated *De re diplomatica* of the Maurist Jean Mabillon.

14

F.L. Ganshof

The death, in Brussels, of François L. Ganshof (14 March 1895-26 July 1980), at the age of eighty-five, caused the world of learning the loss of a great scholar, a great professor and a great academician. Ganshof was a world-famous medievalist who devoted his attention mainly to law and institutions, for which his degrees in Law and in History had specially prepared him. As such he takes his place in the tradition of the great nineteenth-century students of *Staats- und Rechtsgeschichte*, Leopold August Warnkoenig, Georg Waitz, William Stubbs, Fustel de Coulanges, Frederic William Maitland and Heinrich Brunner.

The devotion – even passion – with which many generations of savants have studied the medieval origin and the first development of modern law and institutions was nourished by their faith in the vital importance of law in general and public law in particular. Nineteenth-century belief in the *Rechtsstaat* as an instrument of prosperity and human development was an important motor of political life and assured the history of politics and law of a key position. The medieval origin of the modern state and modern liberties, the role of feudalism and urban autonomy, the organization of the estates, the significance of the medieval legislator and the judiciary for the rise of the rule of law – these were the main themes to receive the historians' attention.

Ganshof's scholarly output, stretching over sixty years, is so impressive both by its quality and its quantity that I will unfortunately have to limit myself to a brief and inadequate survey, in which only his important works can be mentioned. The books on the institutions and the law of the middle ages constitute the most impressive group. This twofold *Leitmotif* can already be perceived in his *Étude sur les ministeriales en Flandre et en Lotharingie* of 1926, whose introduction opens with the words: 'L'histoire constitutionelle fait connaître l'existence au moyen âge ... d'une classe d'hommes dont la situation sociale élevée ne coïncidait pas avec la condition juridique très inférieure: les *Ministeriales*'; the book dealt with aspects of public law and the law of persons, clarifying the problem and referring to an abundant collection of primary sources. This was followed in 1928 by the *Recherches sur les tribunaux de châtellenie en Flandre avant le milieu du XIIIe siècle*, in which the author expressed the hope that he might one day devote a comprehensive study to the judicial organization of the county, and stressed the importance of the subject for 'the general history of institutions'. In 1944 Ganshof published his *Qu'est-ce que la féodalité?* in which he consciously limited his attention to a legal analysis of feudalism; the book proved indispensable from the start, and was translated into several languages. The same can be said of his book *Wat waren de capitularia?*, published in 1955. The author presented it in his Preface as 'a legal-historical monograph on a group of juridical sources, considered as such'. In 1957 Ganshof published, in a collective work directed by F. Lot and R. Fawtier, the *Histoire des institutions françaises au moyen âge*, a comprehensive survey of the institutions of the medieval county of Flanders, which may be considered an unsurpassed *status quaestionis* to this day. In 1968 and 1971 two volumes were published in English with his collected essays on the Carolingian monarchy in general and the institutions in particular, tending, in the author's words, to 'clarify the institutional, legal and ecclesiastical structure of the *Regnum Francorum* under Charlemagne'. They were entitled *Frankish Institutions under Charlemagne* and *The Carolingians and the Frankish Monarchy*.

The fact that Ganshof had a certain predilection for legal history in no way implied a lack of appreciation for its social or spiritual dimensions. If anyone is in doubt on this point, he should read his review, free with warm praise, of Marc Bloch's *Société féodale* (it should be noted that this real eulogy of the work of a Jewish scholar was published in Brussels in 1941, under Nazi occupation) and of L. Genicot's *Lignes de faîte du moyen âge*.[1] Nevertheless, Ganshof believed that it was legitimate and necessary to include the juridical aspect in the study of civilization and to study it with great care and attention to exact detail.

That the great medievalist was fully aware that the study of the past should be comprehensive, and that the institutional development should be placed in a broad social context, appears from his research in the fields of historical geography and urban[2] and agrarian history.[3]

It is understandable that a scholar who studied so many aspects of

---

[1] Published in *Revue belge de philologie et d'histoire*, 20 (1941), pp. 183-93, and 30 (1952), pp. 947-52. The review of Genicot's book ends with the words: 'En le lisant, nous avons évoqué une autre synthèse, une oeuvre très différente de caractère et d'inspiration: *La société féodale* du regretté Marc Bloch. *Les lignes de faîte du moyen âge* ont, à notre sentiment, pour la compréhension des aspects spirituels de la civilisation médiévale, une importance analogue à celle qu'a *La société féodale* pour la compréhension de ses aspects sociaux. C'est dire l'admiration que ce livre nous inspire.'

[2] I refer to his book *Over stadsontwikkeling tusschen Loire en Rijn gedurende de middeleeuwen*, which was published in 1941.

[3] See his collaboration in the *Cambridge Economic History*, i (Cambridge, 1942), and his *Polyptyque de l'abbaye de Saint-Bertin (844-859): édition critique et commentaire* (1975) [in collaboration with F. Godding-Ganshof and A. De Smet].

medieval life and taught at the university a course on Society and Institutions of the Middle Ages, was tempted to write on the general history of that period. This he did on the Flemish, the Belgian, and the European level – three spheres of interest to which we will return later. I refer to his *La Flandre sous les premiers comtes* of 1943 (Dutch version 1944) and his collaboration on Van Roosbroek's pre-war *Geschiedenis van Vlaanderen*. This was followed in 1958 by *La Belgique carolingienne* and his collaboration on the post-war *Algemene Geschiedenis der Nederlanden*. Finally, in 1953, he published the classic synthesis *Le moyen âge*, in P. Renouvin's *Histoire des relations internationales*. Ganshof also lent his collaboration to vast world-histories, starting in 1934 with Gustave Glotz's *Histoire générale*, and followed by *De Pelgrimstocht der Mensheid* and the *Propylaën-Weltgeschichte*. He also compiled bibliographical reference-works for his fellow-scholars, in Pierre Wigny's *Bibliothèque de l'honnête homme* and John Gilissen's *Introduction bibliographique à l'histoire du droit et à l'ethnologie juridique*.

Although these publications could easily have filled several scholars' lives, Ganshof conceived even greater plans. These works, alas, never reached the stage of the printed book, and the vast efforts he invested in them have not led to the envisaged goal. I refer to the stencilled notes for his courses called *Encylopedie van de Geschiedenis*, i, *Middeleeuwen*[4] (Encyclopedia of History, i, The Middle Ages); *Geschiedkundige inleiding tot het burgerlijk recht* (Historical Introduction to the Civil Law); and *De instellingen van de middeleeuwen* (Institutions of the Middle Ages). This last, very detailed and elaborate text was close to being published as a book, without ever reaching that final stage. Another great loss was the fact that Ganshof's fundamental monograph on Charlemagne, eagerly awaited by the learned community and prepared in countless studies on points of detail, has never seen the light of day. Some of those *Vorarbeiten* had themselves reached the stage of a book. The work on the capitularies was one of them, as we read in the preface: 'The history of Charlemagne, especially as lawgiver, has caused us to subject the capitularies to a separate historical enquiry.' It is ironical that the book opens with a quotation from the Oxford scholar H.E. Salter: 'Those who are long past middle age should print their material, if it can be of use to others, and not wait to make it more perfect.' That Ganshof's life's work on Charlemagne was never written is an irreparable loss, for it may be doubted whether there will ever again be a savant who can dominate so profoundly so many data and aspects of that crucial reign as Ganshof.

Ganshof hardly ever expressed his views on methodological questions, but from his books and articles one can infer that his aim as a historian was to achieve the highest possible degree of certainty. In a positive sense this

---

[4] (Ghent, 1951, rev. version 1955). Having been entrusted with the teaching, in Ganshof's stead, of the Encyclopedia of the Middle Ages from 1955 onwards, I published in 1962 a textbook under that title, with Ganshof's collaboration and making abundant use of his material.

meant the exact rendering of the facts, in close contact with the source material. The reader may find an example of this closeness to the texts in Ganshof's paper, read on 17 March 1962, on the international relations in the kingdom of the Franks under the Carolingians, when he said: 'What I study is a complex of facts; I have left out the intellectual currents related to my theme, being content with referring to the relevant bibliography.' The following quotation from Fustel de Coulanges, in Ganshof's contribution to *Karl der Grosse*, i, *Persönlichkeit und Geschichte* (1965), is also revealing: 'Cette question, comme toutes celles que renferme encore l'histoire, ne pouvait se résoudre que par la lecture directe des documents et l'observation attentive des faits.' I also remember in this connection an incident with the late legal historian and professor in the university of Paris, J.F. Lemarignier, who during some conference formulated various hypotheses and invariably met with Ganshof's obstinate reply, 'Il n'y a pas de textes'. In a negative sense this attitude was based on suspicion of imagination and distrust of the speculative, philosophical or sociological approach. Ganshof feared that it might seduce the historian from his proper task, the description and analysis of the phenomena of the past. Here again his motto was a pronouncement by Fustel de Coulanges, quoted among Ganshof's notes: 'Il y a une histoire, il y a une philosophie, il n'y a pas de philosophie de l'histoire.' The American medievalist Bryce Lyon has seen it clearly, where he writes: 'Ganshof seldom speculates or theorizes . . . for each observation and conclusion Professor Ganshof cites the evidence', and he places him in the 'rigorous school of history' of Ranke, Waitz, Monod and Giry, in contrast with the 'various intellectual historians with elaborate theories on Charlemagne and his work', such as Inana-Sternegg, Dopsch, Fichtenau, Lord Bryce and Dawson, Marc Bloch and Huizinga.[5] Sir Frank Stenton also presented Ganshof's work correctly when he spoke of his 'breadth of view, wealth of learning and success of judgment . . . firmly based on recorded facts, not the exposition of a theory, but a synthesis of evidence',[6] and so did the orator, at Ganshof's proclamation as honorary doctor in Cambridge, in elegant Latin: 'maximo autem impetu et ardore, sed accurate etiam et religiose, radicibus tenus scrutatur veritatem'.[7] In private correspondence Ganshof mentioned his being 'little gifted for philosophy'[8] and his limited interest 'in philosophy

---

[5] F.L. Ganshof, *Frankish Institutions under Charlemagne*, transl. by B. and M. Lyon, (Providence, RI, 1968), pp. x and xi. There are no Ganshof articles dealing with methodology proper, see the *Bibliographie des travaux historiques de François L. Ganshof* (Wetteren, 1946), p. 8, where under the heading *La méthode historique*, we find some brief review-articles on the technique of editing texts.

[6] Foreword to *Feudalism*, the English translation of *Qu'est-ce que la féodalité?* (London, 1952).

[7] *University of Cambridge: Speeches of the Orator at the Presentation of the Recipients of Honorary Degrees to the Chancellor* (Cambridge, 1962). It is striking that L. Genicot also used the word 'religious' for Ganshof's respect for the historic text as the basis of truth where, writing about the edition of the polyptych of Saint-Bertin, he says that the Ghent medievalist 'a toujours eu la religion du texte', *Revue d'histoire écclésiastique*, 71 (1976), p. 69.

[8] In a letter to me of 15 Sept. 1971.

and even the philosophy of history'[9] – books on the philosophy of history he gave away to anyone who was interested in them. On the subject of sociology he was, in private conversation, very guarded: he saw it as a danger for historiography, and he talked of historians who, in his judgment, had deviated from the straight and narrow path under the impact of sociological theorizing. This love of exact description implied that Ganshof the historian felt obliged to refrain from value judgments. 'Ce n'est pas à l'histoire, croyons-nous, qu'il appartient de juger', as he put it in his review of de Moreau's *Histoire de l'église en Belgique*.[10] In his *In Memoriam Ferdinand Lot* he sounds a critical note, where he mentions that his Parisian teacher believed that 'distinguer le bien du mal, séparer le faux du vrai, est le premier devoir de l'historien', and adds: 'Il est permis de penser différemment'.[11] If one insists on finding an epithet for Ganshof's method and conception, one could speak of 'positivism', but (to quote Professor Craeybeckx) as a 'positivisme de métier' rather than 'une adhésion voulue aux théories étranges et aberrantes de Comte'.[12] One might also place him among the 'matter-of-fact historians' who (to quote a British scholar) 'look to the particular and stress the uniqueness of each situation and set of events'.[13]

The historical period Ganshof studied with predilection went from the Carolingian era to the thirteenth century. He found the *Quellenlage* ideal: the sources were sufficient to allow a solid historical construction, but so limited as to allow the researcher to comprehend and analyse them in a satisfactory manner. The problems Ganshof worked on were adapted to that situation. He posed questions which could be answered with reasonable certainty and precision; he shied away from the more speculative questions that went beyond that level: what made him famous was the exact formulation of the problems and the profound and exact interpretation of the texts. Ganshof, as we all do, owed much to his teachers and predecessors, particularly Henri Pirenne, whom he has praised repeatedly. This did not prevent him chosing his own path (he, and not Pirenne, was the founder of the legal and institutional strand in the Ghent school) and being critical of

---

[9] Letter to me of 14 Dec. 1974. In a letter of 13 Jan. 1968 he talked of 'the dangers of the history of ideas which is carried too far, too much removed from reality'; in a post-card of 15 Aug. 1965 he repeated his 'conviction that it is more important to write about history than the theory of history'.

[10] *Revue belge de philologie et d'histoire* 20 (1941), p. 729.

[11] Ibid., 30 (1952), p. 1279, n. 2. In Ganshof's 'Monarchie franque et monarques francs: A propos d'un livre récent', *Helinium*, 5 (1965), p. 56, we read: 'Notre rôle à nous, historiens modernes, est non de juger, mais de comprendre', and in his obituary notice on the legal historian from Paris, Olivier-Martin, he counts himself among those 'qui visent – sans toujours y parvenir – à l'objectivité absolue, à l'impassibilité', *Revue belge de philologie et d'histoire*, 30 (1952), p. 1286 and n. 3.

[12] In a review of E. Coornaert, 'Destins de Clio en France depuis 1800', *Revue belge de philologie et d'histoire*, 58 (1980), p. 235.

[13] H.R. Loyn, *The Vikings in Britain* (London, 1977), p. 19.

certain major constructions of his teacher, such as the 'Pirenne thesis' (as one can read in the posthumous edition of *Mahomet et Charlemagne*).

Libros scribere and *alumnos docere* were the twin aspects of Ganshof's life's work. He was a very devoted 'man of the university'. During his very long career in Ghent he taught numerous and diverse courses,[14] among which the General History of the Middle Ages (called officially: 'Society and Institutions of the Middle Ages') which he gave, after C.P. Serrure (1835-71), P.J. Wouters (1871-86) and H. Pirenne (1886-1930), from 1930 till his retirement in 1961. He educated numerous medievalists and was promoter of dissertations on the rise of the territorial principalities in France, the political history of France in the eleventh and Flanders in the thirteenth century, comital and ecclesiastical landowners, judicial organization, criminal law, military organization in Flanders from the eleventh to the fourteenth century, and English law in the eleventh and twelfth centuries.[15] Ganshof carefully followed the progress of all his students and – without any form of paternalism – made every possible effort to help them in their scholarly careers. That their very different political or ideological orientations were irrelevant in this context went without saying: he abhorred any trace of discrimination or favouritism and measured everyone with the same yardstick of talent and diligence. As a 'man of the university' Ganshof played an important role in the life of his Alma Mater. This he did not so much by sitting on numerous committees and councils (he was Dean of the Faculty of Letters in 1937-38), but by moral authority and detailed knowledge of the problems involved: his suggestions and proposals were often followed by the authorities. This was particularly true whenever delicate questions arose in the council of the Faculty of Letters, where he would often, at the decisive moment, produce a draft of a letter or resolution, which he had prepared the day before and which the meeting was happy and relieved to accept. In the Academic Council of the university also his moral authority was outstanding, and his advice was an important factor in

---

[14] Ganshof had started his studies in Ghent in 1913 and became doctor in Philosophy and Letters (1921) and in Law (1922). He was appointed lecturer (*chargé de cours*) in 1923 for courses on Encyclopedia of the Histtory of the Middle Ages and on Institutions of the Middle Ages. He afterwards also taught the Seminar on Medieval History (1924); Historical Criticism (Middle Ages) (1925); Political History of the Middle Ages (1927); Society and Institutions of the Middle Ages (1930); Legal History (1933-1935); Historical Introduction to the Civil Law (1955); General History of the Byzantine and Slav World (Byzantine period) (1958); Fundamental Study of the Political, Social and Cultural History of the Byzantine and Slav World (Byzantine period) (1958); and Art and Culture of the Byzantine and Slav World (1958).

[15] See the list, until 1951, in *Zestig jaren onderwijs en wetenschap aan de faculteit van de wijsbegeerte en letteren der Rijksuniversiteit Gent* (Bruges, 1952) (Werken Fac. Wijsb. en Lett., 114), pp. 51-54. J. Dhondt's book on *Études sur al naissance des principautés territoriales en France* (Bruges, 1948) (102) was not formally published as a thesis, but had been started and written in that perspective and with Ganshof as supervisor.

university politics: his tenure belonged to a period when higher authorities still listened to a certain extent to the voice of the professorial body.

Ganshof was also a 'man of the academy'. He was among the earliest members of the Belgian Royal Academy, and was very active in the Class of Letters. He was also a member of foreign academies – in Paris, Amsterdam, Berlin, Modena, London, Boston, Vienna, Spoleto and Munich – and of numerous scholarly commissions and committees 'quae enumerare fastidium generaret'. I might suffice here with mentioning two that were particularly dear to him, the Royal Commission for the Publication of the Old Laws and Ordinances of Belgium, which he chaired for many years, and the Zentral-direktion of the *Monumenta Germaniae Historica*.

Some scholars love making grandiose plans and launching collective enterprises; others prefer to put their hands to the plough, at the more limited level of individual research. Although Ganshof clearly belonged to the latter category, he sometimes made suggestions for great collective enterprises. I would like to mention here particularly his proposal, made with Professor Strubbe and still valid, to 'prepare and publish a historical dictionary of Dutch legal language'.[16] So far nothing has been realized of the excellent plan then outlined, but it is to be hoped that one day a common initiative of Belgian and Dutch academies and learned societies will fill this void, as such a dictionary would be an essential element for the study of the law of the historic Netherlands.

Ganshof's talent and devotion to research were duly recognized, as appears from the constant flow of distinctions that came his way – without ever going to his head: on the contrary, if ever he mentioned them, it was in connection with some amusing incident or detail. Only the most important can be mentioned here: the Francqui-Prize of 1945 (awarded in 1946) and no less than thirteen honorary degrees in France and Great Britain,[17] the *annus mirabilis* of 1953 alone yielding three, Paris, Lille and Strasbourg. In Germany he received the order 'pour le Mérite'.

Ganshof was not only a savant who taught and wrote, he was also a human being, rooted in his natural surroundings. To what extent personal life is relevant to the appreciation of the oeuvre of artists and scientists is a question to which we would not like to hazard an answer. Ganshof was something else than a first-rate brain that produced regularly and as a matter of course excellent studies, a monument which was with equal regularity and also as a matter of course the object of praise from various

---

[16] *Mededelingen van de Koninklijke Vlaamse Academie der Wetenschappen, Klasse der Letteren*, iii, 3 (1941).

[17] There were ten honorary degrees in France: Algiers (at the time on French territory), Bordeaux, Dijon, Grenoble, Montpellier, Paris, Poitiers, Rennes, Lille and Strasbourg; and three in Great Britain: Cambridge, Glasgow and London. Obituary notices in part of the Belgian press talked of an honorary degree at Berkeley, but this must have been based on a misunderstanding.

corners: he was a fellow human being, a 'brother'. And whereas the majority of the savants only live on through their books and articles, those who knew him retain the memory of his impressive and forceful personality forever in their minds and hearts. Some of them will especially remember his energy, others his emotional nature, which made him wary of public tributes, for fear that 'his cup would run over'. In Ghent, on 11 December 1962, he omitted a passage from a public address, because he feared that his emotion would get the better of him.[18] And on 16 February 1974 he typically wrote that he would not speak at the presentation of Professor Lyon's biography of Pirenne for fear of being overpowered by emotion. Ganshof could react impulsively to stupidity or injustice and would speak harshly of certain top officials who were inspired by political or ideological favouritism rather than regard for qualifications when dealing with appointments. His powerful will could occasionally turn into stubbornness, which reminded his friends of the legendary 'Rocher von Bronze'. They occasionally shook their heads when they heard that he had sent a letter of protest to the Royal Library because its gates had opened one minute late on a certain Sunday morning or that he had protested to the Ministry of Transport because the train that took him from Brussels to Ghent had been two minutes late.

To my mind Ganshof's fundamental quality, from which the others radiated like the spokes of a wheel, the main character of his way of life, was his seriousness, the *gravitas* which the Romans looked for in their magistrates and medieval people in their bishops.

I am thinking of his metaphysical earnestness. The young man who, after deep and even anxious thought, converted to Protestantism from the traditional Catholicism of his time and environment, and remained for the rest of his life a faithful and active member of his denomination – a member of the governing body of his congregation and a supporter of the Faculté de Théologie Protestante in Brussels – clearly was somebody who reflected seriously and deeply on the great questions of life and death. The way in which he defended his point of view alone, independently and on principle, and stuck to it – reminded one, even outside the religious sphere, of the Protestant attitude of the believer who stands 'unmittelbar zu Gott', and of the individual who says: 'Hier stehe ich, ich kann nicht anders'.

There was equally his professional seriousness. I was deeply shocked when he wrote to me, in the early fifties, that he had destroyed the complete manuscript of the first version of his aforementioned contribution to the *Institutions seigneuriales*: upon rereading it, he had found it unsatisfactory and had decided to start writing it all over again. It is equally typical that the English version of his textbook on the 'Institutions of the Middle Ages', about which negotiations were carried on with a publisher in Oxford and

---

[18] He referred to a paragraph about Pirenne mourning at the grave of his pupil G. Des Marez; the passage omitted from the spoken text was printed in the form of a footnote (*De Brug*, vii, Ghent, Jan.-March 1963, p. 25).

through the mediation of a celebrated English medievalist, failed finally to be authorized by Ganshof, because he felt after all that the text was not yet ripe for publication. Even when dealing with subjects with which he had been familiar for a long time, he went about his work with the greatest care. Thus he wrote to me on 15 November 1964 concerning his contributions for the *Karl der Grosse* volumes of Beumann: 'The task was not easy because I *again* [Ganshof's underlining] checked *everything* [Ganshof's underlining] directly in the source material, without taking account of theories or systems.' This same seriousness prevented him, when talking of the 'Ghent School of History', from boasting in the least of that school, let alone his own role in it; this he left to other 'schools', whose ability to blow their own trumpet occasionally led him to critical remarks in private. He pushed his aversion to anything resembling the cult of personality so far as to refuse the publication of a Festschrift in his honour, or even of a collection of his articles, which his friends and pupils would gladly have organized as a homage upon his retirement.[19] The same seriousness of mind caused him carefully to mention the slightest collaboration, even from students, in his publications, and warmly to thank the persons concerned; if one had contributed in a somewhat larger way, one was quickly promoted to the rank of co-author.[20]

There also was the seriousness which allowed him, with the unfailing assistance of a devoted wife, to educate a large family. There finally was the social earnestness with which Ganshof carried out his duties towards society as loyally and well as he could. Just as medieval man was included in the ever-widening circles of family, feudal companionship, county, kingdom and church, so Ganshof lived within three natural communities, three concentric circles – Flemish, Belgian and European – which did not interfere or hinder but effortlessly included each other. Ganshof was born, the eldest of three sons, in the nineteenth-century bourgeoisie of Bruges – his father was a barrister and his grandfather on father's side was an international timber merchant – and was educated in French: he could have been a 'geographical Fleming', without any feeling for the aspirations of the Flemish movement. That this did not happen was because of his understanding of the just cause of Flemish emancipation and his love of Flanders and its culture. Thus we read in the introduction to his *Vlaanderen onder de eerste graven*: 'If we have dedicated this small book to the memory of Mr.

---

[19] However, his fellows on the Editorial Committee of *The Legal History Review* dedicated, without his previous knowledge, a number of articles to him in fasc. 3 of vol. 31 (1963). He also authorized the publication of the aforementioned collections of 1968 and 1971, containing reprints or English translations of articles on Carolingian institutions, but not by way of homage.

[20] He, for example, insisted that his name as collaborator on my *Kurze Quellenkunde* be printed in smaller letters. He found this important enough to devote a letter to it, dated 9 Feb. 1964, from San Antonio, CA, where he was living for a few months, when he was attached to the Berkeley Campus of the University of California.

August Van der Meersch [Ganshof's grandfather on mother's side], during his lifetime a barrister at Bruges, it was because he was the first to introduce his grandson to the history of his people. At the same time as the love of the language and culture of Flanders, he taught him to respect the Flemish past.' Ganshof was a life-long loyal member of the Willemsfonds (a Flemish cultural organization of liberal inspiration).[21] He made an important contribution to the change from French to Dutch in the university of Ghent (from 1930 onwards), helping to guarantee it an honourable and even prestigious place in the European firmament, in spite of financial constraint and falling numbers of students. An insult to any Flemish community was an insult to him, and he left no one in any doubt on this point, even though it was not in his line to issue strident declarations to the press or to sign collective protest motions. When a well-known periodical, published in Brussels, deemed it necessary to eliminate Dutch, the language of the majority of the Belgians, from its title in one issue after the Second World War, Ganshof, who had been its secretary since 1925 and member of its *comité directeur*, reacted to this wounding decision by resigning from the said *comité* in 1946, and for good. And when in 1967 a British author of historical works deemed it necessary to attack in a British weekly paper, under cover of anonymity, the Dutch-speaking Belgian historians – and particularly those from Ghent – because they dared 'out of a spirit of narrow fanaticism' to publish part of their scholarly work in their own language instead of French, Ganshof sharply rebuked him.[22] Just as loyally and unproblematically as he felt himself a Fleming, Ganshof felt himself a Belgian. He served in the army in two World Wars. In the aforementioned introduction to *Vlaanderen onder de eerste graven* he put it, in 1943, as follows: 'This little book was written at the kind invitation of Suzanne Charlier-Tassier, who directs the series *Notre passé*. It seemed impossible to us not to accede to her request since it is meant as a service to Belgium . . .'[23] In the same spirit of respect for national unity and for the equal status of the two national languages in the national capital, he ordained that two Protestant clergymen should conduct his funeral service, one in Dutch and the other in French. His Flemish and Belgian *enracinement* was quite naturally comprehended and taken up by his European sentiment. Nothing European was strange to him, and his admiration for Charlemagne, the first west-European figure of world significance, must have had something to do with it. Ganshof had a perfect knowledge of four living European languages and, from childhood, had travelled extensively, building up a European circle of friends and participating in numerous

---

[21] For the pro-Flemish activity of the aforementioned August van der Meersch, (1845-1912) relating to the Willemsfonds in Bruges see P. Lefevre, 'Le mouvement libéral flamand à Bruges (1872-1940)', *Revue belge de philologie et d'histoire*, 58 (1980), p. 384, n. 1.

[22] In an unpublished letter to the director of the incriminated weekly, to which I hope to devote a note in another context.

[23] The book appeared in 1944, the introduction was dated 14 Sept. 1943.

political developments on the old Continent. I refer, *inter alia*, to his participation in the Conference of Paris and the ensuing signature of the Treaty of Versailles.

His departure has deeply saddened those who knew him, even though we know that all that is born must die. Our sadness is tempered, however, by a warm feeling of gratitude for all that innumerable students and readers throughout the world received from him. Let the poet Guido Gezelle have the last word:

> Neen, geen tijdstip, geen verjaren
> van uw sterfdag mindert ooit
> het geheugen van al 't weldoen,
> dat gij hebt rond u gestrooid.

> [No, no date, no anniversary
> of your death ever diminishes
> the memory of all the good things
> which you have sown around you.]

Index

Aalst 110, 111
Act of Abandonment (1581) 109, 117
Act of Supremacy (1534) 50
Adalard of Ghent 84
Adela, mother of Charles the Good 108
Aethelred the Unready 41
Affligem, abbey of 74
Africa 61
Albert, archduke of Spanish Netherlands 138, 141
alchemists 35
Alcuin of Northumbria 39
Alfred the Great, king of England 44
Alps 39
Alsace 100, 101, 105, 106, 107, 109, 110, 124, 155
American colonies 115, 138
Anabaptists 113
Anarchy of Stephen 102
Anastasius, Byzantine emperor 121
Andrew of Marchiennes 90
Angevin dynasty 40
Angles (*see also* Anglo-Saxons) 38, 55
Anglican Church 115
Anglo-Normans 40, 108
Anglo-Saxons 42-3, 44, 46, 50, 99, 165
Ansbert, St. 81, 83
anthropology and history 21, 29, 31
Antwerp 73, 130, 153, 154, 168
Arabs 147, 148, 174, 175, 176, 178
archaeology and history 23
Aristotelian thought 30, 64, 67, 68
Arnulf I, count 74, 83
Arras, union of 116
astronomy and history 6, 31, 41
Atlantic world 175
Audacer of Flanders 87, 88, 89, 90
Audomarus, St. (St. Omer) 76, 77

Austrians 170, 173
Avignon 149
Azo of Byzantium 127

Backer, Jan de 119
Bacon, Roger 18
Baldwin I, count of Flanders 75, 87, 88, 89, 90, 92
Baldwin II, count of Flanders 78, 88
Baldwin V, count of Flanders 108
Bannockburn, battle of 151
Bartolus 59
Basle, council of 59
Beek, H.H. 1
Belgium (*see also* Flanders; Ghent; Low Countries) 113, 116, 132, 162, 163, 164, 165, 166, 167, 169, 170, 171, 172, 173, 174, 177, 181, 185, 187
Benelux countries 173
Berg, J.H. van den 1
Berghe, Jan van den 129, 130
Bernard, Claude 6
Bernheim 27
Bethmann, L.C. 73
Bill of Rights (1689) 52, 115
biology and history 2, 6, 31
Bisson, T.N. 161
Blackstone, William 52
Bloch, Marc 180
Blok, P.J. 32
Bodin, Jean 140, 142
Bohemia 10, 11, 63
Bollandists 163, 178
Bologna, university of 148
Boniface, St. 39
Boniface VIII, pope 151, 152
Boucault, Jean 124
Boulogne 82-86, 92

Bouvines, battle of 155
Brabant 74, 116, 130, 131, 154, 156, 170, 172
Braudel, Fernand 37
'Braudelian model' 37
British-Celtic civilization 44
Brittany 9
Bruges 100, 103, 105, 124, 154, 172, 187, 188
Brunner, Heinrich 179
Buckingham, duke of 41
Bundere, Maarten van den 127
Burgundy/Burgundians 107, 117, 128, 129, 131, 132, 155, 156, 157, 172, 173
Bury St. Edmunds 138
Byzantine empire 64, 66, 146, 174, 177

Caesar, Julius 38, 66
Calvin, John 113, 139
Calvinists 8, 45, 50, 107, 114, 116, 139
Cam, Helen 58
Cambridge, university of 32, 182
Canute IV, king of the Danes 108
Capetian dynasty 74, 99
Carolingian empire 39, 46, 47, 66, 69, 74, 75, 89, 91, 97, 98, 145, 168, 175, 176, 180, 182, 183
Catholic Emancipation 49
Channel, English 38, 40
Charlemagne 91, 175, 176, 177, 178, 180, 181, 188
Charles I, king of England 41, 57
Charles V, emperor and king of Spain 113, 116
Charles IX, king of France 141
Charles the Bald, king of France 75, 82, 88
Charles the Bold, duke of Burgundy 108, 129, 133
Charles the Good, count of Flanders 75, 78, 105, 107, 108, 111, 148
Charlier-Tassier, Suzanne 188
Chartres 82
China 12
Churchill, Sir Winston 41
Claudius, Roman emperor 38
Cleopatra 20
Clermont, council of 91
Clio 3, 4, 27, 34
Clito, William, count of Flanders 105, 107, 108, 109, 110, 111, 155
Clovis, king of the Franks 175
Club of Rome 27
Cologne 172
Commynes, Philippe de 129-30

comparative history 21-22, 31
Conservative (Tory) Party 46
Constance, council of 59
Constantinople 126, 175, 177
constitutional history 29
Constitutions of Clarendon (1164) 102
Coulanges, Fustel de 179, 182
Counter-Reformation 31, 139
Cromwell, Oliver 42, 138
Crusades 71, 157
cultural history 33-34, 158-59
customary law 119-33, 149

Dampierre 107
Danes 38, 40, 44, 80, 81, 86, 108
Darlington, C.D. 2
Darwin, Charles 53
David, J.B. 169
de Backer, Jan, *see* Backer
de Commynes, Philippe, *see* Commynes
de Coulanges, Fustel, *see* Coulanges
de Draeyer, Rogier, *see* Draeyer
de Lettenhove, Kervyn, *see* Lettenhove
de Liedekerke, count, *see* Liedekerke
de Reiffenberg, baron, *see* Reiffenberg
Declaration of Independence (US) 115
Delisle, Léopold 71, 72, 75, 76, 77, 78
Delrio 140, 142
Denmark 63
Derolez, Albert 72
De Smet, J.J. 169
Destrée, Jules 171
Dhondt, Jan 162
Disraeli, Benjamin 50
d'Olhain, Jacques, *see* Olhain
Douai 99
Draeyer, Rogier de 119, 122
Dubois, Pierre 149
Duchesne, André 76, 79, 80
Dutch civil code (1838) 2-3

Ebel, W. 104
economics and history 1, 2, 3, 4, 19, 28, 29, 30, 31, 34, 54, 158, 162, 164, 166, 167-68, 169, 171, 177
Edward I, king of England 43
Edward the Confessor 43, 69
Elizabeth I, queen of England 45, 50
England, Civil War in 41, 57, 115
—, continental relations of 38-40, 46-48, 149, 150
—, continuity/discontinuity in 42-46, 55-56
—, economic development of 9, 45-47, 48, 52, 69, 111, 155

—, feudalism in 38-40, 42, 44, 46-47
—, geographical identity of 37-40
—, in twelfth century 148
—, law in 21, 37, 43, 49, 50, 52, 68, 102-3, 125-26, 184
—, paradoxes in history of 52-54
—, parliament of 24, 42, 43, 44-45, 46-47, 55-61, 67-69, 154
—, recurrences and constants in 49-51
—, religious history of 39, 40, 45, 46, 49, 50, 51
—, scholarship in 42, 162
—, serfdom in 21
—, witchcraft in 138
Enlightenment 52, 53, 140
ethnology and history 7, 12, 29, 31, 35
Europe, England, role in 38-40, 46-48
—, in the twelfth century 98
—, Islam and 174-77
—, parliaments in 55-70, 154
—, Pirenne's theses on 161-78
—, quality of rule in 29
—, revolutions in, 114-16
—, rise to dominance of 11, 154, 164
—, trends in middle ages 98, 145-59
—, witchcraft in 135-43
European Community 3, 40
experimentation and historiography 6, 15-25

Farnese, Alexander 114
Fawtier, R. 180
February Revolt (Ghent) 107-12
Ferrara-Pisa, council of 59
feudalism 12, 17, 21, 38-39, 43, 46, 47, 52, 58, 62, 63, 64, 65, 66, 69, 97, 98, 108, 110, 111, 127, 148, 172, 180, 187
First Middle Ages 145
First World (Great) War 57, 164, 168, 170, 174
fitz Neal, Richard 64
Flanders (*see also* Ghent; Low Countries), economy of 9, 154, 155, 156, 166, 171-72
—, historical sources of 71-95
—, in twelfth century 97-106, 107-12, 148, 155
—, in fourteenth century 6, 152
—, in sixteenth century 113-17
—, language issue in 165, 170, 171, 187-88
—, law reform in 97-106, 124, 127, 128, 130
—, *Liber Floridus* 71-95
—, origins of 87-90

—, scholarship in 161-78, 179-89
Folcuin of Saint-Bertin 90
France, economic history of 9, 155
—, government of 57, 58, 63, 67, 148, 149, 153, 154
—, historical development of 39, 40, 46, 47, 91, 115-16, 150, 184
—, Low Countries, relations with 78, 108, 146, 151-52, 155-56, 165, 170, 171, 172, 173
—, scholarship in, 131, 163, 166, 167
Frankish empire 39, 46, 63, 66, 74, 81, 85, 88, 91, 109, 122, 126, 135, 182
Freemasons 142
French Revolution (1789) 115-16, 153
Frisia/Frisians 46, 81, 108, 109, 117

Galbert of Bruges 100, 107, 111, 124
Ganshof, F.L. 173, 179-89
Gaul 175
Gelderland 117
Geneva 40, 138
Genicot, L. 149, 180
geography and history 3, 19, 31, 37-40, 180
Gerard of Brogne, abbot 83, 84, 85
Germany, economy of 153, 154
—, law in 29, 47, 98, 126, 131
—, historical development of 5, 39, 53, 55, 56, 60, 63, 154, 171, 173, 175, 176-77
—, religion in 146
—, scholarship in 163, 164, 165, 166, 185
—, serfdom in 10
—, social democracy in 53
—, witchcraft in 135
Gerschenkron, A. 8, 9
Gertrude, mother of Thierry of Alsace 109
Ghent (*see also* Flanders; Low Countries), administration and law in 88, 90, 100, 101, 106, 119, 121, 122, 127, 129, 168
—, historical sources of 73, 74, 78, 80, 93-95
—, relics of 82-86
—, revolts of 22, 107-12, 157
—, university of 37, 71, 163, 165, 167, 169, 176, 183, 184, 186, 187
Gilissen, J. 123
Glanvill, Ranulf de 64, 125
Glorious Revolution (1688) 115
Glotz, Gustave 181
Godfrey, son of Eustace of Boulogne 92
Golden Fleece, order of 5, 157
Golden Spurs, battle of 172
Gothic architecture 149, 159

Gratian 99
Great Britain (*see also* England; Wales; Scotland) 37, 40, 49, 54, 185
Greeks 61, 135, 174
Gregorian Reform 69, 98, 110, 145, 146, 152
Gregory the Great, Pope 40
Gregory VII, Pope 98
Groenewold 18
Groningen 117
Gustavus Adolphus, king of Sweden 141
Guthrum 40

Habsburg dynasty 107, 116, 117, 132, 155
Hague, The 164
Hahn, Heinrich 2
Hailsham, Lord 54
Hainaut (Hainault) 156, 171
Hale, Sir Matthew 138
Harald the Dane 81
Harold Hardrada 38, 44
Hasquin, H. 172
Hastings, battle of 43
Hedemann, J.W. 4
Hegel, G.W.F. 24, 37
Helger, sacristan of Saint-Vulmar 84
Henry the Navigator 153
Henry I, king of England 102, 108
Henry II, king of England 102
Henry VIII, king of England 39, 45, 50, 138, 139
Herlihy, D. 9
Hermann, Gottfried 5
Hintze, Otto 61-62
histoire conjoncturelle 37 n.2
histoire événémentielle 17, 37 n.2
histoire historisante 33
histoire structurale 37 n.2
historiometrics 31
Hitler, Adolf 41, 55
Holland 74, 113, 114, 116, 156
Holy Roman Empire 98
Huftele, Master Lieven van den 121
Huizinga, Johan 32
humanities and history 27-35
Hundred Years War 38, 154
Hungary 10, 63, 67
Huy 128

Iceland 44
iconoclasts (in Low Countries) 21-22, 135
Industrial Revolution 11, 45, 46, 47, 52, 153
Ingelram of Flanders 87, 88, 89

Innocent VIII, Pope 139
Inquisition 113
Investiture Struggle 66, 145
Ireland 44
Isabella of the Spanish Netherlands 138, 141
Islam 63, 113, 146, 176, 177
Italy 39, 56, 58, 69, 167, 168, 174

Jacob, F. 6
James I, king of England 115, 137, 141, 142
Jerusalem 78, 91, 92
Jesuits 138
Jews 142, 180
Johanna of Harcourt 129
John III, duke of Brabant 156, 172
John, abbot of Saint-Amand 99
John, king of England 66
Judith, wife of Baldwin I 75, 92
jurisprudence and history 1, 2, 3, 4, 31, 54, 179
Juste T. 169
Justinian, Byzantine emperor 121, 126, 127, 135

Kekulé, F.A. 162
Koran 148
Kortrijk 128
Kominsky, E.A. 21
Kuttner, E. 21

Labour Party 46, 53
Lambert of Saint-Omer 71-76, 80, 81, 86, 87-88, 89, 90, 91
Latin America 147
'laws of history' 18, 48, 51, 69, 109
Laud, Archbishop 41
Lennoet, Master Gillis van 121
Lemarignier, J.F. 139, 182
Leopold I, king of the Belgians 174
Lettenhove, Baron Kervyn de 169, 171
Leuven (Louvain), university of 131
Levison, W. 77
Liber Floridus 71-95
Lidric of Harelbeke, count of Flanders 72, 75, 78, 79, 87, 88, 89, 90, 91
Liedekerke, count de 171
Liège 129, 133, 166, 170, 172, 173
Lille 108, 125, 175, 185
Linnaeus, Carolus 5
literature and history 19
logic and history 1
'logical extremism' 151

Loire 122
Lot, F. 180
Louis VI, king of France 108, 152, 155
Louis IX, king of France 149, 150
Louis XIV, king of France 57, 138, 173
Louis the Pious 88
Low Countries (*see also* Ghent; Flanders), administration of 157
—, economy of 167-68, 171
—, geography of 39
—, historical trends in 158-59, 173, 174
—, iconoclasm in 21-22, 135
—, in twelfth century 107-12
—, law in 119-33
—, parliaments in 63, 68, 154, 156
—, revolts in 113-17
—, urbanization in 167-68
—, witchcraft in 138, 141
Lütge 10
Luther, Martin 139
Lutheranism 113, 139
Luxembourg 113, 171
Lyon, Bryce 21, 162-63, 175-76, 182, 186

Mabillon, Jean 178
Magna Carta 52, 69
Magyars 147
Maitland, Frederic William 179
Manegold of Lautenbach 110
Marsilius of Padua 59, 68
Mary I, queen of England 45
mathematics and history 19, 33, 41
Mathilda of Flanders 100, 108
Maurists 178
Mechelen (Malines) 128
Mediterranean world 174-75, 177
Meijers, E.M. 2
mercantilism 9
Merovingians 34, 175
Moke, H.G.P. 169
Mommsen, T.E. 31
Montesquieu 171
Münster 113

Namèche, A.J. 169, 171
Namier, Lewis 46
Namur 171
Napoleon III, 170
Napoleon Bonaparte 41
Nazism 5, 56, 164
Needham, J. 12
Netherlands (*see also* Low Countries) 68, 107, 113, 114, 116, 117, 138, 141, 146, 154, 155, 156, 157, 159, 172, 173, 185

Nevelync, Master Joris 121
New Testament 136
Newton, Isaac 41
Nicasius, St. 120
Normandy 39, 108
Normans/ Norsemen 38, 39-40, 42, 43, 44, 63, 78, 79, 81, 82, 84, 86, 90, 108, 147
North Sea 39, 81, 175
Notger, provost at Boulogne 84
numismatics and history 16

October Revolution 8, 55, 116
Old Testament 135, 140
Olhain, Jacques d' 124
Oppermann, O. 82, 83, 84
Orange, house of 115, 116
Otto II, emperor and king 84
Oxford, university of 55, 181

palaeography 16
palaeontology 23
Papenbroeck, Daniel van 178
Paris 124-25, 182
Pertz, G.H. 75
Peter, St. 40
Peter the Great, czar of Russia 11
Peter's Pence 40
Philip, son of Thierry of Alsace 111
Philip I, king of France 78
Philip II, king of Spain 68, 109, 113, 114, 116, 137, 141, 157, 173
Philip IV, (the Fair), king of France 151, 152, 155, 173
Philip of Alsace, count of Flanders 100, 101, 105, 106, 124, 155
Philip the Good, duke of Burgundy 131, 157
philology/linguistics and history 1, 2, 3, 31
philosophy and history 1, 30, 31, 34, 182-83
physics and history 18, 19, 33, 41, 53
Picard, Edmond 169
Pictor, Petrus 74, 91
Pirenne, Henri 31, 161-78, 183, 184, 186
—, Jacques 169
Pirenne thesis 174-78
Pitt the Younger, William 40
Poland 10, 63, 67
politics and history 3, 29, 30, 31
Postan, M.M. 21
Praet, Jules van 174
press and history 3
Protestantism 5, 115, 116, 138, 140, 142, 186, 188

Prussia 61, 171, 173
psychology and history 1, 3, 29, 30
Puritans 45, 138, 141

Raskolniki (Old Believers) 8
Reformation 31, 139
Reiffenberg, Baron 169
Renaissance 153
Renouvin P. 181
Rhine, river 171
Rhineland 154, 155, 167
Richardson H.G. 162
Robert, duke of Normandy 108
Robert II, count of Flanders 78-79, 91, 92
Robert the Frisian, count of Flanders 108, 109
Roman empire 40, 44, 61, 63, 64, 66, 67, 135, 149, 175, 176-77, 186
Roman law 21, 29, 31, 52, 63, 64, 65, 67, 68, 69, 119-33, 135, 136, 149
Rome, Church of 40, 45, 51, 58, 59, 66, 68, 69, 98, 113-14, 138-39, 142, 149, 151, 152, 154
Romein, Jan 62, 126
Roosbroek, van 181
Rorik, king of the Danes 81, 82, 86
Russell, Bertrand 24
Russia 8, 9, 10-11, 55, 115, 116, 164, 174

Saint-Amand 99
Saint-Bertin, abbey of 72, 73, 74, 76, 85, 88, 90
Saint-Denis, abbey of 73
Saint-Omer (*see also* Audomarus) 71, 72, 73, 75, 76, 78, 79-82, 86-87, 89, 90, 108, 111
St. Peter, abbey of 73, 82, 84, 100, 119, 120, 122
Saint-Wandrille, abbey of (*see also* Wandregisilus) 81-86
Salem, witches of 138
Salic law 135
Salter, H.E. 181
Saxons (*see also* Anglo-Saxons) 38, 46, 55
Sayles, G.O. 162
Scandinavia 44, 67, 175, 176
Scheldt, river 120, 146, 152
Schism, Papal 154
Schelswig-Holstein 51
Schmid, C. 24
Scotland 9, 150-51
Second Middle Ages 145-47
Second World War 188
Seine, river 81, 171
serfdom, 9-10, 17, 21-22, 107, 147

Serrure, C.P. 184
Seventeen Provinces (*see also* Low Countries) 114, 116, 117, 153, 156, 173
sex in history 7-8
Sicily 99
Slavs 147
Slicher van Bath, B.H. 9-10
Snow, C.P. 19
social determinism 40-41
social history 28, 29, 34, 158, 162, 164, 167-69, 171, 177, 180
sociology and history 1, 3, 12, 19, 29, 30, 31, 32, 34, 37 n.2, 54, 61, 182-83
Soviet Union 8, 24
Spain 47, 56, 57, 63, 113, 114, 116, 137, 138, 154, 168, 173
Spanish Armada 38
Star Chamber 50
Stenton, Sir Frank 182
Stephen of Tournai 99
Strubbe, E.I. 71, 129, 185
Stuart dynasty 45, 47, 50, 68, 115
Stubbs, William 55, 162, 179
Sweden 63
Switzerland 38, 58, 60

Tanerijen, Willem van der 130, 131
Templars 140
Terlinden, viscount 169
theology and history 1
Thierry of Alsace, count of Flanders 100, 109, 110, 111
Thierry II, duke of Alsace 109
Tornoey, Jacob 120, 121
Treitschke, Heinrich von 31
Tudor dynasty 41, 45, 50, 68
Turks 157
'Two Cultures' debate 19

Ukkel 128
United Provinces (*see also* Netherlands) 115, 117
United States (of America) 115, 163, 165
Ussel, J.M.W. van 7-8
Utrecht 116, 117

value judgment in history 29, 34, 147, 183
van Culsbrouc, Master Jan 121
van den Berg, J.H., *see* Berg
van den Berghe, Jan, *see* Berghe
van den Bundere, Maarten, *see* Bundere
van den Huffele, Master Lieven, *see* Huffele
van der Tanerijen, Willem, *see* Tanerijen
van Lennoet, Master Gillis, *see* Lennoet

Index

van Papenbroeck, Daniel, *see* Papenbroeck
van Praet, Jules, *see* Praet
van Roosbroek, *see* Roosbroek
van Ussel, J.M.W., *see* Ussel
van Werveke, H., *see* Werveke
Versailles, treaty of 165, 189
Verviers 164, 166
Veurne 120
Vico, Giambattista 33
Vikings (*see also* Danes) 38, 82

Waitz, Georg 179
Wales 9, 44, 150
Wallonia 170, 171, 174
Wandregisilus, St. 81, 83
Warnkoenig, Leopold August 179
Wars of the Roses 50
Waterloo, battle of 5
Weber, Max 1, 8, 17
Weber thesis 8-9, 17
Wehemar, castellan of Ghent 111
Weimar Republic 55

Werveke, H. van 82, 83
Wiefrid, bishop of Thérouanne and Boulogne 84
Wigny, Pierre 181
William I (the Conqueror), king of England 20, 63, 108
William I, king of the Low Countries 173
Willibrord 39
Wilmotte, Maurice 172
witchcraft 135-43
Witger of Flanders 72, 74
Woolman, B.B. 6-7
Wouters, P.J. 184
Wuerem, Master Zeger 121
Wulfram, St. 81, 82, 83, 85

Ypres 110, 123, 124, 130
Yvain of Aalst 109, 110, 111

Zealand 114
zoology and history 31

Tabula Gratulatoria

Andriessen, J.
Ankum, Hans
Arnould, M.-A.
Avonds, Piet
Baelde, Michel
Baert, André-Emmanuel
Baeteman, G.
Balthazar, Herman
Bernauw, K.
Bezemer, C.H.
Bijn, Freddy G.
Bisson, T.N.
Blaas, P.B.M.
Blockmans, Wim
Bocken, Hubert
Boone, Marc
Bostoen, P.
Bouckaert, F.
Bourgeois, Jean
Bourgeois-Van Wassenhove, Marie-Christine
Brand, Hanno
Brulez, W.
Buntinx, Willy
Cappon, C.M.
Caruso, Robert D.
Cattoir, John
Cauchies, Jean-Marie
Cloet, M.
Cogen, M.
Collin, Ludo
Cools, C. Hans
Coppejans-Desmedt, Hilda
Craeybeckx, Jan
Croenen, G.
Dauchy, S.
Dauwe, Jozef
De Belder, J.
De Boeck, Frans
De Boos, Georges
De Brock, Tine
De Bruyne, Michiel
Declercq, Georges
De Cock, Patrick
De Grauwe, L.
De Grauwe-Foré, J. and L.
De Hemptinne, Thérèse
De Keyser, Raphaël
De Kok, Harry
Deleeck, Herman
Deleurere, Marie-Thérèse
Delva, Jan Baron
De Maegd-Soëp, Hugo and Carolina
De Mey, Lieve
De Meyer, L.
De Mil, Emmanuel
Demyttenaere, A.
Denève, Leni
Deprez, Ada
De Reu, Martine
De Ridder, Etienne
De Ridder-Symoens, Leo and Hilde
Deroo, Herman
De Ruyver, Brice
De Schepper, H.
De Schrijver, Antoine
De Schryver, Reginald
Deumens, Herwig
Dewachter, Wilfried
De Wever, Bruno
De Win, Paul
De Wulf, Christian
Dierkens, Alain
Diestelkamp, B.
Dubois, Bernard
Duyck, Frederik
Dynstee, Marguerite
Feenstra, R.
François, Luc
Fransen, J. Paul
Fryde, E.B.
Gaus, H.
Genicot, Léopold
Gerlo, Aloïs
Godding, P.
Goode, R.M.
Goossens, J.
Gorlé, Fritz
Hambly, J.C.
Hannon, S.
Heirbaut, Dirk
Herman-Michielsen, L.
Heughebaert, R.
Holvoet, Herwin
Hoste, Anselm
Hoste, Maria
Imbert, Jean
Janssen, Roger
Janssens, Gustaaf
Janssens, Paul
Janssens, Robert
Jocqué, Luc
Joris, André
Küpper, Jean-Louis
Lamarcq, Danny
Lambrecht, Daniel
La Meir, Dirk and Jeanine

Layton, John M.G.
Leermakers, Dirk
Lesage, Xavier
Leupen, Annejet and Piet
Lévy, J. P.
Lewis, A.D.E
Libert, Robin
Lyon, Bryce
Macours, G.
Maertens, Raoul
Magits, M.
Mann, Jill
Maréchal, Griet
Maresceau, Marc
Matton, Guido
McCormick, M.
Meersschaut, Frank
Meester, W.
Mestach, Hilde
Michiels, André
Milis, Ludo
Monballyu, J.
Moorman van Kappen, O.
Mijnhardt, W.W.
Musschoot, A.M.
Neirinck, F.
Nimmegeers, J.
Noël, René
Nycum, Peter
Nygren, Rof and Ulla
Opsommer, Rik
Pairon, Erwin
Papin, Kristof
Peters, Edward
Proost, Greta
Prevenier, W.
Rijksarchief, Ghent
Roelens, P.
Romain, Pierre
Rubens, Christine
Ruyffelaere, Peter
Sabbe, Herman
Sanders, G.
Sandquist, T.A.
Scheerder, J.
Scheiris, Chris
Schnapper, Bernard
Schoups, Inge
Schrage, E.J.H.
Schrans, G.
Schuermans, Frank
Scufflaire, Andrée
Simons, Walter
Sinnaeve, Adinda
Sint-Bavohumaniora, Ghent
Soete, W.
Soly, H.
Spiertz, Mathieu
Spruit, J.E.
Stabel, Peter
Stadsarchief, Ghent
Stadsbestuur, Ghent
Stevens, F.
Storme, Marcel
Strauss, Robert
Szamosvari, Doris
Tamse, C.A.
Tas, Julien
Thoen, Erik
Traest, José
Trio, Paul
Universiteitsbibliotheek, Ghent
Uytterhaegen, Frank
Van Acker, K.G.
Van Bladel, J.
Van Caenegem, Charles
Van Caenegem, Jettie
Van Caenegem, Hendrik
Van Caenegem, William
Van Cauwenberge, Gabriël
Vancoillie, P.L.
Vandekerckhove, J.
Van den Abeele, Dries
Van den Abeele, Raf
Van den Auweele, Dirk M.J.
Van den Berghe, Yvan
Van den Bossche, A.M.
Van den Bossche, Geertrui
Van den Broeck, Jan
Vandepitte, Daniël
Van der Haegen, Herman
Vandersteene, Liesbeth
Van der Wee, Herman
Van de Wiele, Johan
Van Dievoet, G.
Van Eeckhaute-Comhaire, Francine
Van Eeckhoutte, Willy
Van Eenoo, R.
Van Goethem, Herman
Vanhalme, Michel
Van Hecke, G.
Vanhemelrijck, Fernand
Van Hille, P.
Van Houtte, H.
Van Houtte, J.A.
Van Malleghem, P.
Vleeschouwers-Van Melkebeek, Monique
Van Mingroot, Erik
Van Peteghem, C.
Van Peteghem, Paul
Van Poucke, Godelieve
Van Sumere, Chris
Van 'T Dack, E.
Van Tijn, T.
Van Uytven, R.
Van Waesberghe, Lorette
Van Winter, Johanna Maria
Vanwormhoudt, Marc
Verbeke, G.
Verbeke, Werner
Verhaeghe, Frans
Verheeke, Frans
Verhelst, D.
Verhelst, Juul
Verhofstadt, Edward
Verhulst, A.
Vermeir, René
Vervliet, H.D.L.
Voordeckers-Declercq, Prof. Dr and Mrs
Waelkens-Donnay, Laurent and Frédérique
Waterschoot, W.
Weimar, Peter
Wenger, L.B.
Wenger, Leopold
Wijffels, A.
Willems, D.
Wils, Lode
Wyffels, Carlos
Wylleman, Annelies